Boston Publishing Company

President and Publisher: Robert J. George
Vice President: Richard S. Perkins, Jr.
Editor-in-Chief: Robert Manning
Managing Editor: Paul Dreyfus

Senior Writers:
Clark Dougan, Edward Doyle, David Ful-
ghum, Samuel Lipsman, Terrence Mait-
land, Stephen Weiss
Senior Picture Editor: Julene Fischer

Researchers:
Kerstin Gorham (Chief), Michael T. Casey,
Jonathan Elwitt, Sandra M. Jacobs,
Christy Virginia Keeny, Denis Kennedy,
Michael Ludwig, Carole Rulnick, Nicole
van Ackere, Robert Yarbrough

Picture Editors:
Wendy Johnson, Lanng Tamura
Assistant Picture Editor: Kathleen A. Reidy
Picture Researchers:
Nancy Katz Colman, Robert Ebbs, Tracey
Rogers, Ted Steinberg, Nana Elisabeth
Stern, Shirley L. Green (Washington
D.C.), Kate Lewin (Paris)
Picture Department Assistants:
Suzanne M. Spencer, Kathryn J. Steeves

Historical Consultants:
Vincent H. Demma, Lee Ewing, Dr. Donald
S. Marshall
Picture Consultant: Ngo Vinh Long

Production Editor: Patricia Leal Welch
Editorial Production:
Karen E. English, Pamela George, Eliza-
beth Campbell Peters, Theresa M. Slom-
kowski, Amy P. Wilson

Design: Designworks, Sally Bindari

Marketing Director: Jeanne C. Gibson
Business Staff: Amy Pelletier

About the editors and authors

Editor-in-Chief *Robert Manning*, a long-
time journalist, has previously been editor-in-chief of the *Atlantic Monthly* maga
zine and its press. He served as assistant
secretary of state for public affairs under
Presidents John F. Kennedy and Lyndon B.
Johnson. He has also been a fellow at the
Institute of Politics at the John F. Kennedy
School of Government at Harvard University.

Authors: *Edward Doyle*, a historian, received his masters degree at the University of Notre Dame and his Ph.D. at Harvard University. *Stephen Weiss*, an
American historian, has M.A. and M.Phil.
degrees from Yale. He is a former fellow
at the Newberry Library in Chicago. Mr.
Doyle and Mr. Weiss have written other
volumes in *The Vietnam Experience*.

Historical Consultants: *Vincent H. Demma*,
a historian with the U.S. Army Center of
Military History, is director of the center's
history of the Vietnam conflict. *Lee Ewing*,
editor of *Army Times*, served two years in
Vietnam as a combat intelligence officer
with the U.S. Military Assistance Command, Vietnam (MACV) and the 101st Airborne Division. *Dr. Donald S. Marshall*
served in Vietnam as the head of General
Creighton Abrams's long-range planning
group and is currently a consultant for national strategy.

Picture Consultant: *Ngo Vinh Long* is a social historian specializing in China and
Vietnam. Born in Vietnam, he returned
there most recently in 1980. His books include *Before the Revolution: The Vietnamese Peasants Under the French* and *Report
From a Vietnamese Village*.

Cover photo:

Trained to fight, a U.S. Marine finds himself engaged instead in a pacification operation in a
South Vietnamese village south of Da Nang. He
is escorting villagers from an area believed to
harbor Vietcong guerrillas.

Library of Congress Catalog Card Number: 84-
72041

ISBN: 0-939526-12-3

10 9 8 7 6
5 4 3 2 1

The Vietnam Experience

A Collision of Cultures

by Edward Doyle, Stephen Weiss,
and the editors of Boston Publishing Company

Boston Publishing Company/Boston, MA

Contents

Preface

Oh, East is East, and West is West,
And never the twain shall meet . . .
Till Earth and Sky stand presently at
God's great Judgement seat . . .

—Rudyard Kipling

The East is the Republic of South Vietnam, half of a truncated nation, recently freed of colonial control. The West is the United States, most powerful nation in the world. This volume of *The Vietnam Experience* portrays the partnership of the two countries, an effort singular in history but ill-starred from its beginning. *A Collision of Cultures* recounts nearly two decades of American endeavors to promote economic and social development, political reform, and modernization in South Vietnam. The volume focuses on how these endeavors were affected by the escalation of U.S. military involvement in South Vietnam's war with the North. It shows how the means employed to attain victory—massive firepower and more than 500,000 American troops—eventually tore at the social fabric and national unity the Americans had intended to build and to defend. The story of America's partnership with South Vietnam is one of contrasts, idealism and arrogance, ingenuity and obtuseness, exhilaration as well as frustration on both sides. When the Americans left in 1973, South Vietnam's future appeared as uncertain as it was in 1954 when Washington first committed American prestige and power to build a nation and save it from communism.

—The Editors

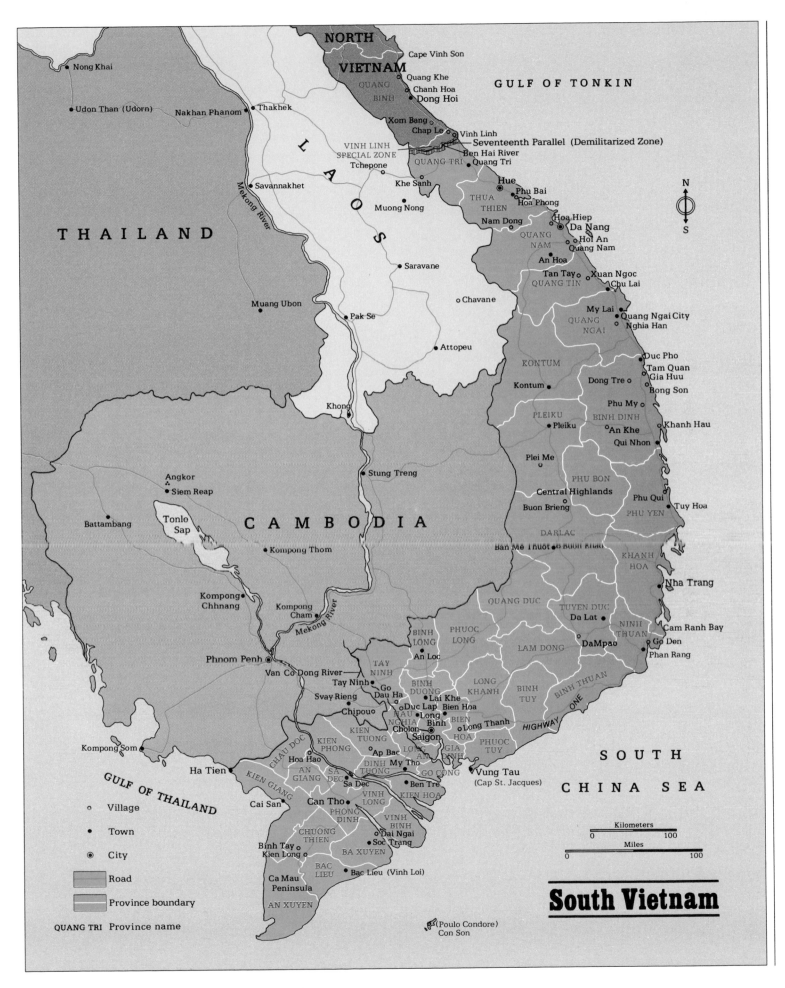

South Vietnam

The War Without Guns

On July 22, 1954, the people of South Vietnam joyously celebrated their independence from French colonial rule. They anticipated better days to come under the fledgling South Vietnamese government of Ngo Dinh Diem, even though the French departure from South Vietnam burdened the Diem regime with deplorable economic, social, and political conditions. According to a study conducted by the U.S. Senate Foreign Relations Committee, "Rarely, if ever, in history has a state come into being amid such inauspicious circumstances; arbitrarily split in two at the end of a bitter eight-year war; suddenly given independence after a period of colonialism during which the colonial power made no effort at all to train civil servants or to prepare the people for self-government ... and with virtually no economic resources."

South Vietnam's economy was a shambles. In 1954 the production of rice, the country's principal export, fell nearly a million tons short of what it

had been in 1929. South Vietnam's few industries were at a standstill, lacking capital and skilled workers. There were less than 100 native doctors for a population of 14 million, and the hospitals were located in the cities. Of 3 million school-age children, less than one-sixth had access to schools.

After a visit to South Vietnam, U.S. Senator Mike Mansfield reported that the outlook was "grim." The Diem regime lacked an adequate bureaucracy to deliver sufficient public services or to address the country's myriad social inequities. Moreover, it faced an influx of 800,000 refugees from North Vietnam, open rebellion by armed Hoa Hao and Cao Dai sect members and Binh Xuyen gangsters, and a power challenge from Diem's military rival General Nguyen Van Hinh. Above all, there was the threat of an invasion of South Vietnam by the Communist government of Ho Chi Minh.

The United States closely monitored what was happening in South Vietnam. Because of its colonial legacy of political suppression, economic exploitation, and social instability, South Vietnam appeared especially vulnerable to Communist aggression either through direct attack by North Vietnam or through a subversive "war of national liberation." According to the "domino theory" propounded in Washington by President Eisenhower and Secretary of State John Foster Dulles, while South Vietnam possessed no intrinsic military or economic value to the United States, its strategic proximity to other non-Communist nations in Southeast Asia made it vital, politically and psychologically, to American security interests in the Pacific. Those interests included the containing of Communist China.

Although the United States viewed the specter of Communist expansionism with a deep concern in the cold war 1950s, Washington's options were limited. The costly, drawn-out struggle with the Communists in Korea had left the United States and its allies reluctant to mire themselves in similar military conflicts elsewhere. In Washington such respected military leaders as Generals Matthew Ridgway, Maxwell Taylor, and James Gavin—known as the "Never Again Club"—issued dire warnings against embroiling the United States in another land war in Asia. As a deterrent to Communist expansion, the United States sponsored collective defense arrangements among non-Communist Pacific nations, such as the SEATO and ANZUS (Australia, New Zealand, and the United States) treaties. As an alternative to military action, the United States also employed an arsenal of political, economic, and military aid to buttress Southeast Asian countries like South Vietnam, Cambodia, and Laos against possible Communist aggression. Americans called this aid strategy "nation-building."

Preceding page. *Members of the MSU group confer in 1957 with top Saigon officials including Ngo Dinh Diem (second from left)* and *to Diem's left MSU chief Wesley Fishel.*

After Diem surprised almost everyone in the spring of 1955 by crushing the opposing sects and exiling General Nguyen Van Hinh, thereby solidifying his power, Washington's partnership with Diem was speedily concluded. In exchange for a broad range of U.S. assistance—money and equipment, as well as political, economic, and military advisers—Diem agreed to establish a representative government in South Vietnam; to institute political, economic, and social reforms; and to maintain an anti-Communist posture consistent with U.S. objectives in Southeast Asia. President Eisenhower granted U.S. aid on the condition that it "be met by performance on the part of the government of Vietnam in undertaking needed reforms."

America's nation-building venture was an ambitious and risky experiment. South Vietnam was a country with no understanding of the political machinery of democracy and representative government. The Americans and the South Vietnamese were venturing into unexplored territory. Could close cooperation and interaction develop between two so radically contrasting countries as the United States and South Vietnam—one militarily powerful, the

Vietnamese army troops suppress an outburst of violence by members of the Binh Xuyen sect on a Cholon street in 1955.

other weak; one wealthy, the other poor; and one technologically advanced, the other underdeveloped? Could the United States delve deeply into the internal affairs of South Vietnam, only just emerging from a century of colonial rule and political suppression, without violating its sovereignty and stunting the very government and society it was seeking to build? Could the Americans, in their effort to influence South Vietnam's economic, political, and social development, avoid the taint of colonialism in the eyes of the South Vietnamese people? It became apparent, years later, that the U.S. had plunged into South Vietnam without careful consideration of such questions.

America's assistance programs in South Vietnam involved several agencies: the Agency for International Development (then called the International Cooperation Administration), the U.S. Information Service, the Central Intelligence Agency, and the Military Assistance Advisory Group. In 1955, the corps of American civilian advisers in South Vietnam included 128 from AID and 10 from USIS. There were also CIA personnel there, but the official figure was still classified almost thirty years later. William

Colby, who served as CIA mission deputy in South Vietnam from 1959 to 1962, has said that there were no more than forty agents there in the 1950s. Although CIA activities in South Vietnam are often shrouded in official secrecy, the agency has acknowledged that it trained Diem's internal security and intelligence units, assisted in developing anti-Communist propaganda campaigns, and supplied the U.S. Embassy with analyses of the political, economic, and military situation in the South Vietnamese countryside.

The more than fifty professors and instructors of a Michigan State University group rounded out the civilian U.S. advisory team. Dr. Wesley Fishel, an MSU professor of political science, headed the group. Fishel had become a close friend of Diem after they first met in Tokyo in 1950. A year later, Fishel arranged for Diem's appointment as consultant to MSU's Governmental Research Bureau. After Diem became premier of South Vietnam in 1954, he, in turn, invited Fishel to come to Saigon to serve as his personal adviser. When Fishel arrived in August 1954, Diem also asked him to organize an advisory team of MSU specialists in public and police administration, as well as economics and finance, to help the South Vietnamese government reform and modernize its administration. That fall, through Fishel's efforts, MSU signed a contract with the Diem government, which hired some MSU faculty members and instructors as advisers. In return, Michigan State, during the seven years its group operated in Vietnam, received a total of $25 million from the South Vietnamese government to pay salaries, travel and living costs, and administrative expenses.

The members of the MSU group represented a new breed of American foreign aid advisers. Harold Stassen, head of the U.S. Foreign Assistance Agency in 1954, had promoted the idea that universities be tapped as "manpower reservoirs" for the extension of "Americanism" abroad. Arriving in Saigon in May 1955, the MSU contingent responded enthusiastically to the call. MSU president John Hannah asserted that the government could contact "his campus specialists, get any answer to most any question for government or research groups within 30 minutes."

By far the largest group of early American advisers were military men. By the end of 1955 nearly 800 U.S. military advisers were in South Vietnam. This was because most U.S. aid to South Vietnam was for training and equipping its armed forces. From 1955 to 1959 three-quarters of the entire U.S. aid budget for South Vietnam went for military purposes. American military advisers felt that the chief threat to South Vietnam was an invasion from North Vietnam and, therefore, military aid should get top priority. Many American civilian advisers, however, believed that what most endangered South Vietnam was Communist-inspired, internal subversion. They argued that military aid could not sustain the Diem regime unless there was substantial progress toward economic and political stability.

The Agency for International Development directed and administered the U.S. economic aid program to South Vietnam in the 1950s and 1960s. By 1956 its field agency in South Vietnam, the U.S. Operations Mission (USOM), was providing Diem an average of $270 million a year—more aid per capita than the United States was then spending on any country in the world except Laos and South Korea. AID disbursed to the Saigon government funds without

The Move South

For many of the nearly 1 million refugees who fled North Vietnam in 1954, U.S. evacuation ships provided their only means to freedom in the South. It was not the last time the refugees would have to depend on American assistance. After their arrival in South Vietnam, the United States provided them with food, clothing, and medical care. Even the land they eventually received from the South Vietnamese government was paid for with American funds. In turn, the U.S. hoped that these staunchly anti-Communist refugees would lend their support to the struggling regime of Ngo Dinh Diem.

Right. *Refugees crowd the deck of "LSM 9052," one of the several boats provided by the United States for relocation to the South.*

Opposite. *Four young crewmen of the U.S.S. Bayfield display an inspirational banner for the northerners en route from Haiphong to Saigon in September 1954.*

which Diem could not have paid the cost of his administration or the salaries of his civilian bureaucracy.

The story of American assistance to South Vietnam was of course more than one of economic programs and political objectives and involved thousands of Americans, their goals, their strivings, their frustrations. They came from across America and from diverse ethnic, religious, and social groups. They differed from most Americans in their desire to live and work in developing countries. Before leaving for Vietnam, one AID employee recalled, her advisory group was instructed, "We have a job to do, it's a big job, it's an important job." *

USAID personnel were well prepared for their mission in such technical fields as agriculture, health, sanitation, economics, and transportation. But they were little trained to understand the Vietnamese people—their language and problems, needs and aspirations. Recalling her orientation, an AID trainee "didn't feel that there was much real awareness on the part of anybody, either the orienters or

* Most of the unattributed comments by AID advisers in this volume are from official debriefing interviews conducted at the end of advisory tours in South Vietnam. Because of AID's policy of confidentiality, the advisers' names cannot be disclosed.

the orientees, about the problems of appreciating the attitudes and the felt needs of the people where we were going. I felt as though the Americans were going to decide what the people needed, and try and get their cooperation to give it to them rather than making it a learning situation and finding out what was really happening." AID training also did not provide sufficient instruction in the Vietnamese language. AID trainees took lessons in the Vietnamese language but only a handful attained even minimal ability to communicate. Regretting the casual attitude toward learning Vietnamese, an AID trainee said, "There was no pressure at all; whether or not a person studies a language would depend on the person's own motivation."

Still, American AID advisers embraced with fervor the effort to save the South Vietnamese from communism. At its beginning, in 1954, the AID mission had difficulty getting underway, partly because of a series of crises besetting Ngo Dinh Diem's regime. The nearly 1 million refugees from North Vietnam presented the most formidable challenge. AID, in concert with Diem's government, supplied the often penniless refugees with temporary shelter, food, and medical care.

AID's role in meeting the refugee emergency was more

than humanitarian. Although the United States did not engineer the great exodus southward, U.S. propaganda certainly encouraged it. American officials decided that the outpouring of refugees from North Vietnam could work to the advantage of South Vietnam. Dramatizing the refugees' flight to the South as a spontaneous quest for freedom from Communist oppression would enhance the legitimacy of and win international sympathy for the anti-Communist state the U.S. hoped to organize around Diem. Both the Americans and Diem saw the staunchly anti-Communist refugees as a political nucleus for the formation of a democratic, pro-American government. Diem, a Catholic, considered the primarily Catholic refugees a power base for himself in the largely Buddhist South where he was not well known.

In collaboration with Diem, AID and other U.S. agencies therefore took steps to exploit the refugee emergency for political ends. USAID helped the refugees in the name of the South Vietnamese government in order to gain their loyalty to Diem. The CIA and U.S. Information Service devised a psychological campaign to lure refugees southward. During the six-month relocation period provided by the Geneva accords, the CIA employed rumors and leaflets to warn about the terror of living under a Communist regime in the North. U.S. Information Service propaganda focused on Catholics. Posters and leaflets distributed in Catholic areas of the North carried such messages as, "Christ has gone to the South" and "The Virgin Mary has departed from the North."

Resettlement of the refugees from the North posed the initial test of one of the principal features of AID's master plan for South Vietnam: land reform. No other aspect of South Vietnam's struggle to form a nation received so much attention from AID and the American press. Land was South Vietnam's most precious commodity, and for thousands of years farming had been the principal occupation of the Vietnamese. Land for growing rice, the staple crop, was also the core around which Vietnamese social, economic, and political institutions had evolved.

Throughout Vietnam's history, the disposition of land had been a major political issue. In the twentieth century, French colonial policies had exacerbated already existing inequities in landownership, forcing an overwhelming number of landless peasants to eke out subsistence as tenant farmers or sharecroppers. In South Vietnam in 1954, 5,300 of the 250,000 landowners possessed 45 percent of the arable land. The Communist Vietminh had successfully capitalized on these volatile conditions to attract peasant support.

USAID advisers correctly saw land reform as necessary to viable government in the South. They knew that for the Vietnamese peasant, the "common man of South Vietnam," the desire to own a plot to support his family superseded ideological appeals for his political allegiance. As Edward Lansdale, a veteran of anti-Communist activities in the Philippines and South Vietnam noted, a peasant's "one real yearning is to have something of his own, a farm, a small business, and to be left free to make it grow as he wishes."

The Americans, therefore, promoted land reform as a vehicle to preempt the chief Communist appeal for peasant loyalty. "An honest land reform," U.S. advisers counseled Diem in late 1954, "intelligently and aggressively applied, may offer the best means available for meeting the Vietminh challenge . . . if a program can be developed that is more than just sham, it will offer one of the best propaganda weapons against the Vietminh." U.S. advisers also pushed land reform because their vision of peas-

Land reclamation was the first step in building resettlement villages for refugees in the 1950s. Here, at Cai San, Vietnamese workers dig drainage canals as a U.S. adviser looks on.

ants owning their own farms reflected American political ideas of individualism and the right to private property. One U.S. land reform expert in South Vietnam during the mid-1950s cited the great faith of Americans in "individualized agriculture as a bulwark of political democracy."

The principal architect of the American land reform project was Wolf Ladejinsky. As U.S. agricultural attaché in Tokyo during the occupation of Japan, Ladejinsky had devised a successful program for breaking up the big Japanese landed estates. Washington considered him the major American expert on land reform, and in January 1955 Harold Stassen, head of the Foreign Operations Administration, appointed Ladejinsky to an agricultural post in South Vietnam.

Phase one of South Vietnam's land reform program began in 1955 with the resettling of 800,000 North Vietnamese refugees. The Saigon government proposed sites for over 300 resettlement tracts and villages. Ladejinsky, his AID staff, and Diem envisioned the largest of them, the mammoth land reclamation of Cai San, as the showpiece of the program. At Cai San alone, AID, through the South Vietnamese government, grubstaked 47,000 refugees until they could fend for themselves. In return for money to build houses, a daily subsistence until harvest time, and a fleet of American tractors, resettlement officials required peasants to clear and drain nearly 20,000 acres of swampland and dig twenty kilometers of canals.

The United States hailed Cai San as a "symbol of South Vietnam's determination to shelter people who linked their future with that of free government." USAID looked upon Cai San as a model for what could be achieved with U.S. aid and technical expertise combined with the will and cooperation of its partner, the South Vietnamese government. To elated USAID advisers, the prospect of tens of

thousands of refugees carving a new home for themselves in a democratic South Vietnam boded well for the whole land resettlement and reform enterprise.

Ladejinsky had no illusions about the difficulty of making land reform work in South Vietnam. "An enormous amount will have to be done if a fair system of rents and land holdings is to be established," he stated. In October 1956, Diem, to much fanfare in the South Vietnamese and American press, enacted broad land reform legislation. The *New York Times* extolled Diem's American-sponsored plan and said it was being carried out "with a determination that is impressing observers." This program built on a 1955 ordinance limiting the often exorbitant rents charged the country's 600,000 tenant farmers. Diem now restricted rice holdings to 247 acres per owner, with the excess to be redistributed to landless peasants for purchase over six years. As a result, more than 1.8 million acres became subject to transfer to landless peasants, with U.S.-supplied funds to be paid landlords for the land taken from them.

"The miracle of South Vietnam"

While the Diem government and AID were addressing the plight of the landless peasant, they also made notable strides toward improving economic and social conditions. American financial and technical assistance enabled Saigon to rehabilitate its war-ravaged highway and railway systems; transport was nearly impossible in some areas. AID helped set up a highway department and trained Vietnamese maintenance crews. It relieved the government's shortage of operating funds and the country's lack of consumer goods by instituting a Commercial Import Program (CIP). The United States purchased goods for import by South Vietnam with foreign aid dollars, which went directly to exporters. South Vietnamese importers paid for these goods with piasters that went into a counterpart fund from which Diem could draw to operate his administration. At the same time, the CIP channeled millions of dollars worth of consumer goods into South Vietnam: food, clothing, pharmaceuticals, bicycles and motorscooters, machinery, building materials, and countless other goods.

In addition, the United States provided an array of agricultural and industrial aid. The agricultural technicians, fertilizers, tractors, and farm implements the Vietnamese received doubled rice production from 2.6 million tons in 1954 to 5 million tons in 1959. The production of other agricultural commodites also increased, and that of livestock and poultry nearly tripled in five years from 11 million to 31 million. Besides modernizing several of South Vietnam's few small industries (producing beer, soft drinks, cigarettes, and matches), American technicians spurred production of goods never before manufactured there, including paper, aluminum wares, plastics, pharmaceuticals,

and glassware. A $6 million AID grant created the Industrial Development Center. On this impetus the Saigon government constructed a coal production plant and hydroelectric facility aimed at meeting the country's rising needs for fuel and electricity.

AID also set about raising the level of health care and establishing an education system, two badly needed primary services. The average life expectancy of the Vietnamese was thirty-five years, then one of the lowest in the world. After Diem's 1956 decree mandating "a rural health program and extended services down to the village level," the Americans strove to establish health centers, as well as medical stations, in 3,300 villages. AID funded a health technicians program to train Vietnamese health workers and a 500-bed teaching hospital to alleviate a chronic lack of doctors and nurses. It also sponsored disease control and sanitation projects. A malaria control project, for example, attacked the main cause of illness and death in South Vietnam. Nationwide over 2,500 Vietnamese health workers began spraying the homes of 6 million people.

U.S. assistance played an important part in renovating the country's outdated colonial educational system. Under the French in 1939 only 5,000 Vietnamese gained admission to high schools, and a mere 700 were permitted to enroll in the country's sole university at Hanoi. Diem made a good start at turning this around. In 1955 South Vietnam founded three new universities at Saigon, Da Lat, and Hue and raised university enrollment to 1,200. By tripling the number of classrooms, the government could accommodate 70 percent of children between five and fifteen.

American advisers stressed that military and economic development alone could not bind the South Vietnamese into a nation. Political democracy and sound government, they felt, were the necessary cement to hold South Vietnam together. An American economist in South Vietnam affirmed: "The economic solution to the problem of economic growth in Vietnam is relatively simple; the real problems, the serious problems, lie in the areas of administration and politics."

At first Americans had doubted that Diem could form a representative government out of the political chaos that engulfed South Vietnam in 1954. Besides the Communist Vietminh, the only active political parties were a hodgepodge of nationalist groups squabbling among themselves. Political rights existed only for those wealthy Vietnamese landowners and bureaucrats who had collaborated with the French colonial regime. Moreover, the country possessed almost no institutions associated with self-government.

Farmers used to wooden plows hauled by water buffalo test out modern farm equipment from the United States at a refugee settlement project south of Saigon.

It was Diem's promises to form a government based on "the will of the people expressed . . . by whatever constituent process they freely choose" that persuaded United States officials to bestow their support on him. This required, in addition to economic and military advisers, Americans who, working within AID and the U.S. Embassy, could help Diem to shape the political reform of his government. The public administration specialists of Wesley Fishel's MSU group were also consulted on political matters. They all came hoping to instill the South Vietnamese with democratic principles of freedom guaranteed by law and of popularly elected government. In pursuit of this, Americans endeavored to help the Diem regime organize national elections, erect a legislative and administrative framework for representative government, train the police and internal security forces, and streamline the bureaucracy. Rarely before had Americans so closely involved themselves in the governmental affairs of an independent ally. Little considering that they might be viewed as the "new colonialists" and exhilirated by the prospect of preserving South Vietnam from communism, Americans charged ahead, confident of their methods and of success. French economist Tibor Mende commented in 1957, "As usual, the Americans go about their business in dead earnest. Having decided to transplant their variety of democracy into this forgotten corner of Asia, they rejoice in every gesture of 'democracy' as only a mother could rejoice in the progress of her child. The greater majority of the Americans in Vietnam very sincerely believe that in transplanting their institutions, they could immunize South Vietnam against Communist propaganda."

To bolster South Vietnam's international standing as an alternative to the "totalitarian" government of North Vietnam, Diem, at the urging of American advisers, held a national referendum in 1955. U.S. advisers watched proudly as millions of Vietnamese elected Diem head of state. The American press, as well as newspapers in Europe and Asia, celebrated the event as the birth of democracy in South Vietnam.

U.S. political advisers then guided Diem to the next stages of nation-building: the 1956 election of a Constituent Assembly to write and vote upon a constitution and the scheduling of elections for a national legislature. Wesley Fishel and his MSU advisory team proffered many suggestions and technical advice to the assembly's constitutional committees. Urged by Fishel's MSU group, AID, and the U.S. Embassy, Diem signed South Vietnam's first constitution into law on October 25, 1956. The constitution had many of the features of a democratic document. MSU political advisers had encouraged Diem to support a constitution with provisions for a president elected by universal suffrage, a unicameral legislature, an independent judiciary, and a bill of rights something like a cross between the constitution of the United States and that of the French Fourth Republic.

The American aid mission, in conjunction with its goal of bringing representative government to South Vietnam, also sought to build among the Vietnamese Diem's image as a democrat. According to one MSU adviser, Robert Scigliano, "Throughout the early period of the Diem government's existence the United States Information Service participated in an intensive propaganda campaign to build up the prestige of the Vietnamese leader. In fact," he went on, "the Vietnamese government's propaganda agency . . . was practically run by American information specialists until 1957." John Mecklin, a U.S. Information Service director in Saigon, related that in 1961 "the U.S. spent some $7 million on a radio network in the hope that Diem would use it to bring his government closer to the people and thus perhaps generate a nationalistic spirit to the detriment" of the Communists. AID distributed hundreds of radios to villages around the country. The U.S. Mission also furnished Diem's propaganda agency with a television network capable of beaming his speeches to about 300 villages equipped with large television screens.

On a trip to Washington in May 1957, Diem was lavishly welcomed. President Eisenhower, flanked by other dignitaries, went to the airport to greet him, an honor Eisenhower had never accorded to any state visitor. "You have exemplified in your part of the world, patriotism of the highest order," President Eisenhower told Diem. Diem thanked the United States for the "faith in my country" that "accomplished the miracle of Vietnam." Some American newspapers and periodicals picked up the theme, calling South Vietnam "the bright spot in Asia" and crediting Diem with performing an "economic miracle."

While Diem acknowledged U.S. aid with "profound gratitude," the U.S. State Department, during Diem's visit to Washington, described South Vietnam "as a prize example of a country reclaimed from chaos by United States assistance." U.S. officials also began calling South Vietnam the "showcase" of American aid. The economic and social statistics the Americans quoted all seemed to point to even more impressive advances in the aid program. All these claims and accolades suggested that by 1957 Diem and his U.S. advisers had indeed worked a miracle in South Vietnam.

The harder realities

The realities, however, suggested otherwise and should have been cause for a comprehensive review by the White House, the U.S. Congress, and the South Vietnamese government. It would have revealed a troublesome divergence of priorities between AID and the Diem government as well as insufficient cooperation by South Vietnamese agencies in administering American-funded aid projects. By 1957, for example, South Vietnamese performance in land reform was lagging far behind the rosy projections of 1955 because the Diem administration had a vested inter-

Speaker Sam Rayburn welcomes Ngo Dinh Diem as he arrives to address Congress, May 9, 1957. Vice President Nixon stands at Rayburn's side, while Senator Lyndon Johnson (left of center in bow tie) prepares for the speech.

est in a land policy that maintained the status quo. A U.S. adviser commented: "The failure of the land tenure program to move forward must still be blamed on the lack of serious interested administrators and topside command. Government officials, beginning with the minister for agrarian reform, had divided loyalties, being themselves landholders."

An American report said that the minister of agrarian reform had not "signed leases with his tenants as provided by land reform decrees and he is most certainly not interested in land distribution which would divest him of much of his property." Furthermore, members of Diem's own family and administration—Truong Van Chuong, his brother's father-in-law, and Nguyen Ngoc Tho, his vice president, among others—fraudulently obtained extensive tracts of land the government had expropriated from their former French or Vietnamese landlords.

The Diem government's actions also hampered the resettlement projects. In the late summer of 1956, the Cai San project director, the nephew of the minister of agrarian reform, demanded that refugees sign tenancy contracts for the land their own backbreaking labor had reclaimed from useless swamp. This outraged the peasants, who had expected to obtain immediate ownership of their land, without having to pay the government over time to obtain title. Peasant resentment swelled as the government refused to back off. In the end, the government and its AID advisers lost much of the good will and political benefit the Cai San project had been supposed to generate. By June 1956 only half of the 100,000 refugees originally expected had resettled at Cai San.

Political mismanagement also bedeviled Diem's pet project, the resettling of refugees and landless peasants in the highlands to form "a human wall" blocking Communist infiltration from the north and west. This would have required encroachment into montagnard territory, and American advisers warned Diem that the montagnards might resist resettlement on their highland domains. For years Diem had been urged to build rapport with the montagnards, who over the centuries had been victims of political and racial discrimination by the Vietnamese. Ho Chi Minh had won the allegiance of northern montagnards by promising regional autonomy and economic aid and could be expected to court their southern cousins with similar blandishments. Diem paid little heed. The resettlements proceeded, with predictable consequences. The montagnards resented the Vietnamese settlers and voiced acrimonious protests. Diem's American advisers described the highland resettlements as "hastily designed" and doomed to "waste money and effort." To the ire of the montagnards, Diem ignored their protests and continued the settlements. "Diem," lamented one adviser, "has given Communist propaganda in the highlands a wider audience than it had before."

Because of inertia, corruption, and bureaucratic bun-

gling, land distribution barely inched along. By 1958 it had ground to a virtual halt. As late as 1962, only about a third of the land in government hands had been redistributed; land reform had to be classified as a failure.

Saigon's mishandling of land reform embarrassed Diem's American advisers. Not only had they participated in drafting the reform bill, but by 1960 they had allocated almost $10 million for its implementation and gambled U.S. prestige on the program. As Wolf Ladejinsky, the program's director, later noted, from the earliest stages of land reform "Americans on all levels played an important, and in many ways a catalytic role." But the Diem government's hesitation and fumblings vitiated a program regarded as most essential to the development of an independent South Vietnamese nation. One of the discouraged U.S. specialists concluded: "We can help stimulate action in a certain direction but we cannot substitute our will for their will."

Diem's refusal to adopt satisfactory land reform gave the United States grounds for rescinding aid to his government. The United States alternatively threatened and cajoled Diem, but Diem took the chance that the United States would not cut off aid, and he was right. Washington hoped for better results in other areas.

The price of the Diem regime's inaction was high, both for South Vietnam and the United States. Saigon was doing poorly in the political contest with the Communists for the "hearts and minds" of millions of peasants. Peasant dissatisfaction with the land reform fiasco invited further Communist agitation. By 1959, Communist propagandists were boldly proclaiming their own land reform program in a bid to win over disgruntled peasants. Within two years, the Vietcong controlled large sectors of the population. John Montgomery, an American scholar who spent two years (1957–58) in South Vietnam studying U.S. aid operations, concluded, "The early implementation of land reform under the Diem regime was ... apathetic by comparison with what the Communists had promised and in part carried out."

More disappointments

Two other highly touted features of American economic aid, the Commercial Import Program and the Industrial Development Project, also fell short of their goals. Although the CIP attained its immediate objectives of furnishing much-needed consumer goods and curtailing inflation, it eventually went out of control. Hundreds of import firms sprang up in Saigon to tap the rising inflow of American goods. Licensed by the government, these firms reaped healthy profits by inundating South Vietnam with American-financed wares. Saigon shops and warehouses bulged not only with consumer necessities but also with such luxury items as water skis, hi-fi sets, automobiles, and air conditioners.

As early as 1956 the USAID, at the request of the Senate Foreign Relations Committee, launched an investigation of reports that the South Vietnamese were using the CIP to import excessively expensive luxury goods. Although sensational reports of U.S.-financed Cadillacs traveling the streets of Saigon proved to be unjustified, extensive evidence of South Vietnamese misuse of American bounty forced USAID to reappraise the CIP. In 1957 USAID declared a number of "luxury items" ineligible for import, but the South Vietnamese discovered numerous ways to beat the system. Unwilling to endanger his popularity by reducing the variety of imports, Diem refused to crack down on importers who flagrantly ignored USAID guidelines. In some cases, crooked government officials granted import licenses to shady firms in return for kickbacks of the banned luxuries.

The CIP was inadequate in other ways. Most of the imports stayed in Saigon, giving the capital a prosperous air, while few made their way into the countryside. Many peasants resented the small flow of consumer goods made available to them. When imports did reach rural markets, they came at artificially inflated prices, well beyond peasant means. South Vietnamese middlemen regularly price-gouged on such things as U.S. fertilizer, milk, plastic goods, textiles, and farm tools. Instead of narrowing it, the CIP widened the standard-of-living gap between city and country and further alienated peasants from their urban-based government.

The CIP also undercut other AID program objectives. Intended as a "quick fix" to stimulate South Vietnam's economy, the CIP gradually made the South Vietnamese too dependent on American-financed goods and gave South Vietnamese businessmen little inducement to invest in local production of consumer goods. The South Vietnamese government became so dependent on CIP dollars that it resisted American suggestions to cut back on imports. The more Diem's government imported under the CIP, the greater the counterpart revenues filling its coffers. In fact, taxes on imports constituted Diem's largest single source of public revenue.

U.S. advisers pressed Diem for tax reforms to raise local revenues for his government and thereby to curb his dependence on funds generated by the CIP. Unwilling to enact tax measures that might antagonize his wealthy political supporters, Diem did nothing. As a result, by 1960, only 15,000 out of 14 million South Vietnamese were paying any income taxes at all. A former U.S. adviser stated that the CIP had "led the Vietnamese government to depend on a foreign power instead of its people for its own support. With less aid, the government would probably have . . . engaged in badly needed administration reforms in its assessment and collection of taxes."

Meanwhile, the Diem government used CIP counterpart funds to accrue a large foreign reserve that it deposited in Swiss banks. Between 1955 and 1960 South Vietnam's foreign reserves jumped from $125 million to $216 million. Milton Taylor, a tax specialist with the MSU group from 1959 to 1960, concluded that during this period Vietnam built up "a financial hoard while using American aid for living expenses." American advisers unsuccessfully tried to persuade Diem to use his foreign reserves to offset part of the cost of U.S. aid programs. They were afraid to press the issue too far with Diem, since publicity about South Vietnam's foreign reserve build-up might jeopardize Congressional support for the entire U.S. aid effort.

Just as the Diem regime's misapplication of the CIP exposed its unwillingness to take responsibility for South Vietnam's needs, its mishandling of industrial development showed it was reluctant to invest in the country's economic future. In taking Diem as a partner, the United States had erroneously assumed that Diem's advocacy of political democracy included a commitment to an economy based on free enterprise. Diem, however, did not share the Americans' faith in privately financed industrial growth and did little to encourage industrialization. Impatient American advisers slowly recognized that behind Diem's foot dragging on industrialization was what MSU adviser Milton Taylor called his "suspicion of private businessmen [and] a fear of foreign capital." Diem's brother, Ngo Dinh Nhu, in fact, equated the "evil" of capitalism with that of communism. "Capitalism on one side," he pronounced, "and communism on the other side are profitable for only one class."

A consequence of all this was that interested American companies had great difficulty overcoming South Vietnamese red tape and regulations to obtain approval for their investment plans. From 1955 to 1959, foreign investment in South Vietnam totaled just $26 million, only $1 million of which came from the United States.

Diem spurned Vietnamese as much as American entrepreneurs. An Industrial Development Center was established with American funds but never fulfilled its function as a lending agency to new or existing Vietnamese enterprises. Vietnamese businesses had to wait months, even years, while their applications wound through the bureaucracy. After three years, the center had still acted on only 4 of 100 applications. A South Vietnamese official informed American adviser Robert Scigliano in 1958 that "delays and special screenings were necessary to keep Communists out of the business life of the country."

Americans fumed as their plans for industrial development withered. But they had neglected to coordinate their priorities with Diem's. They also had underestimated Vietnamese hostility to foreign investment, the result of centuries of exploitation by Chinese and French business and industrial interests. When Saigon did agree to undertake modest industrialization on the condition that the government maintain 51 percent control, American aid officials recoiled at the prospect of promoting socialism with U.S. dollars.

On the political side, faith in Diem turned into disillusionment. AID personnel in South Vietnam did what the agency had always done best: funneling U.S. resources—money, equipment, supplies, and advice—to a recipient government. The American aid operation was concentrated in Saigon, where U.S. advisers worked with the central administration of the Diem government. Except for periodic inspection trips into the "field" outside Saigon, American advisers depended primarily on the Diem bureaucracy to deliver services and materials supplied by the U.S., to execute USAID-funded projects, and to reap the expected political benefits. Confident of South Vietnamese administrative competence, "few Americans," wrote former USAID official George Tanham in his book *War Without Guns*, "went out into the countryside to help the government of Vietnam to ascertain the character of the peasants' problems and needs."

American aid specialists gradually realized their trust in South Vietnamese administrative efficiency was misplaced. USAID rural aid consisted, among other things, of well-drilling equipment, maternity and dispensary facilities, medical supplies and services, school buildings, and plowing machines. But occasional spot checks showed that U.S. aid was seldom being used as American technicians expected. Village nurses and midwives frequently turned clinics and hospitals into their homes, depriving patients of valuable space. School buildings often sat vacant because the Ministry of Education had not authorized their opening or had not yet released funds for teachers and books. If water pumps on wells broke down, villagers, lacking maintenance expertise, simply abandoned them.

Because of political corruption and negligence, AID materials often never left Saigon. An American AID administrator stated: "One of the first things I did when I got to Vietnam was to make an inspection trip of Vietnamese government warehouses and walk around the wharves. In one particular place I found about 5 million dollars worth of medical supplies that had been on the wharf for maybe three years. . . . I also found great quantities of educational supplies and other types of commodities." Sometimes bureaucratic callousness kept U.S. aid from villagers, other times it was channeled to enrich corrupt politicians. When a U.S. technician complained, after uncovering medical supplies wasting away in a warehouse, a South Vietnamese official responded, "You Americans are too sentimental. People here always get sick; they will die anyhow."

The U.S. aid mission asked the South Vietnamese to publicize aid projects in order to foster popular support for what the Saigon government was accomplishing with American assistance. The U.S. Information Service made available millions of dollars worth of audiovisual materials and assisted Diem's Ministry of Information in developing mass communication techniques using posters, leaflets, speeches, radio and television broadcasts, and plays and skits. Surveys of Vietnamese villages, however, showed that the dissemination of information about U.S. aid was spotty. In a typical village fifty kilometers south of Saigon, an MSU advisory group survey in 1958 showed "some storekeepers were unable to give examples of American aid, even when surrounded by shelves full of goods brought into Vietnam as part of that aid." A large percentage of villagers "had never heard of American aid and had no idea, correct or incorrect, of how it worked"; some "had actually received loans through the agricultural credit program, but apparently did not think it was related to American aid."

The Diem government's shoddy information program not only irked American advisers but also undermined the political effect of several U.S. aid projects. While Diem's Ministry of Information dawdled, Communist agents disseminated propaganda to discredit the nation-building campaign. They frightened peasants by claiming the government's malaria eradication spraying was harmful to their health. The Communists also dissuaded peasants from using American fertilizer by spreading rumors that it would poison their crops. Their most ingenious tactic gutted the Tilapia Fish Project, conceived by Americans as "a symbol of benevolence and a triumph of technology." Called a "miracle fish" because of its ability to grow and multiply rapidly, the tilapia, an African freshwater fish, was stocked in thousands of village ponds. But the Communists "proved" that eating the tilapia caused leprosy—by inducing lepers to eat the fish and display themselves—and caused the project to collapse.

Why so often did American attempts to "help" the South Vietnamese government toward improvement run into bureaucratic inertia and undisguised opposition? A USAID official suggested an answer: "Our people immediately ran into the traditional Vietnamese bureaucracy . . . a highly centralized government, an official at the local level who does not wish to do anything without higher instruction, and a communication system which guaranteed an answer only ten or fifteen percent of the time and within a time frame of maybe months. We were dealing with people who had been educated by colonial administrators away from their people . . . who had scarcely been out into the countryside and do not know their own people."

American-proposed reforms met with intransigence from South Vietnamese bureaucrats fighting what they took to be, as one put it, "unnecessary foreign meddling" in their government. When the U.S. aid mission sponsored a study to "assist the [Saigon] government in developing sound organization," the Vietnamese finance minister flatly rejected it. "I have no interest in it," he averred. U.S. aid advisers, one of whom professed "we Americans tend to be perfectionists," began trying to force the Vietnamese into action. They focused their inevitable frustrations on the ineptitude of the South Vietnamese. One U.S. adviser described them as "lethargic, inexperienced officials"; another excoriated them for "too many stupid errors."

American advisers accompany Diem's sister-in-law, Madame Ngo Dinh Nhu (left of center in dark glasses), on an inspection tour of a refugee village, one of many U.S. sponsored projects.

The Vietnamese retort to their American advisers frequently was, why don't you try and do it yourself. It was a characteristically American trait to want to do just that. But Diem would not allow it. He balked at U.S. proposals to post American aid technicians in rural areas "to increase the efficiency of aid projects." Foreign aid expert John Montgomery ascribed Diem's refusal to "fear of what inquisitive Americans operating in the field might uncover and report . . . and the hesitance to risk American activities in the countryside that might discredit the regime or outpace its own services to the rural population."

Tigers in the house

In the South Vietnamese view, American critics were ignorant of their country. They quoted an ancient maxim, "In the hallways of my nation, strangers who see little remain strangers. They are, verily, tigers in my house." For the first eight years of U.S. involvement, until as late as 1962, few American civilians lived and worked outside Saigon. Most resided in the capital and within tightly knit American enclaves. There they enjoyed a style of living far above that of the Vietnamese they advised. In fact, according to MSU's Robert Scigliano, the American community lived "far better than it would in the United States."

In 1959 a Senate committee found that the costs of American housing were "excessive." "Most of the areas in Saigon in which Americans lived and moved about," a USAID worker said, "were spacious and well kept, but this fashionable facade . . . hides a shocking contrast: the extremely crowded and small living places of the vast majority of the population." Chauffeur-driven cars transported American advisers to and from work and on business trips around Saigon. The civilians could shop at the U.S. commissary, where they purchased an assortment of foods at discount prices. They established their own food and supply shops, generally avoided patronizing Vietnamese stores, and tried to re-create as much as possible an American environment.

American civilians were not officially restricted from socializing with the Vietnamese, but most chose to remain inside the social life of the American community, or as one AID adviser described it, "the endless cocktail parties, or parties with the American military." There were some dinner parties and other formal affairs attended by Americans and Vietnamese. A U.S. adviser wrote, "I would say I gave a party at least once a month . . . sometimes the Vietnamese would invite me over to their parties."

More personal, intimate relationships with Vietnamese were frowned upon in American circles. When an AID secretary struck up a friendship with a Vietnamese man, she felt pressure from her fellow Americans to cease dating him. Dating Vietnamese men was something, she recalled in a 1967 AID interview, "that American girls don't usually do. 'Those Vietnamese men,' my friends asked, 'how can you like them?' " Even in their professional interaction with Vietnamese, Americans kept their distance. At AID's Education Division in Saigon, the secretary said, "though the Americans were very friendly and talkative with each other, they frowned upon being talkative with the Vietnamese." She also recalled that when she took the trouble to learn Vietnamese, her boss reprimanded her for speaking it with a Vietnamese coworker. "My supervisor blew his stack," she said. He told her, "Don't you speak Vietnamese in this office anymore." In vain she protested, "But this is Vietnam."

Although few spoke Vietnamese or understood local customs and attitudes, some American civilians tried to demonstrate good will to the people. According to Professor Scigliano, several Michigan State University advisers gave professional assistance in their spare time to "interested Vietnamese." A statistics specialist, for example, aided Vietnamese administrators at the National Institute of Statistics, and an economist served as unpaid consultant to the National Bank. On its own initiative, Saigon's 250-member American Women's Association, formed by the wives of U.S. officials and advisers, engaged in charity drives. For one drive, the women made 300 cloth dolls resembling cats and filled them with beans. They donated them to orphanages for use as Christmas gifts with the provision that any extras would be sold to raise funds for the children.

The women later learned that the dolls, each the product of several hours of painstaking work, had been slit open and the beans removed, washed, and eaten. None had reached the Vietnamese children. The Women's Association, an American later explained, "had been looking at Vietnamese orphans, but seeing American children." Bewildering, discouraging encounters like this tempted most American civilians to pull back into the reassuring world of the so-called "Yankee Ghetto." Members of the Women's Association soon concentrated their attention on bridge tournaments among themselves.

Inevitably the self-imposed isolation of the American community provoked strong sentiments among its hosts. An article in the *Dan Viet* newspaper in 1961, based on a public opinion survey, castigated Americans for "never adapting themselves to local life . . . sharing nothing with and getting nothing from the Vietnamese people. They have their own movie houses, restaurants, clubs and sports grounds completely separate from the Vietnamese

people." "It is sad to know that our food is not accepted," a Vietnamese remarked to an American, "especially since it is not always because the guest dislikes it, but because he considers it unclean. Americans would rather lose a friend than risk having diarrhea."

The Americans' "living manner," stated the newspaper *Nguoi Viet Tu Do* in 1958, "creates a gap and does not help consolidate the American-Vietnamese relationship. . . . The majority still remain aloof and do not try to understand the psychology and aspirations of the local people." For the Vietnamese, the inability of many U.S. advisers even to pronounce the name of their country correctly added insult to injury. John Mecklin, chief of the USIS in Saigon from 1962 to 1964, wrote, "it is pronounced 'Vee-Yet-Nahm.' To call it 'Veet-naam,' as many Americans do, is not only wrong, but insulting. In the Vietnamese language this pronunciation translates as 'sick duck.' "

Criticism of the Americans' conduct in South Vietnam reached the U.S. Congress in 1959. The publication of William Lederer's and Eugene Burdick's *The Ugly American* in 1958 had already created a stir by depicting U.S. foreign aid advisers as "naive and out of touch with the people." In addition, six articles in July 1959 by Albert Colgrove, under the headline, "Our Hidden Scandal in Viet Nam," appeared in newspapers across the country, including New York, Washington, D.C., Cleveland, and San Francisco. Colgrove attacked the American community in Saigon for extravagance and elitism. The articles presented an unflattering portrait of Americans living "high on the hog" while collecting high pay and "hardship allowances." It also attacked the U.S. aid program, charging "waste," "bad judgment," and "incompetence."

Public concern over the Colgrove articles provoked a Senate Foreign Relations Subcommittee investigation. In 1960 the subcommittee recommended that Americans going to Vietnam be given improved language and cultural training, that their wages be scaled down, and various allowances and perquisites be reduced. Vice President Richard Nixon called for a severe curtailment of the U.S. advisory program both in Vietnam and other Asian and African nations. He asserted "that there were too many Americans overseas, that they were too conspicuous and that they consequently often created resentment toward the United States."

As war in South Vietnam heated up after 1960, however, Washington decided to increase, not diminish, the size and scope both of the U.S. aid program and the U.S. advisory team. In 1962, American advisers began fanning out from Saigon across the countryside for the first time. The situation was changed. The long-term economic development programs of the peaceful 1950s had shifted to short-term aid measures aimed at thwarting Communist insurgents active in the villages. Now the emphasis was on providing security. Nation-building had been replaced by "pacification."

"Dr. America"

No one personified American ideals of bringing economic, social, and medical assistance to the people of developing countries in the 1950s and 1960s more than Dr. Tom Dooley. Born in St. Louis, Missouri, in 1927, Dooley received his medical degree from St. Louis Medical School in 1953 and was granted a lieutenant's commission in the U.S. Navy. Dooley was determined, his mother Agnes has written, "to be the best doctor in the fleet." He even dreamed of becoming the surgeon general of the navy.

Life held a different destiny for Dr. Tom Dooley. In August 1954 his ship was ordered from Subic Bay in the Philippines to Haiphong Harbor, near Hanoi, in North Vietnam. Dooley's mother called it the "fateful moment of his life." His ship was to participate in "Operation Passage to Freedom," the evacuation of some 1 million North Vietnamese permitted to relocate to South Vietnam by the Geneva accords. Until November 1955, Tom Dooley and a small team of corpsmen helped direct the U.S. refugee assistance program. The navy provided food, clothing, and medical care to hundreds of thousands of refugees. Despite the high heat and humidity and overcrowding of the evacuation vessels, Dooley ministered to the refugees day and night. His weight dropped from 180 to almost 120 pounds. "I have to get it across to our sailors," he said, "that these people are not a stinking mass of humanity, but a great people distressed."

Newspapers around the world praised Tom Dooley's "mission of mercy." Rear Admiral Lamont Pugh commended him for having done "his level best in a great cause." Before Dooley's departure from South Vietnam, South Vietnamese President Ngo Dinh Diem awarded him the medal of Officier de l'Ordre National, the country's highest commendation. "Your medicine and your knowledge have saved many of their [the refugees] lives and brought comfort to their suffering," Diem told Dooley.

Tom Dooley returned to the United States and to his military medical duties, but his involvement in Southeast Asia was not ended. The publishing in 1956 of his account of the Vietnamese refugees, *Deliver Us From Evil*, turned the attention of millions of Americans toward the struggle in South Vietnam, Cambodia, and Laos between Communist and non-Communist forces. Former Ambassador to Thailand Edwin Stanton wrote, "If other true stories were told as effectively as Dr. Dooley's, we might glean from the minds of many the poisonous, communist-inspired picture of an America intent only on the Bomb, and implant in its place the truth."

If Dooley's experiences in Vietnam captured the interest of America, they also inspired him to return to Southeast Asia and resume bringing aid and sustenance to its poverty stricken peoples. "To me," he said in early 1956, "that experience was like the white light of revelation . . . and would take me many miles back to Southeast Asia, to the very edge of tomorrow, where the future might be made or lost." Shortly after, Dooley resigned from the navy and went to Laos to set up a medical mission.

His mission, called Medico, aimed "to give medical care both to the people of the mountains and of the cities, through the Minister of Health of Laos." Medico depended on royalties from Dooley's book, private donations, and skilled volunteers. Dooley advised his five American assistants, "I don't want you standing on some immaculate pedestal reaching down to pull up the poor dirty Asian. You take off your nice white suit, understand? You get off your pedestal and you get down in the mud with them."

Medico's objective was political as well as humanitarian. "We want to take positive steps for America," Dooley affirmed, "not just denying what the Communists say about it. We shall try to translate the democratic ideals we do possess into Asian realities they can possess. Our instrument for this shall be medicine." Dooley's biographer, Lawrence Elliott, described him as "fiercely proud of his country. Every Medico installation flew the American flag and wherever he went, he made it clear that his medicines were a gift of the American people." Dooley's first mission was at Van Vieng in the Laotian mountains. Its free medical care attracted thousand of villagers who fondly referred to him as "Dr. America." Publicity and Dooley's charismatic appeal brought an increase in donations.

By 1960 Medico had a fully operating hospital in Laos and six more in three other Asian nations, including one in South Vietnam at Quang Ngai. Because of his fervid patriotism and anti-communism, Dooley, according to a U.S. government document, "regularly reported on [Communist] troop movements to the CIA." Radio Hanoi and Radio Peking denounced him as an "American spy." But Dooley, according to his colleague, Verne Chaney, saw himself as simply "a good American who reported to his country" and was not a "paid agent." "There wasn't anyone who worked for us," Chaney added, "who didn't relate any information he could to the Ambassador or whoever was in charge."

On January 18, 1961, news of Tom Dooley's death from cancer at the age of thirty-four shocked many. A year after his death, the U.S. Congress awarded Dooley the Legion of Merit "in recognition of the public service to alleviate suffering among people of the world." Dooley's legacy was more than medals and past accomplishments. His mother established the Tom Dooley Foundation in 1961 "to carry out the ideas and work of my son." The foundation enabled Dooley's colleagues to continue their work in Southeast Asia and to undertake new programs in Nepal, India, Uganda, and Somalia. By 1982, the foundation's staff included over thirty doctors, nurses, and medical technicians and had a $1.2 million budget. Its guiding principle is still that of Tom Dooley: "Help with dignity." And the inspiration for those Americans who carry on his work is the example set by Dooley himself. "His real legacy isn't what he did," said Verne Chaney, Tom Dooley Foundation president, but "what he inspired people to do with their own lives."

A World Apart

April 1966. It had been an ordinary day for Information Specialist Larry Hughes, U.S. Army. An early breakfast had been followed by the regular office paperwork, with a break for lunch. After a shower and dinner, Hughes had dropped in at the enlisted men's club for several drinks. Back at his sleeping quarters, he had settled in for a good night's rest. Hughes's daily routine resembled that of many stateside GIs at posts like Fort Dix, New Jersey, Fort Bliss, Texas, or Fort Ord, California. But he was in South Vietnam, a war zone, at the base camp of the 299th Engineer Battalion, twenty kilometers outside of Qui Nhon, on the coast between Da Nang and Cam Ranh Bay.

The picture most Americans had of U.S. troops in South Vietnam was of battle-hardened soldiers slugging it out, day after day, with the Vietcong and North Vietnamese. Nightly across their television screens flashed scenes of American soldiers and marines dashing out of helicopters onto hot LZs, scrambling up hillsides against enemy

positions, and dodging Communist fire as they traversed flooded paddies. But of the 3 million men and women who served in South Vietnam during the war, most experienced no combat. Like Larry Hughes, they were support, logistical, and clerical personnel who lived and worked in rear areas or base camps, relatively secure from the fighting. If the bulk of American troops saw few of their Vietnamese enemies during one-year tours of duty, they also had little contact with ordinary South Vietnamese civilians. They functioned, as one marine officer observed, like a "temporary American community sandwiched" between the Vietnamese.

When American troops began coming to South Vietnam in 1965, the U.S. military command and the Saigon government were mutually concerned about how the considerable introduction of American combat troops would affect South Vietnamese life. "There was a sensitivity there from the beginning," MACV Commander General William Westmoreland later recalled. "We were in a land that was foreign to us both linguistically and culturally. The American population frankly didn't know where Vietnam was." The South Vietnamese government, according to Westmoreland, was "very cognizant of the problem" of having large numbers of U.S. troops deployed in the country and feared traditional Vietnamese xenophobia might trigger a wave of anti-Americanism. Saigon officials expressed concern that an American military presence might fuel inflation, disrupt their society, and contaminate their culture.

Apprehension about the effect of U.S. troop deployment on the South Vietnamese population even entered into the military strategy debate. In part, Westmoreland rejected U.S. Marine proposals for an "enclave strategy" of restricting American troops to the defense of populated coastal areas because he felt the alternative of deploying them against big enemy units in sparsely populated inland regions "also meant that much less provocation of the xenophobia of the Vietnamese, that much

Preceding page. *Vietnamese women wait to enter the American base at Cam Ranh Bay where they serve as cooks, maids, and interpreters.*

less opportunity for unfortunate incidents between the American troops and the people."

To avoid disrupting South Vietnamese society, MACV located American bases, where possible, away from population centers. In March 1966 General Westmoreland took action to reduce the number of Americans in Saigon, long the site of MACV headquarters and an entry point for incoming troops. Under Operation MOOSE (Move out of Saigon Expeditiously) he ordered several thousand U.S. military personnel stationed in Saigon to remove to barracks outside the city. They relocated to a new base complex at Long Binh, twenty-five kilometers northeast of Saigon. Westmoreland also transferred MACV headquarters to Tan Son Nhut air base, five kilometers outside Saigon. "The relocations," Westmoreland said, "had the effect of moving thousands of American soldiers away

from the [Saigon] population and reducing the likelihood of incidents."

MACV also declared Saigon and Da Nang off limits. It sought to prevent soldiers from circulating American dollars in the South Vietnamese economy by issuing military scrip. For American dollars could be traded on the black market for piasters at an exchange rate higher than the legal limit, causing the inflation of South Vietnamese currency. In addition, MACV ordered that military leaves be spent outside South Vietnam at one of ten designated cities including Hong Kong, Bangkok, Tokyo, and Honolulu, and instituted a savings program with a 10 percent interest rate to encourage troops to deposit rather than spend their pay.

Anxious to keep U.S. troops from behaving in ways that might antagonize the Vietnamese, MACV gave each member of the U.S. armed forces in South Vietnam a card listing "Nine Rules of Conduct." These rules enjoined U.S. soldiers, in their contacts with Vietnamese, to "treat women with politeness and respect," "always give the Vietnamese the right of way," and "don't attract attention by loud, rude or unusual behavior." The generally young, boisterous, and often careless American troops inevitably violated at least one or more of the "Nine Rules." Saigon officials received a litany of complaints from Vietnamese. Vietnamese civilians complained, for example, that U.S. vehicles forced them off the road and roared at high speed through their villages. They also protested about being insulted and mistreated by American troops and being struck by objects thrown by Americans from passing trucks.

In a 1971 poll by U.S. officials of Vietnamese opinions of U.S. troops, the Americans were described as "drunkards, haughty, licentious men who ... seemed indifferent to accidents for which they were responsible." An American lieutenant summed up the problem. "The GI," he said, "isn't tolerant. Never has been. ... I've never seen the place where GIs could get along with the local populace. Our boys are full of fighting spirit, whiskey, women. ... Indeed, they disrupt civilian communities here, in the States, and wherever they are assigned overseas."

Soldiers and civilians

Resigned to the likelihood of trouble between Vietnamese civilians and American servicemen, U.S. commanders decided to restrict the troops to base whenever possible. Engineer Commander Robert Ploger explained, "It wasn't our country. We were there to make the least adverse impact on the population we could, and consequently we kept our people close to home." Sergeant Richard Grefath of the 101st Airborne Division recalls a dozen official warnings by an officer at the 101st's rear base in Bien Hoa that "the only place that's authorized is the battlefield. You

Constructed by RMK-BRJ, the colossal U.S. base at Cam Ranh Bay included a deep-water pier, thirty-six warehouses, and a billeting for 10,000 troops.

have no business in any civilian area. Anytime an M.P. sees a 101st patch on your shoulders and you're walking through a town somewhere, you'll be stopped."

Sergeant Biff Morse, a clerk with Headquarters, 75th Support Battalion, 1st Brigade, 5th Infantry Division, in Quang Tri, remembers being "restricted to base unless it was official duty. The only time we were allowed to go anywhere was on official duty." Official duty for rear base personnel usually meant transporting supplies or equipment. A supply sergeant at Bien Hoa, for example, "had to go into civilian areas like Saigon for laundry runs. Everybody would have dirty laundry and it would have to be brought in to be cleaned."

Travel restrictions were not uniformly applied, nor were they always strictly observed. For one thing, the air force adopted a policy that allowed its personnel to move more flexibly than did the marines. American troops stationed in cities like Saigon, while barred from residential neighborhoods, could enter commercial areas during the day but had to leave before dark. According to marine Lieutenant Charles Anderson, although Saigon "was heavily patrolled by air force and army MPs," curfew regulations "were widely broken." Curfew times in civilian areas often varied, depending upon the judgment of unit commanders and the location. Rank also counted. Noncoms and officers enjoyed more discretion about "going into town." Colonel John Gibney of the 1st Cavalry Division has said "that Saigon might have been restricted partially, but I went in there . . . those regulations had almost zero impact on me." A sergeant, E-5 or higher, said Lieutenant Charles Anderson, could wangle a night off the base at Da Nang if he had "a good reason." But for most soldiers such exceptions, said Sergeant Richard Grefath, were not common: "I was in Vietnam for a year and three months and left base just two times."

Consideration for Vietnamese sensitivities was not General Westmoreland's only motive for trying to confine U.S. troops to base. MACV had not forgotten the grim efficiency with which the Vietcong, since the early 1960s, had terrorized American soldiers with grenade attacks and bombings, even in secure areas like Saigon. After the Vietcong strike against Pleiku in 1967, the military placed all private homes, alleyways, and even an ARVN ammunition dump there off limits. Following the 1968 Tet offensive, MACV enforced even more rigorous strictures on off-duty troops wanting to leave their base.

At Quang Tri, which MACV designated "high risk," U.S. bases observed maximum security procedures. Sergeant Biff Morse was surprised when headquarters forbade his unit even to hire Vietnamese day laborers. "They finally told us straight out," he said, "80 percent of the people in the province were either in the VC or supporting the VC." First Air Cavalry Commander General Harry Kinnard explained the rationale: "My basic policy was that we didn't allow in laundry men, or people who worked in the messes or anything else, and the reason that I made that rule was very simple. It was difficult to tell the differences between the Viet Cong and the friendly, or potentially friendly Vietnamese."

Military commanders constantly reiterated to soldiers the risks of being out among the Vietnamese. During certain alerts MACV ordered soldiers to travel in pairs. It also prohibited soldiers from riding in any vehicles driven by a Vietnamese civilian. Engineer Commander Major General Robert Ploger cautioned his troops, "If you're wandering around at night someplace, you don't know who's a VC and who isn't . . . don't go out and get wiped out by somebody."

Disturbing stories about soldiers wounded or killed by seemingly harmless Vietnamese heightened troop vigilance. Don Luce, an American who worked for the International Voluntary Services, told how "the Vietcong on occasion have sent young girls to lure marines and soldiers off the base and invite them to their death. Near Da Nang three marines saw three girls swimming nude in a stream and went to 'investigate.' A few minutes later one marine lay dead in the stream and the other two were missing, victims of a 'seduce and destroy mission.'" U.S. troops also had to beware of street vendors who occasionally became merchants of death. Vendors sometimes inserted explosive charges under the wicks of cigarette lighters purchased by GIs. When the soldier used the lighter, it would blow up in his face. A young soldier who had a chunk of his face blown off this way said "he had bought the lighter at a good price from an innocent looking lady."

Venereal disease contracted from Vietnamese prostitutes also threatened the health of American soldiers. Since American soldiers often could not get to town, hordes of Vietnamese prostitutes came out to them, working out of shacks and bars just outside American bases. On a rear base, "if a guy wanted a real girl, not a fantasy," a marine stated, "he had to break the rules." Soldiers at Da Nang discovered the guards could sometimes "be counted on to look the other way at night while a hole developed in the fence." A sergeant even started his own prostitution racket just inside the compound. He stationed his prostitute in a storage shed, where "on a typical night [she] made between five and ten trips" with soldiers. "She was allowed to keep half of the ten dollar fee, and the rest went into a [base] club 'Improvement Fund.'" Soldiers at other bases engaged in similar "covert operations."

During the troop build-up, according to General Westmoreland, venereal disease became "prevalent" among American soldiers. By 1966, the VD rate of the 1st Air Cavalry Division was 34 percent. Besides tightening base restrictions, the military commenced an information campaign about the perils of prostitutes. Lurid rumors also floated around about prostitutes secreting broken glass or razor blades in their vaginas. Other stories warned soldiers about contracting a supposedly incurable VD, "the

Culture Shock

"Good bird, lotta words. Lotta words, good bird," insisted an eighty-year-old Vietnamese woman in her crammed Saigon street stall. Towering over her, a black sergeant, among the first combat soldiers sent to Vietnam, haggled over the price of a parrot. But even as the old woman sang its virtues, she revealed "the awful truth": the bird did not know English. The homesick soldier moaned, "A parrot who speaks Vietnamese ain't no good to me. How'm I gonna talk to a bird who don't speak English?"

This kind of bewilderment was shared by most American soldiers stationed in South Vietnam. Transported halfway around the world to a strange Asian country, American soldiers marveled at the startling blueness of the South China Sea, the fiery fanaticism of saffron-robed Buddhists, and the tangled vines of endless jungle that bred dysentery and malaria. They listened, perplexed, to the seeming birdlike twittering of the Vietnamese language. Accustomed to a "sterilized" society of flush toilets and garbage disposals, they recoiled at their first sight of a Vietnamese peasant pulling down her drawers, squatting, and defecating in a rice field; or of a Vietnamese family throwing greasy food scraps on the floor of their crude hootch.

The cultural shock experienced by the GIs had been anticipated by their military superiors long before U.S. combat troops were sent to Vietnam. One early plan to reduce cultural conflicts came from General William C. Westmoreland. In May 1964, Westmoreland recommended to Secretary of Defense Robert McNamara that the U.S. government sponsor some kind of "people-to-people" program in order to foster an emotional bond between Americans and Vietnamese. The city of Boston could "adopt" the city of Da Nang, he suggested as an example, and could organize a Vietnam-

ese-American cultural exchange program. This people-to-people concept was conceived primarily as an information campaign directed at the American home front. An emotional attachment to the Vietnamese people, Westmoreland hoped, might provide an incentive for American perseverance in a long, drawn-out war "that would go beyond any engendered by a strategic American interest in Southeast Asia."

For American soldiers prepped for combat, military requirements dictated a limited amount of time for cultural indoctrination. In contrast to the programs set up for military advisers that stressed language study and lessons on Vietnamese history, instruction on Vietnamese culture for U.S. soldiers was brief and somewhat superficial. Along with the Nine Rules of Conduct, GIs received a small brochure that contained translations of key phrases and a cursory description of Vietnam. Further training was left to the discretion of individual commanders, who received such guidance as "Keep your officers and men well-informed of the Nine Rules of Conduct."

By 1968, MACV's repertoire of "good manners" toward the Vietnamese included corrections of common mistakes made by GIs in years past. For instance, indoctrination officers warned incoming soldiers to respect Vietnamese superstitions, such as the fear that cameras could steal a person's soul and that evil spirits could escape through the soles of feet. They urged soldiers to steer clear of areas the Vietnamese revered, like cemeteries and temples. They informed the troops, "It is not proper to walk hand-in-hand with a Vietnamese woman."

Military instructors occasionally passed on misinformation. Sergeant Biff Morse, a clerk with Headquarters, 75th Support Battalion, 1st Brigade, 5th Infantry Division, remembers that the "so-called military experts ... talked a lot about life not being as important to Orientals as it is to Caucasians. ... And they talked about the water buffalo more as a religious symbol than as an economic necessity." From his own observations, Morse learned that "shooting a water buffalo would be comparable to shooting someone's Mercedes automobile back in the United States, or even worse, destroying a farmer's tractor."

Some information that the military disseminated to American servicemen unintentionally antagonized their Vietnamese hosts. Fearful that South Vietnam's antiquated aqueducts made even city water undrinkable, MACV correctly instructed soldiers to boil tap water at least twenty minutes before drinking it and, when that was not possible, to add an iodine tablet to each quart. Native vegetables and unpeeled fruits were proscribed as possible sources of infection; the United States imported foodstuffs, even bananas and rice, all cleansed and disinfected, in order to satisfy both the sanitary and dietary needs of servicemen. To avoid diarrhea, the soldiers were told, "Put your chopsticks into the steaming rice as soon as it arrives in order to sanitize them."

The Vietnamese observed with amazement and chagrin the Americans' determination to abstain from Vietnamese cuisine and customs. "Who," one confided to an American journalist, "had ever dreamed of so many toilet paper rolls ... so many pills and tablets and stuff to make lettuce safe to eat?" Although many Vietnamese took offense at these measures, others playfully exploited American vulnerability.

In Bao Trai, Hau Nghia Province, local officials invited their American military adviser, Captain Stuart A. Herrington, to a traditional Vietnamese feast of dog meat as a celebration of their recent victory against the enemy. Anxious to please his counterparts, Herrington complied. "As I plowed my way through dog fondue, dog spareribs, and canine cutlets, Sang and his friends observed me gleefully," he recalled. "They were, I knew, engaged in one of the Orient's favorite sports—having fun with a Westerner." After finishing his seventh course, Herrington discovered that the gruesome ordeal had paid off. "Sang's men were full of praise for my performance. I was now the American captain who knew their language and [ate their food]. ... This was no mean achievement in their eyes."

But Herrington was an exception. The average American demanded an English-speaking parrot and had to eat sterilized food. Not surprisingly, the Vietnamese echoed the same complaint. "The Americans spend huge sums of money to assist us," said one, "but they pay almost no attention to our culture."

black, rare Oriental strain." "Once you got it," a serviceman remembers hearing, "it was all over." Another soldier recalled hearing about the terrible fate rumored to befall those who caught it: "The victims would be quarantined for life on a small island in the South China Sea, never to see the States again." Many American troops suspected their military commanders were behind the rumors. "I wouldn't put it past them," surmised Sergeant Richard Grefath. "I wouldn't doubt for one minute that the military started rumors like that as part of their program to discourage civilian contact."

When neither regulations nor rumors could deter troops from the prostitutes surrounding their bases, some military commanders used a tactic formerly employed by the French to abate the VD epidemic. At An Khe, General Kinnard "reluctantly accepted as the best among unhappy alternatives" a proposal by An Khe's chief magistrate to build a separate "entertainment area" exclusively for the 1st Cav troops stationed there. *Time* magazine called it "Disneyland East, a 25-acre sprawl of boumboum (sex) parlors." The Vietnamese women who staffed the parlors had to obtain an ID card proving they had received regular medical examinations and penicillin shots.

"Disneyland East" achieved its objective. The VD count among Kinnard's troops dropped. A few other commanders followed An Khe's example. At Pleiku, for example, a compound called "The Rest Center" featured licensed prostitutes serving U.S. troops. After adverse publicity in American newspapers "tarred" him for legitimizing prostitution, Kinnard defended his actions: "The houses were there, and the girls were there, and since soldiers were going to find access to them, I was trying to give them a fair shot at not picking up some kind of extremely virulent venereal disease."

The comforts of home

While maintaining its policy of trying to isolate American troops from the Vietnamese, MACV also recognized the possible morale problems that might afflict soldiers cooped up on base. This especially applied to the hundreds of thousands of American support troops stationed at rear bases like Qui Nhon, Phu Bai, Bien Hoa, Tan Son Nhut, Cam Ranh, Nha Trang, and Da Nang. There the chief enemy was boredom, the tedium of routine support jobs, and the military regimen. The military instituted a substantial program to meet soldiers' demands for recreation, entertainment, consumer goods, and services. U.S. Headquarters Support Activity Special Services operated recreation facilities throughout South Vietnam. In the Saigon area troops had their choice of an air-conditioned library, a twelve-lane air-conditioned bowling center, a photo laboratory, a swimming pool, a craft workshop, and athletic facilities for handball, badminton, softball, basketball, and tennis. Soldiers could even rent boats for cruis-

ing or water-skiing on the Saigon River. Other large base areas like Da Nang, Cam Ranh, Vung Tau, and Bien Hoa had similar facilities. At smaller bases, however, recreational facilities were much less elaborate.

Except for those in combat, soldiers got three hot meals a day. Sometimes there were stateside-type barbecues. The menu at messes and snack bars listed sizzling steaks, hamburgers, French fries, and ice cream. Military messes near Saigon had adjoining cocktail lounges, and every rear base contained one or more enlisted men's, noncoms', and officers' clubs dispensing potato chips and pretzels to be washed down with liquor and ice-cold beer. When American journalist Desmond Smith joined a group of American soldiers drinking beer at Tan Son Nhut air base at the end of 1966, a tipsy GI quipped, "Just like Fort Benning, isn't it?"

Entertaining the troops became a full-time operation for the soldiers assigned to the Army/Air Force Exchange Service, Pacific. The exchange operated over 300 enlisted men's, noncoms', and officers' clubs in South Vietnam. The U.S. base at Long Binh alone had over 30 officers' clubs. Most servicemen's clubs contained a juke box, a pool table, dice, and pinball machines. The Bob Hope Show toured only once a year, at Christmas time, but American, Australian, and Filipino entertainers performed at U.S. installations year-round. There was a procession of standup comedians, dance troupes, rock 'n' roll combos, go-go girls, and striptease acts. American singer Jan Brinker, unknown in the U.S., was a headliner on the GI circuit. Said Brinker, "We're here for the money, but we also feel an obligation to do what we can for the men out here in South Vietnam."

Soldiers could also see two or three movies a week or listen to the latest pop hits from the United States on Armed Forces Radio. On the larger bases like Da Nang and Tan Son Nhut, American soldiers could tune into favorite shows like "Gunsmoke" and "Combat" on the Armed Forces Television Network. They could also get away from it all with three days at the rest and recreation resort at Vung Tau, on the coast just south of Saigon. Every enlisted man, during his one-year tour, could put in for a three-day stay at Vung Tau. The resort could accommodate 260 men at a time with its bars, gift shops, restaurants, athletic facilities, and a beach protected by barbed wire and armed guards.

As on U.S. overseas bases around the world nothing symbolized the Americanized world on U.S. installations in South Vietnam more than the Post Exchange, the PX. In 1966, the military spent $45 million to expand its PX system to the many new U.S. bases being built in South Vietnam, in the hope of diverting inflationary U.S. dollars from the local economy. The PX system quickly grew into a big business. In 1967 alone, it stocked base PXs with a total of $150 million worth of goods, including all kinds of modern accessories. At most PXs, shelves overflowed with candy,

U.S. enlisted men take advantage of the sun deck and pool at the recreational complex at Long Binh, the army's headquarters in South Vietnam, in September 1969.

A Tonic for the Troops

For many American soldiers in South Vietnam the Bob Hope Christmas show was one of the highlights of a holiday season spent far from home. From 1964 to 1972, Hope's touring group of comedians, singers, dancers, and musicians entertained hundreds of thousands of troops at U.S. bases in South Vietnam. In 1966 alone Hope's show played before nearly half the American troops in Southeast Asia. In addition to the jokes of Hope and Phyllis Diller and the singing performances of Vic Damone and Sammy Davis, Jr., the troops were offered the pleasing sights of Joey Heatherton and Raquel Welch and a dance group called the Golddiggers. After eight years of Christmas shows Bob Hope said, "We'll never forget them ... the "River Rats" of Dong Tam, the "grunts" of Pleiku, the Marines at Danang and Chu Lai, and all the fighter pilots on the carriers in the South China Sea."

Sammy Davis, Jr., and troupe entertain thousands of troops during the Bob Hope Show at Cam Ranh Bay, Christmastime, 1972.

Raquel Welch, one of the performers touring with the Bob Hope Show, dazzles GIs at Da Nang in December, 1967.

A "veteran" of three wars, Bob Hope waits to entertain the troops at his annual Christmas show at Long Binh on December 28, 1969.

cookies, potato chips, peanut butter and jelly, cheese dips, and other foodstuffs, soft drinks by the case, and numerous brands of beer and liquor. PXs also had for sale an array of transistor radios, TV sets, books and magazines, tape recorders and tape decks, stereos and records, aftershave lotions, and many other comforts of home.

The PXs of major bases like Da Nang and Cam Ranh Bay often sold such luxury merchandise as pearl necklaces, opal pendants, ruby earrings, diamond rings, and expensive perfumes. Army Chaplain Robert Falabella explained the symbolism the soldiers attached to the PX. "In some ways," he said, "the PX was a vestige of the world they left back in the States. There in the PX you could do for a few moments what thousands of Americans were doing back home in the States (or the "world" as the troops called it)—namely, buying things—even if you didn't need them. It was the great American way—coming out of a store with a bag filled with goodies."

Lieutenant General Joseph Heiser, former commander of the U.S. Army's 1st Logistical Command in South Vietnam, scolded commanders for "desiring to give their personnel the very highest possible levels of comfort and quality of food . . . far in excess of that authorized by Tables of Organization and Equipment." Retired army General Hamilton Howze in a 1975 article in *Army* magazine criticized "the practice of providing too many luxuries in base camps, including barracks and clubs. We fought

World War II without these and they were not necessary in the soldier's short twelve-month tour in Vietnam. Our base camps became too elaborate, soaked up too much manpower, diverted our attention from the basic mission and lessened our operational flexibility." A November 1971 Senate subcommittee report said it found "almost incredible the vast plethora of clubs, slot machines, steambaths, luxury purchases, and other nonessentials which were flourishing in a war zone."

"Too many luxuries" not only "burdened an already heavily taxed logistical system," Lt. Gen. Heiser said, but spawned military corruption. American soldiers of all ranks contrived to siphon off millions of dollars worth of goods from the military's gushing pipeline. They also misappropriated such necessities as medicines, clothing, gasoline, and construction materials. As logistics commander at Headquarters Support Activity Saigon during the U.S. build-up in 1965 and 1966, navy Captain Archie Kuntze carved out a financial empire for himself through his control of $100 million in government funds. He led the life of a swinging bachelor in an elegant Saigon villa and drove the only official vehicle in South Vietnam with white sidewall tires. The wheeling-dealing Kuntze jauntily proclaimed himself the "mayor of Saigon."

After an investigation discovered "serious personal misconduct on his part," a 1966 navy board of inquiry charged Kuntze with currency violations, misappropria-

tion of military funds, and personal indiscretions, including helping his Chinese mistress obtain a PX card and smuggle cloth into South Vietnam aboard a U.S. military aircraft. The navy dissolved Kuntze's headquarters unit and shipped him out to the 12th Naval District Headquarters in San Francisco. A court-martial pronounced him guilty of "conduct unbecoming an officer" but acquitted him on charges of "perjury" and "exchanging cash for U.S. Treasury checks under false pretenses." Kuntze's punishment was an official reprimand and a 100-place drop on the officer seniority list for promotion.

Corruption also permeated the Army/Air Force Exchange Service responsible for managing South Vietnam's servicemen's clubs. Noncommissioned officers used extortion and bribery to pocket part of $27 million collected annually from slot machines in servicemen's clubs. The army, for example, indicted army Sergeant Major William Wooldridge in 1971 for skimming illicit profits from the club system, physically threatening an officer who probed his activities, and using MACV Commander Creighton Abrams's personal plane to transport whiskey in and out of South Vietnam. He was allowed to retire without trial or punishment. Master Sergeant William Higdon, manager of one of the biggest club systems, was tried and convicted of similar violations. He was dishonorably discharged and fined $25,000. A common scam for NCO club managers was taking kickbacks from talent agents for booking their acts. "You book for $500 and slip $100 back to the manager," admitted the leader of one troupe. "Some of them want to stay honest, but if one plays, everybody has to play."

When the "sergeants' scandal" finally broke in 1971, the U.S. Army's Criminal Investigation Division accused its senior officer, Major General Carl C. Turner, of having refused to permit it to investigate the network of sergeants who illegally profited from their operation of clubs. An investigation that summer by the Senate Permanent Subcommittee on Investigations of Government Operations also castigated the military command in South Vietnam for inadequate supervision of the club system. Although the military could not bring General Turner, who had already retired, to trial, it did revoke his Distinguished Service Medal.

The material abundance at U.S. bases, particularly rear bases, had other detrimental effects. The comfort and benefits accorded the men, coupled with their restriction to base, tended to detach them, psychologically as well as physically, from the war around them. Watching the sights and listening to the sounds of battle off in the distance from the comfortable, secure, Americanized environment of their bases, soldiers had an eerie sense of being involved in an "unreal war."

The impression many rear area troops took home from Vietnam was often the bizarre feeling of having been

Only generals and select colonels could enjoy this "command mess" located at Long Binh. Renowned for its superb service, the restaurant rivaled many first-class night spots in the United States. Inset. *Astronaut Frank Borman (second from right) stops for a command mess luncheon at Long Binh on December 11, 1969, during a worldwide tour to publicize the plight of American POWs.*

mere spectators of a war. Marine Lieutenant Charles Anderson, at Da Nang, wrote of how "once a week someone in the club who was not yet half-paralyzed on a combination of beer and whiskey and thoughts of willing women at home would perceive through loud beery voices and the jukebox the drone overhead of an old converted Air Force DC-3 ('Puff the Magic Dragon') and the muffled staccato of its guns answering the call of a nearby unit in trouble . . . and then lead six or eight others outside. . . . The group would sit and watch and listen through eyes and ears fuzzy with beer a battle less than two miles away. With a cold beer in hand they could watch the area framed by red tracer bullets, the area where frantic men, Vietnamese and American, were fighting and trying to survive and dying."

While the goods and services available on U.S. bases were intended to enhance morale, the incongruity perceived by Anderson had an unsettling effect on many soldiers. "When a man arrived he thought at first that he was going to a war," one of them said, "(but) it was like being on a peaceful assignment in garrison back home. The war itself was a very remote thing occurring only in isolated instances for some troops." An air force major observed that "the whole atmosphere at Tan Son Nhut was rather ludicrous. Here there was a war going on in a country which, as you flew over it, was obviously pock-marked by bombs and destruction of all types. We'd return to our base at the end of a flight and there would be rock bands and go-go dancers and clubs and PXs loaded with all the finery of home. . . . It was a very, very strange contrast that many of us never quite got used to. We had all the comforts of home while the hardships of the war were so vividly and so painfully seen in the faces of the South Vietnamese people."

The good life in the rear not only disconcerted some support troops, but infuriated combat troops forced to spend their one-year tour humping hills or hacking through the bush. Many grunts returning from patrol to base came to despise rear-echelon personnel for not sharing the risks of combat. A former army officer wrote, "After spending a week on an area sweep, sodden from rain, filthy from the mud through which they had straggled, constantly alert to a point far beyond exhaustion by fear of ambush . . . a unit would limp back to base camp. Returning, they encountered soldiers of all ranks . . . wearing clean clothes and smelling of aftershave lotion, men who were secure in mind and body from the damage of war."

"Those REMFs [Rear-Echelon Mother-Fuckers] don't even know what Vietnam is all about," a grunt stated. Special Forces soldier Dave Christian said, "They were collecting their combat pay at our expense, and telling their war stories at our expense." Ironically, while they resented the privileges and benefits accorded rear-echelon personnel, many disgruntled combat soldiers requested transfers from the infantry to a support unit.

Reaching out

Although MACV preferred to isolate American soldiers for economic, social, and security reasons, it did permit "goodwill" contacts under specified conditions. Approved military community programs included Civic Action and County Fairs. Civic Action provided mostly medical assistance—inoculations, cholera shots, and sanitation training to villagers—and helped build or repair community facilities. General Harry Kinnard described the 1st Air Cavalry's version of Civic Action: "What we tried to do was to find out what it was that they thought they needed, rather than what we thought might be good for them."

GIs also distributed emergency food and clothing throughout South Vietnam. From 1965 to 1969 military units conducted numerous civilian assistance drives. In one week in April 1966 the 3d Marine Amphibious Force in I Corps supplied needy villagers with 11,289 pounds of food and 240 pounds of shirts and pants. In II Corps the first and second brigades of the 1st Cavalry Division (Airmobile) sponsored a Boy Scout jamboree and provided toilet facilities and 450 bars of soap to nine different villages. The 101st Airborne Division in III Corps gave medical care to 1,305 villagers, repaired three kilometers of roads for rice harvesting, and conducted English classes. And in IV Corps American military advisers vaccinated 350 people, offered both cement and engineering expertise for the building of a new village marketplace, and built a playground.

The Civic Action program also treated Vietnamese villagers to entertainment, such as concerts, and gave games and toy kits to children. The County Fair Program, a joint U.S. Marine–ARVN effort, conducted similar operations. Several platoons of U.S. Marines and Vietnamese soldiers would surround a hamlet while other platoons searched it for VC. Then the marines would distribute food to villagers and administer medical treatment, and South Vietnamese officials would organize dramatic skits and show movies. MEDCAP was a more specialized form of Civic Action. MEDCAP teams, made up of several navy corpsmen escorted by a marine rifle squad, regularly held sick calls in villages near marine bases. They dispensed medicine to villagers and trained local volunteers in rudimentary health care practices.

Many soldiers made informal gestures of friendship toward the Vietnamese. Marine Sergeant John D. Moss, for example, bought a pony in mid-1965 near Da Nang and offered free rides to Vietnamese children. At Phu Bai, marines periodically organized "scrub-ins" for nearby villagers' babies. Army Captain Ronald Rod, before a sniper killed him in December 1965, collected enough money and supplies to fund an orphanage. Soldiers with children at home found giving a helping hand to Vietnamese children particularly rewarding. "Kids are the same everywhere," one soldier said. "It makes us feel good to be constructive."

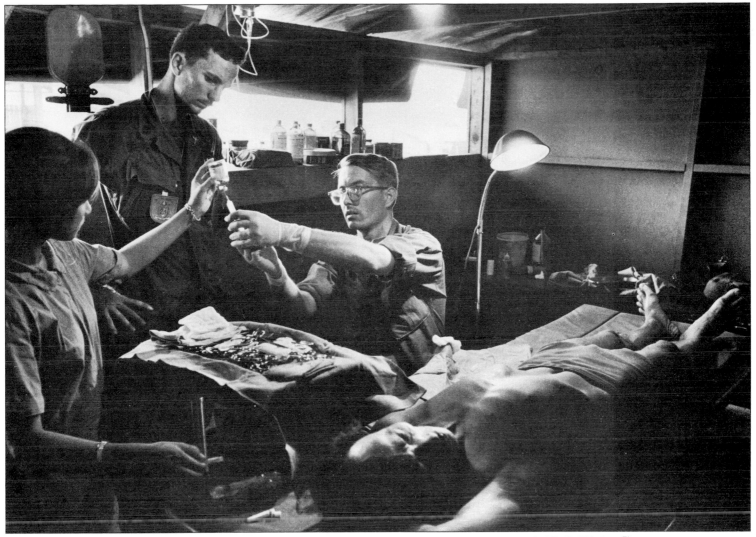

Dr. Kenneth R. Case, Jr., (with glasses) and his assistant Specialist Robert Smith of the 29th Civil Affairs Company, prepare for surgery. The montagnard patient lost his thumb when he was hit by shrapnel.

Inefficiency, cultural obstacles, and misunderstandings, however, robbed these American initiatives of much of their good will. Lieutenant Colonel Robert Chandler, a former air force intelligence officer in South Vietnam, found that "problems plagued the civic action activities. Projects had to be abandoned before completion when they were interrupted by combat requirements, and schools were constructed when no teachers were available. In other cases, soap, candy, gum, coins, clothing, and similar items were handed out in the spirit of charity, but those acts sometimes caused friction because those most in need were often overlooked." Matters of custom and belief also interfered. For example, Americans sometimes dug wells for villagers in places the Vietnamese believed were haunted by "ancestral ghosts." In such cases, the wells were not used.

The major stumbling block to mutual good will was the Vietnamese attitude toward the assistance the Americans were dispensing. American correspondent Neil Sheehan, in a 1966 article for the *New York Times*, gave this analysis: "The Vietnamese live in a relatively harsh society where charity is not a common phenomenon. Thus since the Vietnamese normally do not entertain charitable notions themselves, they do not attribute them to others." American studies of Vietnamese villagers confirm this. In the Mekong Delta hamlet of Khanh Hau, James Hendry, an MSU economics professor, found "little sense of community spirit" among the villagers he was studying. Another study of a village near Saigon noted: "Neighbors and relatives outside the immediate family do not appear to tend each other's business, nor do they frequently get involved in helping each other—even in times of emergency."

Not surprisingly, then, the Vietnamese often viewed American giving with suspicion and hostility. Even GI friendliness toward children was sometimes resented. Parents, for instance, felt if a child accepted gifts the entire family lost face. The sullen response of many Vietnamese toward U.S. generosity befuddled and offended American soldiers. Why were people they were trying to help so ungrateful? This question was on the mind of Army Chaplain Robert Falabella in 1967 after he accompanied a GI, who wished to adopt a child, to a Vietnamese orphanage.

The Vietnamese orphanage director, said Falabella, told them, "Come back tomorrow." When he asked, "Couldn't you at least give him [the GI] some printed information he could read?" the director replied curtly, "We are closed. Come back tomorrow." Falabella grew angry and said, "Is this all the consideration you can give this American who has such concern and respect for your people?" The director ignored him.

Some soldiers bristled at instances when Vietnamese repaid intended kindness by taking advantage of them. One soldier recalled numerous occasions in which youngsters that the GIs befriended stole from them. Another soldier derided the Vietnamese as "nothing but thieves." Psychiatrist Robert Jay Lifton during interviews with American veterans of the war detected the Americans' "sense of estrangement among ungrateful and viciously sly people . . . squeezing out the Yankee dollar." Unfortunately, the more material assistance American soldiers allotted to the Vietnamese, the more frustrating and unfulfilling the experience. Noncombat contacts with Vietnamese, in Lifton's words, became "characterized by hopeless contradictions and deceptions."

A deep culture gap made it difficult for soldiers seeking personal encounters with Vietnamese. The Americans had inadequate understanding of Vietnamese language and customs. General Charles Timmes, deputy and then chief of the Military Assistance Advisory Group in Vietnam from 1960 to 1964 and special adviser to the U.S. Embassy in Saigon from 1967 to 1975, has stated that few American soldiers "knew the first thing about the Vietnamese language, the country's nationalism or its policies, its culture." Chaplain Falabella recalled the orientation briefing he attended after arriving in South Vietnam. "It turned out," he said, "to be a boring repeat performance of what we had learned from our Vietnam orientation back in the States. Slides were shown of Vietnam as if we were coming to the country as tourists."

General Westmoreland explained the limitations involved. "You've got to get in so much in a relatively short time, you've only got the men for two years. . . . How do you allocate that time? . . . You've got a soldier, seventeen or eighteen years old. You put him in a lecture hall and try to teach him the culture of Vietnam. The chances are it goes through one ear and out the other. He doesn't give it much priority." The comments of Sergeant Richard Grefath reflected the feelings of many soldiers. "The training was to teach you how to fight a war," he observed. "I really don't remember a lot of details about lessons on Vietnamese language and culture. . . . At the time I was distracted from really learning. I was thinking more about staying alive."

Even when individual soldiers did bridge the culture gap between themselves and the Vietnamese, feelings of anti-Americanism and the exigencies of war often made personal relationships difficult. A navy NCO, who said he was "critical of sexual exploitation [of Vietnamese women] on the part of the American military," developed a close friendship with a woman. Although, according to the NCO, they experienced "mutual sensitivity and consideration," the woman had to break off the relationship. She told him "that her seeing me made her a prostitute in the eyes of her country." A GI who cultivated what he called a "caring relationship" with a middle-aged Vietnamese woman and her daughter found "that breaking out of the gook syndrome was going against the system." The Vietnamese woman he befriended was killed by the VC because "she associated with the Americans." The bitter GI concluded, "It's better to leave them alone."

A U.S. serviceman and a Vietnamese woman who desired to marry confronted official restraints and red tape. MACV would not grant soldiers permission to marry until ninety days prior to their date of departure. Even though the process of obtaining a marriage license was tedious, more than 6,000 Vietnamese-American marriages—most of them involving U.S. military personnel—took place between 1965 and 1972. Relationships between American soldiers and Vietnamese women that did not end so happily often left the sad legacy of an unwanted Amerasian child. Although the U.S. State and Defense departments have kept no statistics, unofficial estimates of Amerasian children born during the war varied in 1984 from 15,000 to as high as 200,000. Donald Scott, executive director of My Friend's House, a nonsectarian orphanage, put the figure at 35,000. Singled out by their curly or light hair, long noses, and fair skin, and ostracized by the Vietnamese as *Bui Poi*, or "dust of life," Amerasians suffered severe discrimination. Amerasian children not lucky enough to find a home in an orphanage had to survive as beggars, trapped in a cultural no man's land.

Crooked noses

Like the Americans, the Vietnamese also had trouble understanding their allies. However assiduously it tried, the U.S. military could not dispel the image of American troops, in the eyes of xenophobic Vietnamese, as the "new French colonials." Nguyen Than Bi, a schoolteacher in the district town of Can Giouc, remembered his town's first sight of American troops: "One morning a convoy of large GMC trucks loaded with American soldiers arrived. . . . Most of the (people) were curious. They came out of their houses to look. . . . They wanted to see what the difference between the Americans and the French was, but to them it was difficult to detect any difference at all. Like the French Expeditionary Force, the Americans were both black and white. All of them were tall and big." Vietnamese racial prejudice reinforced this negative first impression of the "foreigners." While U.S. troops stigmatized them as "gooks" and "dinks," the Vietnamese referred to the Americans as "monkeys" and "crooked noses."

An Amerasian child in Saigon, March 1970. All too often, GIs left their Vietnamese families behind once their military tours of duty ended.

The relatively "luxurious" standard of living enjoyed by American soldiers, compared to the deprivation of many Vietnamese, especially in rural areas, widened the gulf between them. Vietnamese working at U.S. bases gazed on the material affluence of the "American world" with awe. The editor of the Saigon *Daily News* wrote: "From a strictly military point of view, not philosophical or cultural point of view, the systematic insistence that American troops in the field must be provided with as many facilities of home as possible is really ludicrous. The U.S. military command has had to solve the terrible problem of logistics to give hot meals and cold drinks to all of its half million troops." For the American military, his editorial concluded, "refrigerators, electric generators, air-conditioners, radio networks, newspapers and *Playboy* magazines are a must just the same."

The stark contrast between the Americanized world of U.S. troops and the ugly realities of the war around them jarred some Vietnamese. Ly Chanh Trung, a Saigon University professor, expressed his sentiments thus: "Observe the American pilots, tall, handsome, athletic, with such precision as the electronic computer. They eat breakfast at some military installation ... then they fly away for a few minutes, push a few buttons and fly back. Death is the immediate result of all this button-pushing activity. ... They return to their base, eat, drink, relax, play sports, and on Sunday they go to church." Other Vietnamese critics argued that if the U.S. did not "squander" so much money on amenities for its troops, more money could have been available to benefit people harmed by the war.

Most dealings between the Vietnamese and the American soldiers did little to mitigate the mistrust and animosity between them. South Vietnamese Major Le Van Huong commented, "Most Vietnamese would rather not have foreign combat troops in their country. ... The presence of free-spending, boisterous Americans brings countless little frustrations and irritations to Vietnamese." Those "little frustrations and irritations" included the troops' "free spending," their indifference to local customs and sensibilities, and their "shameful"—Huong's word—behavior toward women.

The lowliest American private was rich by Vietnamese standards. While Vietnamese shopkeepers, bar owners, taxi drivers, and waiters eagerly solicited GI dollars, at the same time, behind a thin veneer of Asian politeness, they often hid contempt. Specialist 4 Michael Guthrie, who served in Vietnam in 1970, reflected: "There is no doubt in my mind that the Vietnamese didn't like Americans. They made it clear that Americans were assholes, a lot of them." Said Major Le Van Huong, "Americans are not discreet spenders. Everywhere they want the best food, the best housing. ... But I guess that is the price we have to pay for their protection."

That price ran higher than bruised Vietnamese pride. Vietnamese struggling to make ends meet resented the American soldiers because of the 170 percent inflation rate caused by their presence in the country. American soldiers with money to burn for amusement did not easily comprehend the complex reasons for the enmity Vietnamese harbored toward them. Like Specialist 4 Poe Price, a clerk in the 173d Airborne Brigade, many GIs attributed Vietnamese rancor merely to "jealousy because we spend a lot of money here. ... Of course," he added, "the GIs don't help it any. They simply don't respect the women in the country."

In South Vietnam the soldiers, when they could get off base, often fraternized with local women. This aggravated the already simmering hostility of Vietnamese toward Americans. Centuries of Confucianism and Buddhism prescribed an almost puritanical public demeanor for Vietnamese women, who were expected to display extreme modesty, formal etiquette, and discretion. Many young American soldiers seeking female companionship frequently, and probably unknowingly, flouted these time-honored moral values. One attractive Vietnamese woman "especially tired of having her fanny pinched everytime she went downtown for errands," said, "I sympathize with these young boys and they are good for coming here. But now I am really disgusted by them. I can't stand them. Why must they be so rude?"

Seeing Vietnamese women even holding hands with American soldiers in public enraged a Vietnamese doctor who said "he would never hold his wife's hand outside their home." Thich Huyen Minh, a Buddhist monk, spoke in 1967 of "how many parents come to see me complaining that their fourteen- or fifteen-year-old daughter has run away with an American soldier." He complained about the Americans' "reversal of moral values." The sight of American soldiers with Vietnamese women convinced many Vietnamese of the "foreigners'" almost complete disregard for their culture. Journalist Ton That Thien expressed his people's wish that the "Americans would be more discreet and considerate of Vietnamese sensitivities." Said a university student, "They pay almost no attention to our culture."

From the Vietnamese vantage, the Americans' seeming obsession with sex smacked of "barbarism." American Chaplain Falabella bemoaned the "image of Americans being given [to the Vietnamese]. The image of the 'ugly American' is bad enough without adding to it ludicrousness by its exaggeration of sex, as manifested in the frantic acclaim and wild clamor of troops at a performance by some female dancer. Their reactions seemed 'unreal, unnatural, excessive, overdone,' according to some Vietnamese. Another said that if that reaction was representative of Americans, in general, then they must be 'sex-obsessed barbarians.' " It is no wonder, therefore, that the Vietnamese so deprecated American soldiers for the contagion of prostitution that followed them. The Vietnamese judged prostitution as not just a social malady but a degradation of their race and culture. Some saw in it the prostitution of their entire country by the Americans. A Vietnamese doctor growled, "What can we say to you Americans—*merci bien*—for turning our women into a nation of bar girls."

Illustrating the debilitating psychological impact of prostitution were stories Vietnamese men circulated about mysterious outbreaks of impotence among them. Even many educated Vietnamese men believed that American troops were carriers of what was called the "shrinking bird disease," which was said to cause the slow shriveling of a Vietnamese man's genitals after he came in contact with a woman who had slept with an American.

Chaplain Falabella thought, "What was really bothering the Vietnamese male was that these nonyellow foreigners were coming into his country, ostensibly to help him against a common enemy, while in fact they were humiliating the Vietnamese male by taking away his women. I used to remind the troops in the field that an added reason for refraining from playing around with the Vietnamese women was to lessen the reason for the VC and North Vietnamese to fight with such stubbornness. It is one thing to fight for some political principles and another to fight to vindicate your manhood."

The propaganda value of this was not lost on the Communists. An American in a small hamlet heard villagers repeating VC rumors about how the women "who are captured when the Americans come in helicopters and surround our villages are taken back to be concubines." Moreover, the idea of vindicating your manhood had a powerful emotional appeal to many young Vietnamese men. In 1967 four Vietnamese students approached their teacher to say good-bye. "We must fight for our country," they told her. "We must fight the Americans . . . because their presence is destroying our native land . . . culturally and morally. To fight now is the only way to prove our love for our country, for our Vietnamese people."

An American takes his Vietnamese girlfriend for a ride down a beach road in Vung Tau, 1972.

Away from the War

American combat troops in the field in South Vietnam had no "off-duty" time. At the end of the day's patrol, they barely had a chance to gulp down their C-rations, dig a foxhole for the night, and catch a few hours sleep in between guard duty on the perimeter. In rear areas, however, support troops had at their disposal a wide variety of amusements—military clubs where they could drink, play cards or slot machines, listen to music, and participate in a variety of sports, such as tennis, basketball, and golf. On large bases like Long Binh, sol-

U.S. officers and guests enjoy the sun and sand at "Air Force Officers Beach" at Cam Ranh Bay in spring, 1969. Below. Lieutenant James Welch tours one of Hue's ancient sites, the tomb of Emperor Thu Duc.

Off-duty in I Corps at Camp Eagle, Phu Bai, headquarters of the 101st Airborne Division. Above. *Second Lieutenant Harry Tuthill lunges for a volleyball.* Right. *Late night poker.* Inset. *First Lieutenant Jim Cummings and Second Lieutenant Peter Costello catch some rays.*

diers could do what millions of Americans did every night: watch television.

In addition to their off-duty time spent in Vietnam, all of the more than 2.5 million troops who served in South Vietnam were entitled to R&R (Rest and Recuperation) leaves. Soldiers could spend a week in one of ten cities throughout the Pacific, including Hong Kong, Bangkok, Sydney, Tokyo, or Honolulu. The U.S. military provided free transportation on chartered commercial jets that made an average of three flights a week to every city.

The host cities constructed American-style hotels for the more than 500 soldiers arriving each week. Catering to the wants of the troops became big business in R&R cities. Thousands of people found work as waitresses, taxi drivers, and entertainers. The souvenir industry boomed. So did prostitution. By 1967 Bangkok and Hong Kong were each taking in over $100 million a year from R&R.

Honolulu was the first R&R choice of married soldiers. It was a relatively inexpensive location for reunions with their

wives flying in from the mainland. Wherever they went, many young soldiers, temporarily released from the pressures of war, turned their R&R into daily rounds of drinking, eating, and sex. Many soldiers dubbed the experience "I&I," for "intoxication and intercourse."

Some, of course, took time for sightseeing in such exotic locales as Bangkok, Hong Kong, and Tokyo. Combat troops, recalled John Parrish, a navy doctor, considered R&R "heaven." For men who had been in "blood and mud for months without bathing or eating a hot meal," R&R offered "women, beer, lights, bars, music, laughs."

The millionth R&R couple, Staff Sergeant and Mrs. Lester R. Hudson, admires Volcano National Park, Hawaii, April 1969. Below. A GI tours Bangkok on R&R, 1967. Inexpensive and close by, Asian sites appealed to single GIs. For a few dollars, soldiers could hire a guide or, more frequently, an "R&R girl."

The Other Americans

As the number of U.S. military personnel increased in South Vietnam in the 1960s, so did the number of civilian advisers. Total USAID personnel, for example (not including dependents and contractors), rose from 189 in 1963 to 1,674 by 1967. The U.S. Information Service also increased its civilian contingent from 48 in 1965 to 117 in 1967. Besides these official advisers, there were a variety of other American civilians in South Vietnam: volunteers from private assistance organizations, missionaries and Christian service workers, and journalists and photographers. Despite their separate missions, all of these groups faced the common challenge of living and working in a country and culture vastly alien to their own. Inevitably, these American civilians became embroiled in the controversy of the war. And at times, in the pursuit of their objectives, they would find themselves in conflict with the South Vietnamese and U.S. governments, the American military, or even among themselves.

The swelling American civilian community during the 1960s in Saigon outstripped the city's ability to accommodate it. From 1963 to 1968, the price of Saigon's modern houses and apartments leapt upward as Americans bid against each other. Many Vietnamese, unable to keep up with spiraling rents, were squeezed out of the housing market. A Vietnamese journalist reported in 1967 that "several Vietnamese tenants received eviction notices from their landlord, who thought he could rent his house to Americans for twice the price." Support facilities for American civilians—commissaries, clinics and hospitals, stores, recreation areas, and entertainment spots—expanded the carefully sequestered urban enclaves in which the Americans preferred to live.

There was some reason, of course, for the enclaves. Americans were subject to terrorist attacks. John Mecklin of the USIS has described how American civilian advisers in Saigon preferred to drive their cars "with windows nearly closed, despite the heat, rather than invite a grenade. . . . The Embassy Security Office reminded us repeatedly not to establish regular patterns in our movements. . . . Packages of any sort, including ladies' handbags, were banned from all American installations unless they were first inspected by a U.S. Marine guard for concealed grenades. . . . Armed M.P. guards rode the buses carrying children to and from the American School in Saigon."

While in the early years USAID confined itself to Saigon, the agency decided in 1962 to send more civilian advisers out into rural areas. By mid-1964 USAID's newly formed Office of Rural Affairs had sent about 100 advisers into the field. The Office of Rural Affairs, according to its first director, George Tanham, sought to recruit "hard-driving, imaginative, dedicated men . . . from all walks of life." The Rural Affairs approach was one of active participation, a departure from USAID's traditional reliance on local government to carry out AID-financed projects and deliver services. "From the beginning," one Rural Affairs official asserted, "we had a concept of operations that was very different from anything the United States normally does. This was more or less a gung ho type of thing—an esprit de corps idea."

The Rural Affairs workers considered themselves a "different breed of cat" from colleagues safely ensconced in Saigon. "From the Vietnamese point of view," one of them explained, "the typical American that they had seen before would arrive at around ten o'clock in the morning, get out and look around a bit, drink a little tea and shake hands, and then they would have a big lunch and some beer. Then maybe at two o'clock in the afternoon they would go out and look around a bit further; and, after that,

the American would get into his airplane or car and drive on. . . . There were very few Americans who went out and stayed out for any length of time." Rural Affairs advisers were given a per diem and were expected, as their supervisor said, "to manage the rest of their own house, their own food, and everything else. In other words, they were going to live off the economy out there."

Still, the advisers did not exactly have to rough it. "So far as housing is concerned, even in the rural areas, we lived quite well when I was there; and, if anything, things have improved since then," an adviser reported in 1965. Vietnamese villagers warmed to the Americans willing to live among them, mingle with them, and submit to the dangers of the war-torn countryside. A USAID official said that when the "Vietnamese suddenly saw young Americans get into working clothes and actually work with the

---

Preceding page. *AID refugee affairs assistant, Bob Resseguie* (center rear), *supervises the loading of bulgur wheat for refugees at Pho An, Quang Ngai Province, 1965.*

people, when they saw how knowledgeable these Americans were, that they traveled throughout the province and did so without fear, when they saw this sort of spirit, this thing rubbed off on a number of Vietnamese, and we had much closer contact with them."

Rural Affairs people tended to learn the Vietnamese language and adapt to native customs. Adviser David Garms, in Go Cong Province from 1967 to 1968, found the Vietnamese to be "impressed by my small degree of fluency [and] remarked that few Americans in Vietnam took the time to learn any of [their] language . . . within a few days word got around the province that 'there is this new American and he can speak Vietnamese.' . . . An American who exhibited the slightest degree of interest in and respect for the way of life in Go Cong was likely to be stunned by the response." If speaking the language re-

Rob Warne of the United States Operations Mission looks over a partially destroyed school at Trung Hiep in 1964. Inset. His wife, Susie, strolls through the streets of Vinh Binh while a Vietnamese strokes the chin of their daughter, Robin Jane.

duced the villagers' mistrust of the "foreigners," it also relaxed American advisers in their strange and sometimes hostile Vietnamese surroundings. A U.S. provincial representative declared, "I think you are more secure, safer if you speak their language. ... I feel secure in traveling around. I enjoy it. In traveling with the Vietnamese, my security stemmed from them. I really didn't have much to worry about because I understood what was happening around me."

Higher Vietnamese officials in Saigon interpreted U.S. advisers' attempts to communicate directly with villagers as a threat to their authority. The U.S. advisers' involvement in rural affairs also set them at odds with their own U.S. bureaucracy in Saigon. A USAID adviser in I Corps Tactical Zone discovered that "pretty soon one begins to identify with the people, with their reactions toward the central government. ... It's the feeling that people back at headquarters just don't understand our problems. ... We often found that the guidance from Saigon was quite unrealistic, not at all tailored to what actually existed." An AID representative in Kien Phong Province in 1966 complained that USAID officials in Saigon were too unfamiliar with conditions in rural areas to provide adequate guidance. He called them a "bunch of generalists ... who lost sight of what is really happening." Another AID worker commented, "There was recrimination, charges of incompatibility within the USAID community and with the Vietnamese officials." For example, in the Vietnamese bureaucracy, an AID official charged, "all the common faults were there: divided responsibility, improper delegation of authority, and, of course, inexperienced people."

Sometimes USAID's civilians clashed with U.S. military officers. A civilian adviser recalled a run-in with a U.S. Special Forces unit at Kien Phong that indiscriminately razed villagers' timber to construct a post: "They cleared an area of about 500 meters around the post, set up artillery and began to fire indiscriminately. ... The people have all moved away because of the Special Forces personnel. ... They have either gone over to the VC or moved in to other government secured areas." A Rural Affairs representative in An Giang Province protested to MACV that a U.S. Navy installation there "had a very disruptive influence. ... Westmoreland sent his deputy down there to investigate the situation," he stated, "and confirmed that what we were reporting was correct."

The principal victims of incessant bureaucratic tussles among U.S. civilian advisers, the South Vietnamese government, and the USAID administration usually were the villagers. Then, too, there was the war, which gradually eroded the American-Vietnamese cultural rapport and understanding U.S. advisers had tried to nurture. The destruction caused by the combatants—the Communists, Americans, and South Vietnamese—created new barriers of fear and distrust between U.S. advisers and the rural people. Soon many villagers worried, as one of them put it, that while Americans "might bring food they might also bring death."

American know-how in Asia

AID representatives were not the only Americans offering social and economic assistance to the South Vietnamese. From 1957 to 1971 more than 400 men and women of the International Voluntary Services (IVS) lived and worked in villages throughout the country. Founded in 1953 as a nonprofit organization, IVS sought to recruit idealistic young Americans, with skills in such fields as agriculture, education, and community development, to help people in undeveloped countries. IVS volunteers had a self-help philosophy, regarding themselves as "dispensers of ideas, attitudes, and skills, not things." In 1960 IVS administrator Dr. Daniel Russell instructed the volunteers, "Your job is to bring your great American know-how to Asia."

IVS personnel in South Vietnam served a minimum of two years. In 1967 the number of IVS volunteers there peaked at 170. They were required to study the Vietnamese language and familiarize themselves with cultural traditions before entering the country. Each volunteer received an allowance to cover living expenses plus $80 per month. Both private and U.S. government funds financed IVS projects. Because of their fluency in Vietnamese and rapport with the villagers among whom they worked, IVS volunteers impressed both USAID officials and touring congressmen who became familiar with their activities. As a result, IVS obtained regular and generous financial support from Washington. "IVS had political clout in Washington," explained a USAID official responsible for submitting aid requests to Congressional committees. "The IVSers had guided senators and congressmen during their Vietnam junkets. They had seen villagers call the volunteers by name. This folksy, people-to-people relationship proved excellent public relations. They had seen [the International Voluntary Services] in action. They favored giving it what it needed."

Despite the support from USAID funds, IVS volunteers viewed their function as separate from the politics of the nation-building and pacification effort by the U.S. and South Vietnamese governments. Don Luce came to Vietnam in 1958, after receiving his master's degree in agricultural development and farm management from Cornell University. In 1961, he was appointed IVS director in South Vietnam, a post he held until 1967. Luce explained IVS's politically neutral stance in the controversial struggle being waged in South Vietnam: "When we decided to cast our lot with IVS in Vietnam, we were simply seeking an experience in which we could both help others and learn ourselves. ... Politics, in fact, seemed quite irrelevant, and the challenges and reward of our work were such that we decided to stay well beyond the initial two years of our contracts."

After 1965, when the destruction of rural areas wrought by the war dramatically increased, some IVS members began criticizing the U.S. military and the political policies under which it operated. They cited the harmful effects on South Vietnam's rural society caused by U.S. bombing, combat operations, and the widespread use of Agent Orange and other defoliants. Wrote Don Luce, "The sufferings of the Vietnamese increased as warfare returned to the country. As the range of our own experiences also broadened, we began to see unnecessary mistakes being made by our American government in response to the new conditions. Our early humanitarian motives for wishing to serve in Vietnam were being thwarted. . . . It became inevitable that our commitment to Vietnam would take on political overtones."

In July 1967 IVS's Vietnamese Advisory Board pressed the American volunteers to take up these concerns—such as the refugees created by the U.S. military—with the U.S. Embassy in Saigon. The Vietnamese Advisory Board members told them not to worry about compromising their neutrality by assuming "a political role. . . . It is the function of IVS," the board asserted, "to work toward the improvement of social conditions, is it not? Well, that is a political activity. Politics and social participation are not independent processes." That summer, Don Luce, John Sommer, and several other IVS volunteers met with U.S.

Ambassador Ellsworth Bunker to discuss their concerns. "The ambassador," said Luce, "was cordial and correct, but the session produced no satisfaction for us in our concerns. It would not be proper to speak out on these matters, Bunker said. The role of volunteers is to help in economic, not political matters. The refugee problem, he said, was a political matter."

Frustrated and disillusioned, Luce and three other volunteers resigned from IVS in September 1967. They wrote a letter to President Lyndon Johnson that forty-nine IVS members signed. It protested "the free strike zones, the refugees, the spraying of herbicide on crops, the napalm." The volunteers informed the president, "a villager lives peacefully under Viet Cong control. Government or American forces arrive to 'liberate' the population. Violence ensues, refugees are created, but the Viet Cong vanish. If the military decides not to plow the villages under, the Viet Cong will come back and resume their authority." After resigning, Luce and his three colleagues returned to Washington, hoping to see the president, but were unable to arrange a meeting. Luce said that Assistant Secretary of State William Bundy "expressed the view that those of us who had resigned from IVS could not see the Vietnam issue in its proper perspective."

The issues surrounding the American military's conduct of the war divided IVS but did not shake its commitment to

IVS Director Don Luce (center) takes a break from his work with Dick Peters (at left) and Nguyen Van Dung at the site of an irrigation system in Phan Rang in September 1961.

At an agricultural experiment station, a Vietnamese farmer and an International Voluntary Services volunteer work side by side to irrigate a sweet potato field, 1961.

continue operating in South Vietnam. The IVS volunteers who remained refused to allow the problems raised by Luce to prevent them, as one said, from "continuing the work which had brought them to Vietnam." But no matter how much IVS attempted to disassociate itself from the war, the dangers to its volunteers steadily increased. Even though IVS kept its people away from heavy combat zones, Martin Sisk left the organization in 1966 because he would not accept the insecurity of working in the highlands. By the end of 1967, four IVS members had been killed by enemy fire. During the 1968 Tet offensive, three more lost their lives. On January 26, 1968, the Vietcong killed David Gitelson near Tan Tay. The people of Tan Tay mourned Gitelson, whom they had called "*My Ngheo*" ("the poor American"), because of his simple clothing and Spartan ways. His dedication to their welfare had earned him the respect and affection of Tan Tay villagers. "My people love that man," a Vietnamese man had once told Don Luce. "He helps my people very much." At Hue, three other volunteers—Gary Daves, Marc Cayes, and Sandra Johnson—were captured by Vietcong guerrillas. The Communists released Sandra Johnson after two months. Daves and Cayes were never seen again.

According to Hugh Manke, who replaced Don Luce as

IVS director in South Vietnam, the casualties suffered by the organization during Tet "forced IVS to completely rethink its program. It was necessary to ask 'What in the world are we doing here in the middle of a war?' so we changed accordingly." Manke cut IVS personnel significantly, from 151 to 87. Disagreements with USAID and the South Vietnamese government further diminished IVS operations. IVS emphasis on promoting long-term agricultural and economic development in the villages conflicted with the objective of USAID and the South Vietnamese government to win the political allegiance of peasants through short-term relief projects. IVS volunteers resisted AID pressure to engage in more politically oriented aid programs. By the late 1960s, Manke observed, "We definitely became far removed from what AID and the South Vietnamese government wanted done." This steadily diverging approach led to bitterness between IVS and USAID. In March 1971, according to an IVS history by Winburn Thomas, "USAID informed IVS that the South Vietnamese Ministry of Agriculture was displeased with its performance." Then in August, Saigon announced its decision not to approve any more IVS projects. The time had finally come, Manke decided, "to close up shop" in South Vietnam.

A different mission

In addition to the civilians of the U.S. advisory program who had the political mission of winning the hearts and minds of the Vietnamese people, there were other Americans who came to South Vietnam to show their Christian concern for the sufferings of the Vietnamese. Some came as missionaries on a spiritual mission to win souls for Christianity. Others came chiefly to provide relief and services to Vietnamese in need. Christian missionaries were not new to Vietnam. Roman Catholic missionaries first visited the country in the sixteenth century, converting many. Threatened by the "subversive teachings" of a foreign religion, Vietnam's Confucian emperors slew missionaries and persecuted their followers. In the nineteenth century France used the emperors' persecution of French missionaries as a pretext for invading Vietnam. Throughout the colonial era many Vietnamese shunned Christianity as the religion of the French oppressors and their Vietnamese collaborators, but by the end of French rule in 1954, nearly 1.5 million of Vietnam's 33 million people were Roman Catholics.

Protestant missionaries entered Vietnam much later. In 1911, three members of the Christian and Missionary Alliance settled in Da Nang. It was not until the 1960s, however, that Protestant missionary groups, moved by the trials of the war-wracked Vietnamese, arrived in greater numbers. Mrs. Gordon Smith of the United World Mission felt that "war plows up hearts and makes an opportune time for sowing the Gospel seed." In addition to the Christian and Missionary Alliance, there came in 1966, among others, the Seventh-Day Adventist World Service, the Wycliffe Bible Translators, and the World Evangelization Crusade. Christian relief organizations included the American Friends Service Committee, Catholic Relief Services, Vietnam Christian Service (Church World Service, Mennonite Central Committee, and Lutheran World Relief), and the World Vision Relief Organization. Nearly 200 Americans worked for these missionary and service groups in South Vietnam.

Unlike most U.S. civilian advisers, many missionaries and Christian relief workers tried to adopt the lifestyle of the Vietnamese they had come to help. They patiently studied the Vietnamese language and assimilated the country's culture. Mennonite Earl Martin stated, "many people in the Mennonite Central Committee wore the local dress, the pajama shirt, as well as the rubber tire sandals. As much as possible we tried to go places on bicycles. When my wife and I worked in the refugee camps, we would ride the four miles on bicycle because it brought one in much closer contact with the people. You had a much better feel of what was going on around you when you were on the level of the local folks and going at the speed that they were."

Adjusting to eating goat's blood and sauce made of rotten fish (*nuoc mam*) was not easy for the Americans. Some yielded to the temptation to be "comfort-loving North Americans." During his orientation at Vietnam Christian Service Headquarters in Saigon, Douglas Hostetter "was somewhat shocked at the standard of living in the missionaries' big houses in the wealthy section of town with big walls, servants and iron-barred gates. I just can't seem to reconcile this to the Christian message and life." He "really longed for the day when I can get out among the people. Life here is so unreal."

Most missionaries and relief workers did brave the adversities of working in the countryside. Although giving spiritual rather than material aid was their overriding concern, missionaries administered food, clothing, and medicine to needy Vietnamese and refugees impoverished by the fighting. "Man is composed of body and soul," an American missionary once said. "Our responsibility is in regard to need, in whatever form it takes." The Seventh-Day Adventist Welfare Service, for instance, raised $268,000 in 1967 to fund a thirty-eight-bed hospital and a nursing school.

Christian service groups provided most of the material aid. Catholic Relief Services dispensed $11.5 million in 1966 to purchase supplies for schools, hospitals, and orphanages. The Vatican's Caritas International sent $3 million to assist more than 1 million refugees to obtain food and clothing. The Vietnam Christian Service, principal agent for Protestant relief, spent $500,000 to support seventy-three foreign workers, mostly doctors and home economists, and operated some sixty projects, including the distribution of bread to supplement a Saigon school lunch program.

The missionary and relief groups directed their spiritual and material efforts toward all Vietnamese, Communists or non-Communists. Like the early IVS workers, they generally sought to disassociate themselves from the politics of the Vietnam conflict. "We are social workers and Christians," said Neil Brendan of Lutheran World Relief. "We're here to do a job," Earl Martin of the Mennonite Central Committee in Quang Ngai commented. "We saw our presence in Vietnam not as being representatives of the United States but of the Christian Church, which as we see it, transcended all nationalities." A few Protestant missionaries in South Vietnam did take a political stand. A missionary stated "that the survival of Christianity in Vietnam depends on the victory of American forces in Vietnam." "If the Americans withdraw," another missionary said, "the Christian Church (in South Vietnam) is finished." One missionary even advocated "using nuclear weapons in North Vietnam . . . so that Christianity could survive in the South."

Catholic Relief Services and World Vision openly aligned themselves with the American nation-building program. American Catholics who opposed the war criticized Catholic Relief Services for helping distribute U.S.-

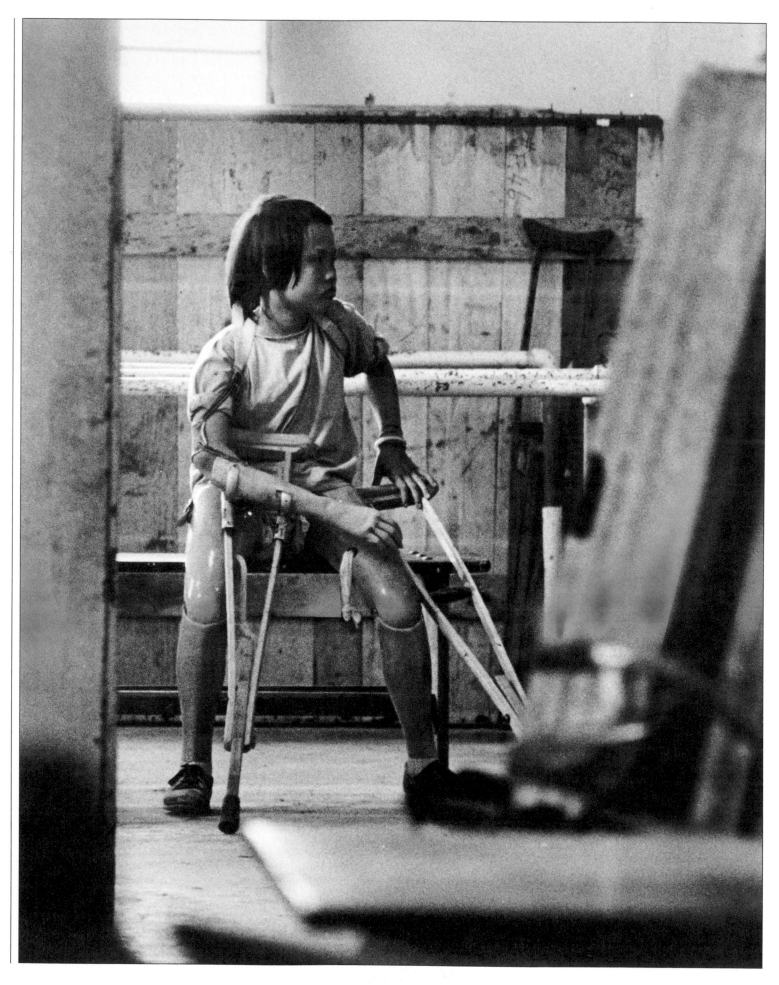

Swords into Plowshares

The American Friends Service Committee, among its many relief efforts in South Vietnam, developed a program to help civilians maimed by bombs, mines, and booby traps. At their Prosthetics Center in Quang Ngai, a team of American doctors, therapists, and nurses fabricated artificial limbs and provided them without charge to amputees in need. "Our methods are sometimes less sophisticated than would be seen in the States, but equally effective," said one doctor. "Lately, we've been using Plexiglas from the windshield of a wrecked helicopter to make limbs. Sort of turning swords into plowshares."

Left. *At the Quang Ngai Prosthetics Center, the face of a young victim mirrors the bitter tragedy of war.*

Above and right. *The staff train Vietnamese how to fashion and fit artificial limbs.*

supplied food to families of South Vietnam's 700,000-man local militia at General Westmoreland's request. World Vision Director Bob Pierce in 1966 built a Christian embassy in Saigon "as a symbol of both our confidence in the future of Vietnam . . . and in the faithfulness of Almighty God . . . here we shall train young men and women to better serve their country and its people."

Some missionary organizations extended offers of aid to people in VC-controlled areas. The American Friends Service Committee, for example, dispatched medical supplies to a VC village. The VC, however, rebuffed them. "We want to thank you," a VC spokesman wrote, "for sending these medicines to us, but we must ask you to return them to the Americans. . . . Although we lack many things, we still have more than enough strength to fight the Americans for another 10, 20 or more years until we defeat them. Please let the Americans know this." The VC wanted no part of Christianity. This was, in part, the result of Ngo Dinh Diem's ardent Catholicism and his use of Catholic refugees as a base of political support for his repressive regime in the 1950s and early 1960s. The VC also associated Christianity with the political ideology of the United States and the South Vietnamese government. "The NLF feel that Christianity is an American religion," wrote Douglas Hostetter. "This is often supported by the fact that American chaplains often visit with [Vietnamese] pastors. Also, the village pastors receive American goods, often from the military, for distribution to their church members." Above all, the NLF and North Vietnamese opposed Christianity because they judged its values and practices to be inconsistent with Marxist doctrine.

Since missionaries frequently relied on U.S. military transport to deliver their aid, neutrality was difficult to maintain. According to Earl Martin, the U.S. military took it for granted that missionaries were "contributing to the whole war effort and were therefore allies. . . . One afternoon in Quang Tri . . . we were talking to this colonel and telling him that we were working with the refugees and just interested in relieving the difficult situation of the farmers. The colonel responded, 'The more VC we kill, the better we're doing our job. We also need to win the hearts and minds of the people and that's where you come in. We're glad about what you're doing because it makes our job more effective. We're glad you're part of the team.' That left us feeling most uncomfortable."

Refusing to cooperate with the military could be costly for Christian organizations. Douglas Hostetter recounted an attempt by U.S. military officers to use religion for pacification: "A U.S. officer in MACV decided it would be a good idea to stage Christmas parades [in a village], bring in gifts for all the children and a large Marine band. When the missionaries refused because it was basically a

The 1st Infantry Division Band entertains South Vietnamese villagers as part of the U.S. pacification effort, 1966.

Keyes Beech of the Chicago Daily News on a patrol with ARVN troops in the Mekong Delta, 1965.

political operation, the colonel who was in charge of MACV was furious. He said that from then on, all the traitors who refused to cooperate in that parade would not be given any concrete or steel or corrugated tin for building their schools, clinics, and orphanages."

Neutrality could not guarantee the safety of missionaries out in the combat arena. The VC treated them as "spies" and American "lackeys" and attacked them as enemies. Throughout the war the list of slain missionaries kept growing: thirteen from the Christian and Missionary Alliance and two from the Wycliffe Bible Translators. Christian service groups also suffered losses, two from the Mennonites and one from the Vietnam Christian Service. In 1966, John Haywood of the Worldwide Evangelization Crusade was slain by the VC, who cut him down with six bullets to the head and chest. He was operating a sanitarium for lepers near Da Nang. The day after his funeral his widow gave birth to a daughter. Eugene Evans of the Christian Missionary Alliance reported that during the 1968 Tet offensive "[the Communists] killed six of our people in cold blood and three of them were in nurses' uniforms. They later killed four others who were also in the medical service." The Mennonite Central Committee said the "danger of having the organization's relief and service efforts identified with the U.S. government's total military and psychological strategy to win the war continues to pose serious problems."

Despite the threat to their lives, the missionaries persevered. They hoped to create vital indigenous churches that would endure beyond the Americans' departure and no matter what political course the Vietnamese chose. "We were never the great white fathers," Eugene Evans maintained. "It was our intent to establish a self-supporting, self-governing, self-propagating church." Protestant congregations contained 100,000 members. Yet the missionaries still had difficulty convincing the country's non-Christian majority that the God Christians worshiped was not "white, western, and capitalist." Doug Hostetter declared that "Vietnamese brought up Catholic [or Protestant] are not Easterners. ... Protestant and Catholic churches in Vietnam were all built with Roman and Gothic architecture. Missionaries felt there was something inherently pagan about Oriental architecture. The music in the Protestant Church was also totally Western, you know, good old Handel and Bach. ... What they did actually was to take good 'Christian', Western music and translate the words into Vietnamese."

Because of the Western, American overlay to the religion the missionaries preached, hundreds of Vietnamese Christians also opposed the Communists and became martyrs for their faith. In 1968, American journalist David Kucharsky reported, Vietnamese Protestants were "now losing their lives with sad regularity." As U.S. troops began withdrawing in 1969, American missionaries wondered if Christian concern for the Vietnamese would van-

U.S. journalists (left to right) *Neil Sheehan, Ray Herndon, and David Halberstam* listen to a briefing from a South Vietnamese military official, 1962

ish with the last helicopter. Some Vietnamese felt that Christianity had no future in a peaceful Vietnam "free" of westerners for it was built on slim pilings. A Buddhist student wrote, "I know that Jesus entered Vietnam along with the artillery and bombs of the French. The result of that was the destruction of our homes and gardens, and the defoliation of our land. . . . I cannot accept a kind of love which is so destructive and has left such a scar on my heart."

Getting the story

Others whom the American involvement brought to Vietnam were the men and women of the news media. From 1954 to 1975 more than 2,000 American correspondents converged on South Vietnam in order to report and film the activities of those Americans who were advising, fighting, or ministering to the needs of the Vietnamese people. The importance of the military and political struggle in South Vietnam and the breadth of U.S. involvement irresistibly attracted journalists and photographers. Peter Arnett of the Associated Press, who began covering the war as a photographer and became one of its more notable

chroniclers, found it to be "the longest running front page story going on anywhere in the world." The journalists shared with the other Americans in Vietnam a sense of mission: to report what they saw, to capture, in words and pictures, the truth of what the United States was doing there. Most saw the American involvement as a worthy cause, though many came to be critical of how that cause was being served.

The members of the American press corps in South Vietnam were of diverse backgrounds. There were old hands like Homer Bigart of the *New York Times*, Robert Shaplen of the *New Yorker*, Marguerite Higgins of the *New York Herald Tribune*, and Keyes Beech of the *Chicago Daily News;* and correspondents from small-town newspapers, including an elderly lady from an evangelical journal in Duluth, Minnesota. There were also ambitious young reporters eager to make names for themselves, such as Neil Sheehan of United Press International, Malcolm Browne of the Associated Press, and David Halberstam of the *New York Times*. Obtaining accreditation as a journalist in South Vietnam was not difficult. A correspondent had only to get an entry visa and a letter from his or her newspaper, periodical, or news agency requesting certification. Free-lancers were required to have two backers, but they were easily obtained. The Associated Press and United Press International, for example, accredited almost anyone willing to pack a camera to South Vietnam and who held promise of sending back newsworthy stories or photographs. Once "in-country," correspondents received an identification card from MACV, which entitled them to military transportation when available.

Only a few American journalists spent time in Vietnam during the 1950s and early 1960s. The country was relatively peaceful then and there was little interest in the activities, economic or military, then underway. Even in 1963, when the expanding Communist insurgency in South Vietnam alarmed Washington, and Buddhist demonstrations threatened to topple Diem's U.S.-backed regime, the pace for the twenty or so American journalists there remained, as Phillip Knightley put it, a "leisurely, almost unreal one." The modest group of American correspondents following political developments in Saigon could be comfortably seated at one large table at Brodard's, the restaurant on fashionable Tu Do Street where they regularly met for lunch. They could take a taxi from Saigon in the morning out into the countryside, discuss the military situation with a South Vietnamese military officer or a U.S. adviser, and return to Saigon by dusk for cocktails and dinner at the Caravelle Hotel.

When the war intensified after 1963 and Washington deployed more combat advisers and then troops, the American press corps also grew. In 1965 the number of accredited U.S. correspondents in South Vietnam jumped from 20 to 131 and two years later reached 207. The news they sought was increasingly found in the rice fields, bush land, and hills beyond Saigon, where U.S. and South Vietnamese forces battled Vietcong guerrillas and North Vietnamese regulars. Free-lance photographer Tim Page, among others, has pointed out that some journalists stayed in Saigon, reluctant to move from behind their desks to cover the fighting in the countryside. They contented themselves mostly with secondhand information and the military briefings provided at the Joint U.S. Public Affairs Office in Saigon. These briefings consisted of communiqués from units on operations and soon became notorious for squabbles between correspondents and officials over enemy body counts and other details. The daily event came to be designated "the five o'clock follies."

To get the facts firsthand, to see for themselves what was happening on the battlefield, many journalists accompanied American units into combat, visited lonely outposts and firebases, and checked out areas where extensive sweep operations were underway. Gavin Young of the London Observer likened this pattern of combat coverage to the activity around a ski resort: "Correspondents bustle out at dawn from bacon and eggs, some to the 'nursery slopes' of a routine patrol, others to the major peaks of a full-scale brigade assault." The conditions jour-

nalists experienced in the field varied. As Charles Mohr of the New York Times described them, "a reporter may spend a night in the compound of an American advisory group long established in Vietnam. In that case he can have a comfortable room, a good meal, a drink and see a movie. On the other hand, he may sleep in a hole on a battalion perimeter. . . . My own worst nights," Mohr said, "were spent in Plei Me Special Forces camp, where rats kept running over our chests all night, and in a flooded sugar cane field in Hau Nghia Province, where Jack Foisie of the Los Angeles Times bitterly contested the single, tiny, hip-size patch of dry ground I had found." David Halberstam recalled, "I kept going out to the boondocks, to isolated posts. . . . A couple of times I got so sick I thought I was going to die. But that's where the story was."

An important fact about the Vietnam War is that no censorship was imposed on reporters by the American or South Vietnamese governments. Correspondents could write about and transmit anything they could witness, any rumors they heard. Photographers could photograph any action they could find. What is more, because of their access to military transport, journalists and photographers were able to travel wherever the soldiers went. They were so ubiquitous that the MACV Information Office in Pleiku had a cartoon on the wall depicting a squad deep in the jungle calling for air support because it was surrounded by correspondents. "The troops never understood the correspondents," a journalist remarked. "They always said, 'What are you doing out here? You must be crazy!'" Crazy or not, some reporters and photographers never passed up a chance to document the course and tempo of the fighting. Life photographer Larry Burrows, two-time winner of the Robert Capa award for "superlative photography, requiring exceptional courage and enterprise," epitomized reporters of this caliber. Burrows once said, "I will do what is required to show what is happening. I have a sense of the ultimate—death. And sometimes I must say to hell with that." Capa had been killed in 1954 while photographing combat in the French Indochina War.

Dickey Chapelle of the National Observer, one of eighteen women correspondents in South Vietnam, was respected by her colleagues for her guts and determination in combat. They admired her pluck and willingness to take punishment. "In fatigues and helmet," said a marine corps commander, "you couldn't tell her from one of the troops, and she could keep up with the best of them." One time Chapelle parachuted into Vietcong territory, returning safely with the story and photos she had gone after. Chapelle traced her fascination with battle and danger to her quiet childhood in Wisconsin. "Violence was so unthinkable [to me]," she explained, "that it became as much a mystery to me as sex seemed to other teenagers."

Over the entire war, at least sixty-two reporters and photographers never returned from the field to file their stories. Forty-four were killed, and eighteen were listed as

Freelance photojournalist Sean Flynn runs for cover during street fighting in Da Nang, 1966.

missing and presumed dead. They died in South Vietnam, Cambodia, and Laos from helicopter crashes, gunfire, mines, and mortars. In November 1965, while covering a U.S. Marine operation near Chu Lai, Dickey Chapelle was blown up by a land mine. Charles Eggleston of UPI was shot dead in May 1968 while with a company of South Vietnamese paratroopers engaging the VC on the outskirts of Saigon. After covering the war for nine years, Larry Burrows was killed in February 1971, when the helicopter in which he was flying over Laos was shot down by the North Vietnamese.

A few American reporters deliberately courted danger in their continual coverage of combat. Henry Kamm of the *New York Times* described them as "proto-journalists" out for the "thrill." Sean Flynn, son of actor Errol Flynn, quit his job with *Paris-Match* in 1966 to become a free-lance reporter in South Vietnam. He told his editor at *Paris-Match* that he wanted to take part in "the greatest adventure—that of war and death." When Flynn arrived at the *Time* bureau in Saigon seeking work as a stringer, he was dressed in full combat gear, with two hand grenades hooked to his web gear. Dana Stone, a photographer,

came to Saigon a few months after Flynn. They met shortly afterward and quickly became friends while free-lancing for UPI.

Flynn and Stone soon acquired a reputation as a "daring duo" who took incredible risks for the sake of a good story or photograph. According to their colleague and friend Perry Deane Young, they "enjoyed the war . . . finding the personal courage to edge right up to death while staying calm." The marines called the five-foot six-inch Stone "minigrunt" because he took so many risks to take his photographs. "How does it feel," a correspondent once asked Stone's wife Louise, "to be married to a death wish?" Together Stone and Flynn did the camera work for the CBS documentary "Charlie Company," which won the prestigious Peabody Award for broadcasting. Wrote David Greenway of *Time* magazine, "There may be other more famous photographers with greater skill in Vietnam but there are none with more courage and initiative than Stone and Flynn."

By 1970, Dana Stone was tiring of combat photography. In a letter home he had told his parents the war had become "dull and frightening. . . . It looks," he added, "as though the war will last a while, a long while, but I'm not sure that I would." His words were prophetic. On April 6, 1970, Stone and Flynn set off on identical bright red motorcycles for the Cambodian border. It was just three weeks before the U.S. and South Vietnamese launched their invasions of Cambodia, and the Communists' border sanctuaries were buzzing with activity. Three kilometers outside the town of Chi Pou, on a lonely road, Stone and Flynn encountered a Vietcong roadblock. They were never seen again. Whether they were immediately killed by the Communists or died in captivity remained a mystery. For a while there was hope that Flynn and Stone might still be alive in a VC prison. By 1972, most of Flynn's friends presumed him to be dead. Stone's wife went to Saigon on the slim chance her husband might suddenly appear. On Tu Do Street, near Stone's old apartment, she showed his picture to a Vietnamese man who read faces. After examining the picture, however, the Vietnamese told her, "This man is dead."

Of the American press in South Vietnam, military journalist John Steinbeck IV wrote, "It was not so much that these people were remarkable as individuals, but rather that their mission had reached such giant proportions that reporting the war became almost as large as the operation of war itself." Certainly journalists and photographers maintained a high profile in South Vietnam. Moreover, the role they assumed in reporting what happened became a major source of contention. Most reporters and photographers professed adherence to principles of objectivity and neutrality. Photographer Philip Jones Griffiths asserted, "Your job out there is to record it for all history. You can't not feel involved, but you have to steel yourself and do your job."

However much they attempted to remain emotionally disengaged, correspondents—as Americans—were drawn into the passionate debate the war generated. John Pilger, a British reporter for the *Daily Mirror*, understood the American correspondents' dilemma. South Vietnam, he

"At Bearcat"

by Richard Young

Two of us at the Long Binh replacement center had orders to report to the 1011th Service and Supply Company at a place called Bearcat, forty kilometers east of Saigon. The other guy, a bear-like Vermonter named Hugo Bailey, and I waited a long time before a jeep came for us. The driver was covered with dust and looked like something out of the Wild West. He sported a thick handlebar mustache, and his jungle hat was tied rakishly up on the sides and looked more cowboy than army-issue.

In fact, he and everyone else from the 1011th were from the Wild West. The men of the 1011th, one of a handful of reserve

units in the entire U.S. that had been deployed in Vietnam, came from right near Dodge City—Emporia and Lawrence, Kansas. When Hugo and I arrived in January of 1969, they were serving as advisers and suppliers for 10,000 soldiers of a Royal Thai Army "Black Panthers" unit that was stationed at Bearcat. The Thais were in Vietnam as part of the Free World Military Assistance Force, serving in the same way as an American infantry unit in the field and patrolling the area around Bearcat with the same kind of search and destroy tactics the Americans were employing.

The driver helped us with our gear, then we drove at rake-hell speed past paddies, rubber tree plantations, and jungle, the beautiful late afternoon sunlight turning ominous as it slanted through the nearby greenery. When we finally reached the line at Bearcat, the first thing I noticed was that Asian soldiers were walking in pairs and holding hands or strolling along arm in arm. The driver did not pay any attention, but Hugo and I exchanged a glance of wonder. Wonder gave way to astonishment when we saw a giant American lieutenant, with a handlebar bushier than the driver's, walking arm in arm with a Thai soldier.

The first sergeant, who was outside the

company HQ, saw our astonished looks and said, "They ain't queers—it's just a custom with them. At least they ain't tried to queer me yet." He launched into an unintentionally hilarious briefing about Thais and their customs, and the kinds of things we should watch for and avoid. We were told never to point a finger or toe at a Thai or to cross our legs or feet in their presence. We certainly should never put our feet up on a table, because to show the sole of the foot was considered a grave insult. As far as I was concerned, most of it was no problem, but the idea of walking hand in hand with another soldier seemed very strange.

Most of the Kansans were uncomfortable with the Thais and did not have much contact with them outside of duty, for the same reason they did not seek out the Vietnamese villagers of nearby Long Thanh: they were foreigners with a foreign language and strange customs. The reservists belonged to a close community of friends and relatives who had grown up together, and they were not interested in much outside their unit. The Kansans were wonderful scroungers and found materials to build their own little version of Emporia, complete with colorfully painted, tin-roofed hootches, a canvas-covered movie theater where we drank twenty-five-cent beers, and a club that said, was a new type of war, "impossible to cover without becoming part of it yourself, and when you become part of it you have to decide where you stand." Stanley Karnow, formerly of the *Washington Post*, has said, "To suggest, as some critics have, that the Saigon correspondents behaved irresponsibly, is to miss the mark. They have been reproached for their 'emotional involvement' in the Vietnam situation, and they do not deny the charge." "I defy anyone to spend six months in Saigon without becoming emotionally engaged," another journalist stated. "After all, we're human beings, not jellyfish." Inevitably, the ranks of the press, like the American public, divided into hawks and doves. The hawks accused the doves of being excessively critical of the military and the South Vietnamese government. The doves, in turn, charged the hawks with unquestioning acceptance of American military and political policy. The military and the White House joined the fray. MACV urged critical journalists to "join the American team." And the White House blamed the declining public support for President Johnson's Vietnam policy on pessimistic reporting.

David Halberstam, one of the most outspoken critics of the way the war was fought, has defended the journalists: "It is not much fun to be pessimistic. . . . It is not much fun being shunned and cursed by high officials of your country in Saigon and Washington. It is not much fun to write grim stories about a country which means a great deal to you and in which your friends are dying." For years to come after the war was over, the actions of journalists in South Vietnam, like those of the American civilian advisers, aid volunteers, and missionaries, remained a matter of controversy and some bitterness. The question still lingered whether the members of the U.S. press in South Vietnam, as Pulitzer Prize winner Peter Arnett wrote, "performed the classic American press role of censuring government policy or . . . botched the whole job and aided and abetted the enemy."

echoed late in the night with the music of Hank Williams and Johnny Cash. The Thais were not part of that vision of home, so the Kansans did not go out of their way to include them.

They all understood how lucky they were to be with the Thais, however, because the Thais were tough fighters who relished a battle and appeared almost disappointed that the Vietcong usually made a wide arc to by-pass Bearcat. Firefights were common in the two sectors on either side of us, one manned by the South Vietnamese and one by the American "Big Red One" (the 1st Infantry Division), but the Thais were given a wide berth. One story may have been apocryphal but it was nevertheless persistent. The rumor circulated that the Thais disposed of all their prisoners with the ceremonial swords that many carried with them. One of the Kansans who spent some time in the field with them did show me a picture of a Thai officer holding a sword high above a kneeling Vietcong soldier. It may have been posed, but it seemed sickeningly real.

The Thais looked fierce as they moved out, all of them wearing several chains with Buddhas encased in plastic around their necks. They considered it a talisman against danger to wear every Buddha given to them by friends and family, so some wore as many as fifty when they went smiling and waving into battle. There was something frightening about the good cheer they exhibited as they went to war. I had a sense that this must have been the way that Ghengis Khan's warriors must have looked when they started riding west.

After the Kansans went home, the 1011th was filled with replacements no one else wanted—druggies and incompetents, shammers and psychos. These guys were dangerous, and life became a nightmare for those of us who had come to rely on the hardworking, honest and trustworthy Kansans. Hugo and I and our friend Mac Trull from North Carolina began to spend more and more time with the Thais.

We became regulars at the banquets that some of the Thai units gave when they returned from the field. These banquets were all-evening rituals that included several exotic dishes, each one different from the others, most of them hot and full of spices I had never even heard of, much less tried. The Thais would pour an extra bowl of chili in vinegar over some dishes that were already so hot that the Americans were teary eyed. Once, after several Singha (Thai) beers, I made the mistake of boldly following their lead and pouring a bowl of the chili sauce on a chicken dish. My reddened face and my bulging eyes produced roars of laughter as I reached frantically for the water pitcher.

The Thais' food was so good that I had no reason to mistrust them another evening when they told me they had been lucky enough to shoot a rare delicacy that I should try: monkey. One of the Thais, smiling broadly, cut off a goodly portion of a skinny little leg and handed it to me with great fanfare. The others watched and waited for my reaction as I put it in my mouth and started chewing. I am not a finicky eater, but this was too much to bear. Monkey tasted to me just the way I imagined rat would taste. The saliva started running, and for just a moment, I thought I might vomit. They were still smiling, waiting for my reaction, so I tried to smile and nod and say, "Mmm, good." Their attention then went from me to the monkey, which they proceeded to carve and eat with great zest. This gave me time to put my hand surreptitiously to my mouth and remove the stringy meat that was still stuffed in my cheek like a wad of tobacco.

We were not the only Americans who went out of our way to make friends with the Thais, but there were not many of us.

Saigon U.S.A.

They did not come to South Vietnam to fight like the soldiers, to advise like the civilians, or to preach like the missionaries. These Americans, over 5,000 contractors, construction workers, and businessmen, converged on South Vietnam in 1965 because that "was where the action was"— and the money. "You rarely know what's going to happen next," said an American business executive, "but that's the thrill of it."

Never before had U.S. businessmen followed American troops to war in such numbers. The opportunities were lucrative, a businessman explained. It was "a high rolling game for big stakes." By the end of 1965 the U.S. Defense Department had contracted with American construction firms to build $300 million worth of military installations, including air bases, hospitals, warehouses, and harbor and docking facilities. And the Pentagon had projects costing another $200 million already planned for 1966 and 1967.

Because of the immense technical, material,

and logistical requirements of this colossal military building program, four private U.S. construction and engineering firms—Raymond International, Morrison-Knudsen, Brown and Root, and J. A. Jones—combined to form a consortium called RMK–BRJ. Employing 4,200 Americans, RMK-BRJ worked quickly to construct the enormous physical infrastructure needed by U.S. military forces in South Vietnam. By the spring of 1966, it was building three airfields and logistical complexes the size of San Francisco at the same time.

The consortium's three largest undertakings were at Da Nang, Cam Ranh, and Saigon. At Da Nang it tackled some sixty projects totaling $120 million, including a 10,000-foot paved runway and taxiway, a spacious aircraft parking apron, and three deep-draft piers. At Cam Ranh Bay, one of Asia's great natural harbors, RMK-BRJ embarked on a $110–million venture to build a deep-water pier, a half-mile long causeway, thirty-six warehouses, 380 ammunition storage pads, a 10,000-foot airstrip, and billeting for 10,000 troops. Near Saigon RMK-BRJ fabricated three additional piers, a "New Port" with four deep-water piers, and a second 10,000-foot airport runway. The consortium was certain it was making an essential contribution to a successful war effort. Said one of the conglomerate's executives, "[President] Johnson wouldn't build all this for the Communists."

Hundreds of other companies, large and small, joined RMK-BRJ in South Vietnam. Foremost Dairies, for example, built a factory near Saigon that produced 300,000 cases of condensed milk each year, one-third of total South Vietnamese consumption. The Parsons and Whittemore paper plant in Bien Hoa filled 25 percent of the country's printing and writing paper needs. Johnson International Corporation of New Jersey established the Vietnam-American Textile Company, which expected to double its output after just two years in operation. Major importing firms from the United States, like the American Trading Company and Brownell Lane Engineering Company, sold and serviced heavy equipment such as bulldozers and locomotives.

One of the more unusual aspects of the American business build-up in South Vietnam was the profusion of companies pursuing the GI dollar. Cars International sold cars to servicemen for delivery when they returned home. Because U.S. troops did not have to pay sales taxes, a new 1966 Ford station wagon with a factory list price of $2,573 could be purchased in South Vietnam for only $2,065. Cars International's sidewalk placards enticed GI buyers with such slogans as "All cars, all ranks, all ages." In 1966 its car sales hit 100 a month.

Other U.S. companies seeking the soldiers' dollars ped-

dled everything from machetes to mutual funds to real estate lots in Florida. Investor Overseas Service, an international broker for eighty U.S. mutual funds, did business out of a two-room office in Saigon. General Development Corporation of Miami, Florida, vended 10,000-square-foot Florida property lots for $2,395, each only $25 down. "Once we sit down with a client," General Development manager William Weldon said, "50 percent of them reserve a lot."

Most of the American companies and business investors did well in South Vietnam. George Calfo of the American Trading Company turned a 1-man, machinery-selling operation into a 200-man organization grossing $10 million annually. He also served as principal South Vietnam distributor for International Harvester, General Electric, and Du Pont. "Calfo," an American journalist wrote, "has a reputation for being as inscrutable as any Asiatic. He maintains painstaking attention to 'face' and bows to all his Asian clients." *Fortune* magazine announced in March 1966 that "soaring demand for their products" and "lush profit margins" enabled U.S. companies in South Vietnam "to recoup an investment in two to four years." In 1967, *Business Week* magazine reported "that the investor in Vietnam can expect profits of from 20% to 30% a year in a wide range of industries."

To handle the financial needs of the budding American business community in South Vietnam, the United States government encouraged American banks to open branches there. Between 1966 and 1972 Citibank, Chase Manhattan, Bank of America, and First National City Bank took the plunge. Charles Bradley, assistant marketing vice president for Citibank, stressed South Vietnam's investment potential: "Americans have a completely erroneous idea about South Vietnam. The war hasn't wrecked the country ... there has been enormous technological progress." John Graves, vice president of First National City Bank's Asia-Pacific Division, said, "Sure you'll find a lot of bullets flying around, but there is a lot of money floating around too. And if you're a bank, you go where the money is."

The quest for profit lured not only big companies but small businesses and entrepreneurs. Magazines and newspapers at the time carried many stories about enterprising Americans who started successful businesses in South Vietnam. Charles Munro, for instance, arrived in Saigon as a young engineer in 1965. He later married a Vietnamese woman and decided to remain there. He started a securities consulting business and helped Saigon's Ministry of Finance organize the country's first securities market. James Swanson, a native of Brownsville, Texas, made a name for himself in the town of Ben Tre selling shrimp. The Vietnamese nicknamed him "Ong Tom" ("Mr. Shrimp"). After serving as an infantryman and adviser until 1971, Swanson was determined "to make himself rich" by buying shrimp from Mekong Delta fish-

---

Preceding page. Wartime Saigon was a hodgepodge of sights and sounds, a whirl of crowds, garish signs, honking vehicles, and, as this photo shows (at center), *pickpockets.*

A Vietnamese woman feeds her baby in front of the Saigon branch of Bank of America on Tu Do Street, November 1969.

ermen and reselling it in the profitable Saigon market. He expected to double his income in less than three years. Although Ben Tre was a bit too quiet for Swanson's taste, his friends back home kept him well stocked in his favorite jalapeno peppers, pinto beans, and Gouda cheese. "Once I get rich," Swanson said, "I'll get good cigars shipped in from San Antonio."

American engineers and contractors on field projects risked attack by Vietcong snipers and guerrilla units. In 1966 an American construction worker operating an earth scraper at a quarry outside Saigon was shot and killed by a VC sniper. Contractors who specialized in field maintenance of equipment near Da Nang and Pleiku were assaulted repeatedly by the Communists in 1966 and 1967. Most American businessmen and construction personnel, however, from executives down to drillers and crane operators, found life pleasant and, for the most part, secure. RMK-BRJ salaries were generally higher than those paid for identical work in the United States. A construction foreman could make up to $200 per day on top of subsistence payments and bonuses. All contractor employees were also entitled to the privileges and bargain prices of the U.S. military PX.

American businessmen lived in former French villas and were served by cooks, houseboys, and maids. In 1967 John Steinbeck IV wrote of American company executives, "There's no question that ... most of these men had the safest and easiest job any middle-aged soldier of fortune could have hoped for." Ralph Lombardi, who came to South Vietnam to sell securities, said, "There's a feeling of complete freedom here. A man with a little money in his pocket can do anything—smoke opium, sleep with three girls, meet interesting people. The charm of Saigon is not to be denied."

American business interests, despite the uncertainties of the war, were in those days bullish about South Vietnam's economic future. First National City Bank President Henry Sperry said in 1966, "We believe we're going to win this war. . . . Afterwards, you'll have a major job of reconstruction ... that will take financing, and financing means banks." Even the upheaval caused by the 1968 Tet offensive did not cool the ardor of the American investors. "A lot of people are wondering when is the best time to get in on the ground floor," an American stated. *Business Week* reported in 1969 that "stepped-up business interest reflects both the swift recovery of the South Vietnamese economy from the Tet offensive and increasing security in the countryside." As late as 1973 securities broker Charles Munro was optimistic about long-term economic prospects in South Vietnam. "By 1975," he speculated, "there should be a rush to invest in everything from rice, fruit, and fish to

The American–owned Foremost Dairies plant on the outskirts of Saigon, 1971. First produced in South Vietnam in 1964, Foremost milk went primarily to U.S. PXs.

rubber, timber, and oil. There are tremendous long-range business opportunities. It's like frontier California; there's a great potential for growth."

Like every facet of the American presence in South Vietnam, the activities of U.S. business interests kindled controversy. Radio Hanoi regularly vilified American companies as "neo-colonialists" and "imperialist capitalists." In 1966 American Jules Henry, an anthropology and sociology professor at Washington University in St. Louis, called South Vietnam "capital's last frontier." He accused the United States of "increasing the immensity of our military commitment there" to keep it "free for American investment." In 1971 some Vietnamese even suggested the United States was prolonging the war to protect recently discovered petroleum deposits off the South Vietnamese coast for U.S. oil interests. "Oh, it was oil you were after," a Vietnamese said to an American. "Why didn't you tell us in the first place? That would have made it much easier to understand why you were spending billions of dollars a year on our little country."

But these charges were unfounded. Although American economic investment had profit motives, its expansion to South Vietnam was not the objective of U.S. military and political intervention. Nor does it appear that it was the goal of U.S. business simply to "rip off" the Vietnamese by exploiting the American military presence. The U.S. Departments of State and Commerce advised American businessmen "if you find any investment opportunities that look interesting, get a Vietnamese as a partner. Don't compete with the Vietnamese." American companies often provided capital for joint ventures with Vietnamese businessmen. Parsons and Whittemore and Foremost Dairies, for instance, founded their operations in conjunction with South Vietnamese investors. And James Swanson bankrolled his shrimp business with capital put up by Vietnamese partners.

Neither U.S. corporations nor the U.S. government acted in collusion to monopolize the economic market in South Vietnam. Americans competed with energetic penetration by the Japanese, Thais, French, South Koreans, and Taiwanese. If there was to be an oil bonanza, the Japanese rather than the Americans stood to gain most from it. "Japan," according to a 1971 Newsweek article, "desperately wants other sources of oil to use as leverage against the rising price of Mideast crude." An official at the U.S. Embassy in Saigon pointed out, "It would be much easier for us to get out of here without a catastrophe if they [the South Vietnamese] could earn a lot of foreign money by selling petroleum."

Working for Americans

The South Vietnamese government welcomed the presence of RMK-BRJ and other private American business concerns. By 1968 the giant construction consortium alone was providing jobs for 60,000 Vietnamese, while other U.S. businesses employed tens of thousands more. Nguyen Huu Hanh, governor of South Vietnam's national bank, said in 1966 that "RMK-BRJ not only is raising the income of our working classes, but also is giving them an education." The Vietnamese who worked for RMK-BRJ performed a variety of tasks: unloading ships and trucks, operating winches and fork lifts, and driving thirty-ton flat-bed rigs. American stevedore Dick Adair described Vietnamese stevedores as "skinny little men, half naked in striped droopy drawers or loincloths. ... Each carries a few pieces of French bread wrapped in newspaper, and rice for lunch in little tin buckets."

But they did the job, enduring backbreaking physical labor. Under a scorching sun and in stifling humidity, they hefted big bags of cement, lugged steel beams and wood pilings, and pushed wheelbarrows brimming with wet concrete. Despite the arduous labor, Vietnamese anxiously lined up to apply for positions. Because of the military draft's drain on manpower, women, old and young, occupied most of even the physically demanding jobs. In June 1965 an American, P. T. White, then writing for National Geographic, watched a group of women stevedores at a dockside warehouse carrying bags of grain. "Women do the really heavy work here," an American informed White. "The bags are put on their shoulders and they walk about 200 feet to the truck. Each bag weighs 50 kilos, 110 pounds." At Cam Ranh a labor contingent of Vietnamese war widows became known as the "little tiger ladies."

Vietnamese received lower pay than Americans. Still, unskilled Vietnamese laborers could make much more from the Americans than most Vietnamese employers could offer. "I talked to a woman stevedore with gold teeth and black pajamas," said P. T. White. "She had no husband now, but she had eight children, and she was glad to have the job. It paid 65 piasters [less than a U.S. dollar] for eight hours, enough to feed her family if her daughters shopped wisely." Some American contractors staffed their work crews with laborers recruited by the Saigon government. "We have an agreement with the South Vietnamese Army's Joint General Staff," an American businessman wrote, "to take a number of men who have been wounded in action—we call them category two veterans. We give the government our needs. We say that we need 50 bricklayers, 75 stonemasons, or so many forklift operators or truck drivers."

American employers dismissed allegations that they engaged their Vietnamese workers in "coolie labor." They claimed an impressive record of teaching the Vietnamese new industrial and technical skills and training them for management positions. Foremost Dairies gave on-the-job training to 100 Vietnamese workers at its Saigon factory. At Engineco, importers of U.S. equipment, manager Linden Brownell said his company was bringing "American know-how to Vietnam." Beyond that, he added, Engineco "has painstakingly trained Vietnamese mechanics to repair everything from baby incubators to diesel engines." An American businessman stated that U.S. firms "had access to the top people in Vietnam. Anyone with a technological background could join American firms at a preferable salary level and a very commanding title. They were able to work with very expert American engineers, equipment operators, and trainees."

Some United States companies shied away from hiring Vietnamese. "There are problems because the Vietnamese, though willing and intelligent, simply aren't big physically. ... It would take three or four of them to use a wrench, and the handle just isn't long enough to get that many hands on it," an American engineer explained. In a few American businesses tokenism was evident. Vietnamese were often placed in trainee positions just for show. "A man might be called a personnel assistant," an American businessman acknowledged, "when the only function he carried out was interpreter; a man might be called an engineer trainee when, in fact, the only thing he [did] was drive a vehicle."

Next to private business, the largest employer of Vietnamese was the United States government. Most American military bases around the country took on Vietnamese men and women to carry out a myriad of services and manual labor tasks. It was the policy of General William Westmoreland "to hire Vietnamese civilians to do the menial jobs and some of the skilled jobs. We would train them and put them through schools to drive trucks, tractors, and bulldozers. And they were good. Without them we probably would have needed 100,000 more troops." Fifty-year-old Le Van Dau, for example, worked at gardening and maintenance in the U.S. military advisers' compound near Go Cong. In Phan Rang Province, 300 kilometers northeast of Saigon, farmers near a U.S. Air Force base worked there as day laborers. It is estimated that the U.S. military employed over 90,000 Vietnamese in similar capacities. General Westmoreland wrote, "It might be initially amusing to watch a Vietnamese, dwarfed by his machine, operating a big American bulldozer or roadscraper, but the Vietnamese learned quickly and worked efficiently."

U.S. civilian agencies also employed Vietnamese as secretaries, messengers, clerks, interpreters, personnel assistants, administrative trainees, bookkeepers, receptionists, chauffeurs, and maintenance workers. A select num-

Vietnamese employees of the RMK–BRJ consortium spread gravel along Plantation Road near Saigon in August 1970.

ber of well-educated, highly skilled Vietnamese obtained management posts. Although their pay was less than one-fifth that of the Americans, the Vietnamese still enjoyed higher incomes than their counterparts in the South Vietnamese government. Their major complaint was that they felt shut out of any substantial role in decision making. They also resented the American notion that a Vietnamese could not be trusted because one could never be sure he or she was not a VC spy.

The American dream

The sheer magnitude of the American military and civilian presence indirectly created tens of thousands of occupations for job-hungry Vietnamese. Most involved service-oriented work, catering to the wants and needs of Americans who could afford to indulge themselves. This was particularly true of Saigon. Even though MACV policy was inclined toward sequestering U.S. troops from the Vietnamese, it was impossible to achieve this in a city that had become home to as many as 60,000 troops, inhabiting at least 500 buildings. Thousands of American civilians were their neighbors. The American colony in Saigon, in fact, was large enough to require a separate telephone directory.

Vietnamese attached themselves to American households as maids, butlers, cooks, house boys, and gardeners. They waited tables, washed dishes, and groomed the grounds at posh recreation haunts like the Cercle Sportif. Entertaining Americans became an industry in itself. Saigon teemed with movie houses featuring the latest Hollywood films, cafés, bars, restaurants, discotheques, steam baths and massage parlors (thin covers for brothels), and any other establishment that Americans might frequent. The hustling Saigonese devised some ingenious ways to earn a dollar. In 1967 Dinh Thanh Chinh rode his motor scooter each night to the gates of Tan Son Nhut air base and waited, along with scores of other competitors, to ferry U.S. airmen into the center of Saigon. Young Nguyen Qui "inherited" a valuable parking place just across from Saigon's USO. If he saw Americans cruising for a parking spot, Nguyen directed them into his space, yelling, "I watch! I watch!" He would then exact a fee from the driver for guarding his car.

Many shrewd Vietnamese found ways to profit from the Americans. Saigonese home owners capitalized on the city's critical scarcity of the kind of housing Americans wanted. By renting rooms to five American soldiers and their Vietnamese mistresses, Vu Van Phan supplemented his $70 a month salary. Despite warnings from his neighbors that Americans might draw VC terrorism and endanger his family, Phan believed that the risk was worth it: "To keep abreast of the rising cost of living caused by the war and the Americans, you have to deal with Americans if you want to maintain a decent standard of living." A Mr.

Ly, recalled Barbara Evans, wife of a British doctor, "assembled an array of labourers who demolished [his] cycle hut [motorcycle garage] overnight and began to build a warehouse with flats on top for foreigners. All over Saigon private building of this sort was proceeding at a phenomenal rate. Homes rose in weeks, not months."

The average landlord, like Vu Van Phan, profited only modestly off American rents. As Phan said, "I'm not making a fortune or exploiting anyone. I'm just holding my own." Many Vietnamese entrepreneurs were women whose husbands were off in the military. Of Saigon's labor force of 330,000, 250,000 were women. A Mrs. Danang owned a villa she rented to Americans, several restaurants, and a movie theater, as well as a lavish home of her own. Mrs. Nguyen Duy Luong owned pharmaceutical laboratories, directed the Nam Bo Bank, and managed the Park Hotel in Saigon, where the U.S. military held briefings. Huynh Thi Nga ran her family-owned Saigon car dealership. At least a dozen enterprising Vietnamese women in Saigon were said to have amassed fortunes estimated at $5 million each.

Because of its bustling, dollar-fueled economy, Saigon had a prosperous air. In 1965, American nurse Marva Hasselbad marveled: "The mood was infectious and it was hard to remember that the country was at war. Beautiful Vietnamese girls in lovely and often expensive aodais walked along the streets . . . looking into shop windows full of all kinds of merchandise—stereo sets and radios, and cosmetics and clothes mostly imported from Europe and the United States. . . . There was heavy traffic along all the main streets, and from the number of shining new vehicles one could scarcely credit the reports of waiting lists of several years for new cars." GI Larry Hughes was amazed on seeing Saigon for the first time: "As we drove through the streets of Saigon I stared out [at] blue and white taxicabs darting in and out of streets and alleys in swarms. Motorized pedicabs buzzed along . . . thousands of motor bikes and bicycles filled in when the space was available. . . . We passed banks, embassies, fine restaurants, department stores, auto showrooms, movie theaters, and beautiful boulevards."

In 1967, army Chaplain Robert Falabella "was surprised to see how large a city Saigon was. But what especially impressed me was that the city people gave no indications a war was going on. As we drove through the city it seemed we could just as well have been driving through almost any large city in the United States." Not even the destructive thrust of the 1968 Tet offensive into Saigon's heart could bridle the city's careening economy. U.S. military adviser Stuart Herrington remembered the astonished reaction of a North Vietnamese POW, Do Van Lanh, to his first glimpse of Saigon in 1971. "Lanh had never imagined," Herrington said, "that Saigon would be the colorful, fascinating collection of sights, smells, and sounds that unfolded before him. . . . [Lanh] was awe-

The Papillon Bar, Tu Do Street, one of the many establishments catering to the needs of American soldiers, March 1966. A group of bar girls sits opposite the American at the bar.

struck by the wealth of consumer goods for sale in Saigon's shops. He had been unprepared for such signs of prosperity and abundance."

Financially well-off Saigonese, particularly business people, attained an unprecedented standard of living. Mrs. Danang surrounded herself with luxuries, including paintings and sculptures, and made excursions to Switzerland to buy diamonds. Former South Vietnamese Brigadier General Nguyen Duc Hinh wrote, "High income and quick wealth turned these people into a new privileged urban class, a class by itself that never existed in Vietnamese society before."

The abundance of dollars and goods in Saigon's economy raised the living standard of some middle- and working-class residents too. Ordinary households usually owned a radio and one in ten a television. In 1967 Saigonese possessed 100,000 motorbikes, 25,000 motor scooters and motorcycles, 25,000 trucks, and 7,000 automobiles. Even unskilled laborers fortunate enough to be on an American payroll owned such appliances as electric rice cookers or transistor radios. A young cocktail waitress who made a decent salary was able to take taxis to and from work and had a maid to do the housework. A twenty-two-year-old Saigonese woman generally despised Americans "but loved what the Yankee dollar" was doing for her lifestyle. "I've saved enough to make most Americans look poor," she said to an American journalist before driving off in her pearl-white Toyota.

Off to the big city

Saigon's boom-town atmosphere attracted hundreds of thousands of rural Vietnamese. During the period of U.S. involvement, the city's population more than tripled from 800,000 in 1957 to 3 million in 1970. By 1972 its population density of 70,000 per square mile surpassed that of Hong Kong, Tokyo, and New York. In a 1972 U.S. government poll of urban residents, only 25 percent of the Vietnamese questioned "were native to the city they were living in." Most of the rural migration to Saigon occurred from 1965 to 1970, when its population doubled.

Nguyen Huu Khoa was typical of thousands of villagers whom the war drove from their villages toward the city in search of security and a chance to make a living. Khoa sold his house and garden in Long Thoi Village, 200 kilometers south of Saigon, after the VC mined the roads and

Pigs share a Saigon street with new owners of a television set, 1968. As American consumer goods flooded Saigon's markets in the 1960s, one out of ten households came to own a TV set.

put his farm produce transport operation out of business. Then he and his family headed for Saigon. "We didn't know what to expect," Khoa's wife said. "It seemed like such a big city, filled with strangers who never paid any attention to each other."

Khoa's scrappy family did better than just get by. Khoa went to work in a car wash, his wife opened a vegetable stall in the Central Market, and four of their twelve children took jobs. Together their salaries were enough to purchase things never available to them in their village. In their three-room house, electricity enabled them to have a sixteen-inch color television, two radios, and a sewing machine. Mrs. Khoa treasured her chrome-plated electric coffee pot, which she reserved for special occasions. Many other war refugees, like Khoa, made a reasonable living in their new urban environments. A U.S. study found that many "refugees have found means of support either directly because of U.S. troops or indirectly by providing the troops with needed services."

Not all who joined the mass flight to the cities were peasant refugees forced off their land by the fighting. The urban enticement of higher wages and modern conveniences drew hundreds of thousands of villagers hoping to find the good life. Dr. Gerald Hickey, an authority on Vietnamese society who worked for the RAND Corporation, indicated that "a good percentage of the people who flocked to the cities are not actually refugees. ... People came in to get jobs, to earn more cash than they ever had in their lives. They had found an entirely new way of life. ... If you have just a little money in the city you have electricity. Even a twenty-watt bulb is better than an oil lamp. These are services people do not find in the countryside."

Although Saigon was the first choice of villagers relocating to the city, they also migrated to such cities as Da Nang, Cam Ranh, Nha Trang, Hue, Qui Nhon, and Bien Hoa. Like Saigon, the populations of these cities markedly increased. Because Da Nang, Cam Ranh, and Nha Trang were extensions of U.S. military installations rather than separate metropolitan areas, Americans referred to them not as cities but as "urban complexes."

Residents of these "urban complexes" existed almost exclusively by working for Americans. A South Vietnamese soldier described what "working for the Americans" did for one Da Nang family. The wife "went to work for the Americans" as "a way to furnish their house with refrigerator, television set, record player, radio, electric fan, and other things they could never have afforded. After only a few months, their house was full of American and Japanese appliances." USAID adviser Joseph Salzburg found Da Nang "filled with displaced persons who came [as] job–seekers [and] who abandoned agrarian pursuits to find in Danang more salaried occupations." Duong Tam was a refugee from a village outside Qui Nhon who hoped to get a job at the U.S. military base nearby. "I would make more if I worked for an American construction firm," he said. "The Americans have many soldiers in Qui Nhon and so they are doing a lot of building."

South Vietnam's urban migrants unable to find formal employment with the Americans earned their livelihood by catering to the demands of American soldiers. Near the large U.S. base at Bien Hoa migrant Huynh Thanh opened a car wash with a colorful sign: "Car washing. Excellent service." Around Cam Ranh Bay Vietnamese businessmen and women set up bars, barbershops, and laundries to accommodate U.S. troops. A Vietnamese woman stated, "Everyone in my village was saying how easy it was to make a living in Cam Ranh, so I decided to join the gold rush." In Qui Nhon Vietnamese sold souvenirs and newspapers and pushed carts loaded with cold drinks for thirsty soldiers. In Da Nang Vietnamese did laundry and washed jeeps and trucks for American GIs. Others made money by beating brass shell casings gleaned from artillery positions into bowls, trays, and statuary and selling them to Americans as souvenirs.

"The urban revolution"

The Vietnamese rush to the cities and the American base areas was not discouraged by U.S. and South Vietnamese authorities. The migration from the countryside brought more Vietnamese under government control and deprived the Vietcong of the people or some of the "water" in which, according to Mao Tse-tung's saying, their guerrillas, or "fish," would "swim." U.S. adviser John Paul Vann saw urbanization as "the solution to guerilla warfare." In 1969 Vann observed how the "urban strategy" was useful. "Often we visit a hamlet that we thought was under Viet Cong control and we find it empty. Its population has been added to the three million Vietnamese farmers who have taken the trail to the cities in the past three years."

While in the French Indochina War approximately 85 percent of the people lived in rural villages, by 1970 about 40 percent of South Vietnam's 17 million people lived in urban areas. The dark side of this rapid urbanization was starkly dramatic. There were insufficient housing, sanitation, transportation, social services, and jobs to accommodate the tens of thousands of newcomers who settled in each month. In Saigon this provoked a state of emergency. Huge shantytowns encircled the city's prosperous center. At least half of Saigon's 3 million people lived in squalor, crunched into hovels slapped together from sheets of tin, cardboard, and mud. In some sections, 2,000 squatters crowded onto three or four acres of land. It was, a Vietnamese remarked, "as if the contents of a cookie jar had been squeezed into a sardine can." Authorities tried to expand public housing but completed only 2,000 new units a year, far below the 10,000 to 15,000 houses a year it needed just to stay even with its population increase.

Sewage and other sanitation facilities hardly existed for Saigon's huge "fringe population." Two-thirds occupied

buildings or shacks lacking even water. One American soldier, Ronald Bayless, recalled seeing people "living in cardboard shacks made out of Coca-Cola cartons, and I remember watching them go outside in the mud into a little bucket and take a bath there." People often bathed, urinated, and washed their clothes in the same meager amount of water found in gutters, puddles, or drawn from wells. Disease was rampant. Saigon during the war had the highest combined incidence of cholera, smallpox, bubonic plague, and typhoid of any major city in the world. Saigonese children had a one-in-three chance of reaching the age of four; in 1968, children under five accounted for half the city's deaths.

Uncollected garbage piled into mountainous heaps. In 1965 only a dozen antiquated French garbage trucks operated around the city, mostly in affluent commercial and residential districts. They dumped most of their refuse at sites within the metropolitan area. Don Luce of the IVS remembered seeing "enormous piles of refuse [on] the streets, causing the rat population to multiply and incidence of plague to increase." The dearth of hospitals

and clinics made it impossible to prevent epidemics. Saigon contained only 6,000 hospital beds, and there was just one trained doctor for every 8,000 residents.

Because the city possessed no adequate public transportation system, some 100,000 vehicles, burning low-grade gasoline and kerosene, choked the streets and fouled the air with a polluting blue haze. Saigon's forty-four primary schools could handle but 144,000 children, one-half of the city's school-age population, so up to 150,000 Saigonese children from poverty-stricken families scouted the streets in hope of earning some money. Thousands who could not find gainful employment joined the mobs of youthful beggars roaming the streets and alleyways. Triple-digit inflation made it difficult to procure the basic necessities. Throngs of adults, unable to get jobs, and lacking unemployment insurance or any kind of welfare help, hit the streets to survive. Some scavenged garbage dumps for scraps of food and salable items, and according to the South Vietnamese government, as many as 300,000 women resorted to prostitution, plying their trade on streets in nearly every city in South Vietnam. Saigon's

The other half. Left. *A Saigon slum abuts the city's prosperous center and comfortable U.S. military housing complexes.* Inset. *A food peddler washes her clothes in the gutter of Tu Do Street in March 1966.*

city budget totaled $8.7 million—equivalent to that of Lynchburg, Virginia, or Allentown, Pennsylvania, whose populations were at least twenty-five times smaller.

British journalist Richard West, in his book *Sketches from Vietnam*, called Da Nang a "dirty, filthy slum city." Residents of its urban slum, which the American soldiers called "Dogpatch," subsisted mainly on the U.S. military's garbage and rubbish. Marine Lieutenant Charles Anderson wrote, "Discarded soft drink and beer cases and pallets were salvaged and reappeared as the walls of shacks, giving only the barest protection from the weather. Scraps of sheet metal became roofs. Worn tires became playpens. Used aircraft fuel tanks became water tanks."

American and South Vietnamese officials combined their financial and technical resources to attack the country's urban blight. USAID built 12,000 new classrooms in Saigon, supplied them with desks and books, and trained new teachers. In 1969 the Saigon government conducted a nationwide urban immunization campaign that significantly reduced the incidence of diseases like cholera and bubonic plague. The United States supplied Saigon with

135 trucks to help remove its 60,000 metric tons of garbage a month and established a program to train sanitation mechanics to maintain them. MWK International of Seattle, which in 1967 had contracted with Saigon to construct new steam and gas generators, began producing 30,000 additional kilowatts of electricity. The United States financed water purification systems for Saigon and Da Nang. It also provided Saigon's fire department with modern pumps that cut from 300 to 50 the average number of shacks razed by a single blaze. More U.S. funds paid for twenty-nine public health clinics.

In spite of these efforts, urban disease still afflicted hundreds of thousands of people. When Saigon's new purification plant opened at the end of 1967, the city's worn and rusted iron pipe system recontaminated the water supply. The new garbage trucks could handle, at best, two-thirds of the garbage stacking the streets. The city's electrical service was insufficient to prevent daily brownouts and blackouts. Furthermore, municipal governments saw legions of their trained administrators "defect" to American agencies and businesses for better pay and benefits.

A black market operation in Saigon, February 1970. The markup of contraband ranged from 40 to 500 percent. With the exception of whiskey, which was often diluted with rice wine, black market goods were usually genuine.

Crime does pay

The most intractable urban ailments throughout the war were crime, black marketeering, drug dealing, and official corruption. Thousands of boys with neither jobs nor schooling formed mobs of juvenile delinquents who committed burglaries, muggings, and petty theft. Because the legitimate economy of South Vietnam's cities could not provide their people with enough jobs, services, and income, tens of thousands of Vietnamese supported themselves buying and selling goods and currency on the black market. In 1969 Robert Parker, former attaché to the U.S. Embassy in Saigon, testified before a U.S. Senate Permanent Investigating Subcommittee that "black marketeers and illicit money changers have built a racket which has been estimated overall as running over $150 million a year in Vietnam." The black market dealt mainly in goods stolen from American military or economic aid shipments. According to Phillip Knightley of the Sunday Times of London, pilferage cost an American subcontractor $118 million in one year. In 1967, Knightley reported, half a million tons of imported U.S. rice reportedly "disappeared."

In the black market at Qui Nhon thousands of cases of army C-rations, clothing, liquor, television sets and other appliances, guns, and ammunition brought black market operators a cool $10 million. Former South Vietnamese General Tran Van Don said a "large source of black market supplies was the American PX. . . . Many of the goods destined for the American soldiers never reached their destination. . . . Some big [Vietnamese] operators even published catalogues listing the PX goods for sale. If you wanted a Sony tape recorder, for example, you simply picked it out of the catalogue."

In long rows of sidewalk stalls Saigonese black market dealers openly displayed hair spray, watered-down Scotch, cartons of cigarettes, and all sorts of wares from the United States. USAID adviser David Garms observed, "From the muddy city of Cau Mau in the south to Quang Tri near the Demilitarized Zone, the black market was widespread and stunningly well-organized. I might go into any of the U.S. military exchanges and still not be able to find what I wanted in liquor, cigarettes, or razor blades, but there was certainly not a single street in any city or town in South Vietnam where I would not be able to buy these things openly."

American soldiers and civilians also participated in the black market. Vietnamese journalist Van Minh wrote, "I wonder if any Vietnamese, however cunning and resourceful they may be, could afford to steal so many goods as to regularly feed the innumerable open black markets without the connivance of the Americans themselves. . . . It is a well-known fact that some American guards at U.S. warehouses often come to a deal with Vietnamese crooks. In exchange for a certain amount of money or for some

cute girls, those guards agree to let the crooks have absolute freedom to steal everything." James Lilly, general manager of RMK-BRJ, said in 1966, "A GI can drive up to a supply yard in his six-by-six truck, wave a carbine at the Vietnamese guards, order them to open the gates and load up with everything he wants. . . . U.S. servicemen support and sustain the black market for PX goods and troop commodities."

One of South Vietnam's biggest black market profiteers was General Nguyen Huu Co. Co had held several important positions in the South Vietnamese government, including corps commander, minister of defense, and deputy prime minister. In addition to his black market dealings, Co once fired a province chief because the chief refused to give Co's wife a "gift" of a large piece of real estate in the province. He justified his shady dealings in a letter to a friend. "In our careers as generals," he wrote, "once we are turned out to pasture, it is very difficult to change profession." The American black market and smuggling kingpin was an American named William Crum. Crum began his business career as a liquor distributor to American PXs in Korea in 1950. By 1960 he had expanded into supplying goods to military installations throughout the Far East. Crum, known as the "money king," got started in South Vietnam by bribing three officials of the Army-Air Force Regional Exchange in order to obtain military contracts for slot machines, juke boxes, and other coin-operated devices. In addition to buying himself a monopoly of amusement sales to U.S. military clubs, Crum engaged in smuggling and black market currency transactions. His philosophy, people who knew him recalled, was simple: "No one is honest. Everyone has their price . . . whether it is a four star general or a private."

In 1970, the Senate Permanent Subcommittee of the Committee on Government Operations began investigating reports that Crum was reaping nearly $40 million from his illegal operations in South Vietnam. U.S. government investigators offered the subcommittee substantial evidence of Crum's corrupt financial empire. As a result, in June 1970 the U.S. Army punished General Earl Cole because of his involvement in Crum's illegal military activities by demoting him to colonel, placing him on involuntary retirement, and stripping him of his medals. As for Crum, he disappeared on his yacht in the South Pacific before he could be apprehended by U.S. authorities. He was killed in a Hong Kong fire in 1977. During the subcommittee hearings, when Senator Abraham Ribicoff asked Jack Bybee, a former employee of Crum in South Vietnam, "Are there many Mr. Crums operating in Vietnam?" Bybee replied, "To be honest there are many, many crumbs."

In 1966 U.S. authorities prosecuted over 400 servicemen and civilians for black marketeering. Because of the black market's prevalence, however, most Vietnamese and Americans involved were never punished. "Vietnamese black marketeers are so well organized," American Robert Parker stated, "that they have legal services departments that promptly pay the fine of any money changer caught and set him back up in the business." Sergeant Richard Grefath of the 101st Airborne Division said, "There were some guys stationed in Saigon who had rackets going all over the place. A friend of mine had what would be considered a villa. He had his own jeep, a beautiful house, and owned three bars. He was making a fortune!" Some American deserters also used the black market, supporting themselves by selling goods purchased from PXs. A GI deserter in Saigon said, "You get up late, you smoke a few joints, you get on your Honda and ride around to the PX, buy a few items you can sell on the black market, come back, blow some more grass, and that's it for the day."

Although in South Vietnam there existed, as General Westmoreland acknowledged in 1967, "a strong temptation for embezzlement," the majority of U.S. troops resisted the lure of black marketeering. Thousands, however, did succumb. "Be alert," Westmoreland urged his commanders, "for [military] crooks and grafters." Despite MACV's vigilance, the black market remained a persistent problem. In 1969 the Senate Permanent Subcommittee of the Committee on Government Operations found that the black market in South Vietnam was costing the military $2 billion a year.

Besides the black market, beginning in 1968 South Vietnamese urban centers became marts for marijuana, heroin, cocaine, opium, amphetamines, and LSD, most of it sold to American soldiers. They could purchase any drug from men, women, and even children. Urban drug entrepreneurs also established fancy drug parlors, or "shooting galleries," where soldiers could "snort" cocaine or "mainline" heroin. In Saigon's "skag bars" a GI could order heroin stirred into his beer. In "Mom's," near Tan Son Nhut, soldiers could buy LSD, mescaline, heroin, or marijuana "joints" rolled on electric machines.

By 1970 South Vietnam's urban drug business had ballooned into an industry more profitable than any legitimate trade in the country. Between 1968 and 1972, drug moguls raked in more than $1 billion, according to U.S. government estimates, because of high demand, even though the opiates and marijuana they sold were cheap. A heroin habit, for example, cost an addict $2 to $6 a day compared to $200 or more in the United States or elsewhere. The drug culture was so extensive that Lieutenant General Walter Kerwin, deputy chief of staff for army personnel, suspected that "some of the people who were volunteering to go back to Vietnam for maybe the second or third time did that for the specific purpose of drugs."

Illicit traffic in black market goods and drugs thrived because of pervasive corruption at high levels of the South Vietnamese government. After a fact-finding trip to South Vietnam in early 1968, Senator Edward Kennedy charged that "South Vietnamese police accept bribes" and "offi-

cials and their wives run operations in the black market." Former General Tran Van Don, in his book *Our Endless War*, wrote of government officials and their wives who prospered by dealing in the black market and drugs: "One thing that deserves close scrutiny by historians who want to seek out the roots of South Vietnam's social and political problems is the incredible clout exerted on our political leaders by their wives. There were a thousand ways, both legal and illegal, of making money in war-torn Vietnam. And the wives of our leaders mastered all of them." A study by a Vietnamese political group in 1975, Don added, "estimated that between 1954 and 1975 these mighty wives pocketed an equivalent of $500 million. There is an old saying in our country calling the wives 'the generals of the internal affairs.'"

Mrs. Nguyen Ngoc Quy stepped off a flight from Thailand in 1971 with 19.8 pounds of heroin hidden in her suitcase. She was the daughter of a senior official in South Vietnam's Senate. A week later, Pham Chi Thien, a government deputy, was caught smuggling 9 pounds of heroin from Laos. To reduce, much less eradicate, such official corruption was difficult to the point of impossibility. It so permeated the South Vietnamese government that proof was difficult to obtain and prosecution therefore rare. "One reason corruption's so hard to prove," an official at the American embassy, who wished to remain anonymous, said, "is that investigations are extremely dangerous. When so many people are making so much money, they aren't going to stand by and let someone ask a lot of embarrassing questions."

For officials like General Nguyen Duc Thang, head of the South Vietnamese government's Revolutionary Development program, running an honest program meant bucking a very powerful system. "It is very hard," he said. "If you are not one of them you become a threat to them and very dangerous." Education Minister Le Minh Tri discovered how dangerous. While investigating a graft scandal at the National Medical School in 1967, Tri made enemies who decided to put him out of the way. As Tri was on his way to the office one January morning, an assassin on a motorcycle tossed a hand grenade into his car, killing him and his chauffeur.

An uncertain future

After witnessing the alarming social and economic problems besetting the country's cities, in 1969 American and South Vietnamese officials began to feel that their experiment in encouraging urbanization had created a monster. "What's going on here in South Vietnam is a revolution," a senior U.S. official told a *Newsweek* reporter in February 1970. "And it is making what is happening out there in the jungles between us and the Communists passé. . . . What are we going to do with all these people once the fighting stops? I don't think for a moment that anyone has given

Some of Saigon's many homeless children try to nap on a sidewalk, March 1966. The war generated refugees faster than relief efforts could house them, and many of them ended up in Saigon.

this much thought." Policymakers had assumed that when security conditions in rural areas improved, as they did after 1968, most refugees would return to their village. But they had misjudged. "I don't think these people are going to go back to the countryside," the American social scientist Gerald Hickey said. "Luxuries they never heard of have become necessities and I don't think they're going to give them up. As a result, the cities are going to be hopelessly overpopulated."

"I might go back when the war ends," fifty-one-year-old Nguyen Huu Khoa told *New York Times* correspondent Terrence Smith in early 1970. "But we old people are the only ones who care anymore. My children will never go back. I remember what it was like—no electricity, no running water, no TV set, they wouldn't like that." Khoa's oldest daughter added, "We're city people now."

What of the poorest Saigonese who had none of the "luxuries" the Khoa family had grown used to? The Saigon regime had optimistically gambled, said a South Vietnamese government official, "that if conditions were bad enough, the squatters will gladly go home." But many impoverished city dwellers—even those in the most squalid conditions—showed no signs of packing their few belongings and returning to the country. "Once they've seen the glamour of the cities," a U.S. official remarked, "they'll take a shack with television in a slum rather than ten acres of rice in Dullsville."

The biggest worry for Americans and South Vietnamese who were planning for the future concerned the economic impact the U.S. military withdrawal would inflict on a population that—rich or poor—relied so heavily on the foreigners' dollars. Under 10 percent of the urban work force, for example, was employed in local industry. South Vietnam's urban society, once deprived of the U.S. dollars it fed on, could fall apart, with disastrous economic and political consequences. "Our cities are parasites which produce nothing and import everything," a South Vietnamese official said in 1969. "And we—not the Communists—are manufacturing them."

Persistent Vietcong agitation and propaganda in urban ghettos induced additional anxiety. Many Americans and South Vietnamese regarded South Vietnam's overcrowded cities as potential time bombs. Don Luce wrote, "The allied forces have helped to create a rootless urban

Pop Culture Abroad

Inset left. *The dance floor at the Baccarat discotheque, March 1966. A popular Saigon night spot, the Baccarat was billed as "Paris After Midnight."*

A Saigon billboard advertises the American movie Love Story.

Inset right. *A Vietnamese rock band, CBC, performs in a club in Saigon.*

While their parents complained about the American foreigners' "rebellious teen-agers" and "crazy music," young people in Saigon avidly imitated the clothing styles, long hair, and rock 'n' roll music then popular among teen-agers in the United States. Saigonese "hippies" gathered in cafés where they smoked marijuana and listened to American protest songs by Bob Dylan and Joan Baez. Teen-age girls jammed movie theaters to see the latest teen idols. Along with half a million U.S. soldiers, the "generation gap" had come to South Vietnam.

society. Such an unstable society not only promises little tactical support to the side that has created it, but is also likely to pay bitter dividends of social discontent for years in the future." Gerald Hickey said of wartime Saigon: "This city is a prescription for disaster."

While government authorities pondered the ramifications of the urban revolution, many Vietnamese brooded over its deleterious effects on their society and culture. Some, for example, saw "reckless economic disruption" and blamed it on the Americans. A South Vietnamese soldier whose family lived in Da Nang asserted, "If they [Americans] see a relatively new house that looks to them halfway decent, they snap it up on the spot. The landlords take the Americans' money, buy more houses with it, fix them up, and rent them to more Americans. . . . The more Americans there are, the worse it is for everyone who doesn't have much money." The American presence, one Vietnamese lamented, "has created pockets of insolent prosperity widening still further the economic gap between the cities and the countryside."

In addition to the dangerous distortion of the economy, there was also the distortion of traditional Vietnamese society. The fact that those who flourished on American dollars—earned legally or illegally—lived better than those who did not pitted Vietnamese against Vietnamese. A policeman, for instance, made only $25 a month, an American-employed construction worker up to $300. Most infuriating to many, a civil servant with twenty years experience earned $85 a month, while a young bar girl or prostitute could take in ten times as much. A prostitute's income sometimes exceeded an ARVN major's or even a cabinet minister's. A university professor complained, for example, "There was a time when the scholar was the most respected member of Vietnamese society . . . but no longer. Why, when my wife goes to the market with her flat purse, the merchants look down on her. Their best pieces of pork or chicken are saved for the taxi girls who can pay the American prices."

"The main problem with the American presence [in the cities] is that the man in the street, along with our government, has developed the habit of leaning on Americans for everything," a Vietnamese publisher in

Saigon said. "Today, Americans are paving the streets of Saigon and everybody is happy about it. If tomorrow the U.S. decided to take over garbage removal in Saigon, most people would find this perfectly natural too. . . . The American presence has become a kind of opiate."

A Vietnamese student leader in Saigon railed at urbanization as a menace to moral values. "You Americans are the real revolutionaries," he told Tom Buckley of the *New York Times* in 1971. "You gave us Hondas that we didn't need or want. The North Vietnamese are conservatives in comparison to you." The crass materialism they believed the Americans fostered angered many Vietnamese as well. A city engineer in 1971 said, "Many people believe things were better in 1961 than they are today. The morality of our society is declining sharply. Our spiritualism has given way to materialism." Few Vietnamese seemed willing to accept responsibility, at least in part, for the urban

revolution in their country. The money and jobs generated by the American presence may have caused people to rush to the cities, but there is no doubt that many of them enjoyed urban living and the economic and social opportunities it afforded. While for some Vietnamese, life in the city was chaotic and oppressive, for others it provided a new sense of freedom from the social constraints of the village and the excitement of change.

Vietnamese abhorred the endemic corruption in the cities—crime, black marketeering, drugs, and graft—yet even some of those involved in it held American aid responsible. In March 1968 Saigon's *Cong Chang* newspaper charged that "American aid is entirely responsible for the current corruption. Americans have earned more animosity than sympathy from the Vietnamese people." *Saigon Daily News* columnist Van Minh took the more reasonable position that the corruption of the people was, in part, a self-inflicted wound. He placed some of the onus on the Vietnamese people for not resisting "the many opportunities for corruption caused by the Americans' tempting display of riches." Even those who accepted the necessity of the U.S. presence mourned what it was doing to their country. "Of course I want the Americans to stay," a Vietnamese stewardess said. "I don't want the Viet Cong to take away my freedom. But I can't help hating the Americans for the way they are corrupting my country."

Looking to the future, older Vietnamese—parents and teachers—attributed a growing generation gap in urban society to American cultural influences. American popular culture, spread by the presence of so many youthful soldiers, had a distinctive effect on Vietnamese teenagers. They imitated almost every element of the youth culture then thriving in the United States and elsewhere, including "free love," rock 'n' roll, jeans, drugs, and rebelliousness.

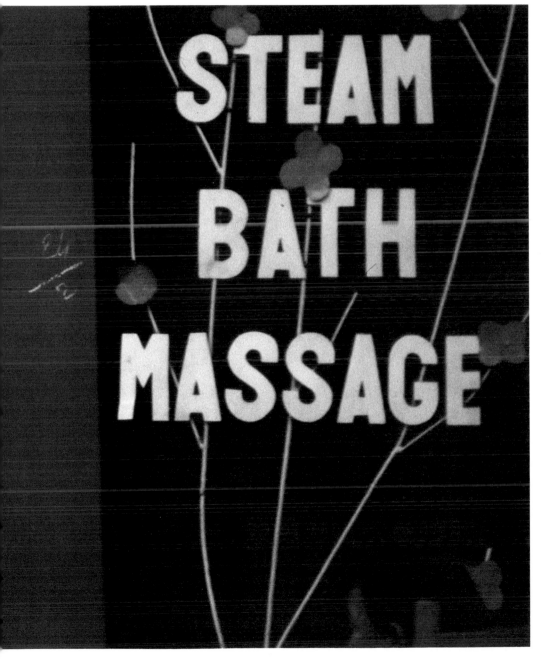

"The young people have lost their faith in the older generation," observed Nguyen Van Trung, faculty dean of Saigon University. "This is why the youngsters have given up the ideal of a life of struggle and are now in pursuit of pleasure." Gerald Hickey explained, "Young people [in the cities] have their Hondas and their Western clothing and they really like it all. They listen to rock music on their transistors. The cities have little cafes where they can go and drink coffee, and have some companionship away from the old family constraints. They have formed an entirely new world and they won't leave it."

For better or worse, the Americanized urban environment in South Vietnam exposed many Vietnamese to a very different world than most of them had known before. How they would resolve the conflicts—traditional versus modern, spiritualism versus materialism, village serenity or city excitement—depended on the outcome of the war. A Saigon elder put it this way one day in 1969: "Our situation borders on the schizophrenic. Our feet are deeply rooted in an agrarian and traditional past—and our hands firmly resting on an electric rice cooker."

An American brothel for servicemen on Tu Do Street.

Saigon

A City in Transition

The French called it the "Paris of the Orient." They prized Saigon for its stately French architecture, tree-lined boulevards, splendid hotels and villas, and cozy cafés. But by the peak of the U.S. military build-up in the 1960s, Saigon was rapidly losing its identity. Its famous boulevards were widened and their trees cut down to accommodate big American trucks and vehicles. U.S. combat boots scratched the glazed tile floors of elegant French villas. Noisy jeeps and motorcycles crowded out the cyclos and pedicabs of Saigon's placid past.

For the Vietnamese, the coming of the Americans heralded an era of modernization, growth, and unprecedented affluence. The U.S. presence meant new

The intersection of Tu Do and Tran Hung Dao streets, Saigon. Inset. At one of sixty checkpoints in the city, a Vietnamese soldier examines I.D. papers of cyclists.

businesses and tens of thousands of jobs for Saigon. The city's shops soon overflowed with U.S. subsidized imported goods. Services like electricity and water, previously available only to the wealthy, now reached the homes of many of the city's poorest residents.

Saigon used its newly acquired affluence to insulate itself from the terror and suffering imposed by the fighting on rural villagers. According to a South Vietnamese government survey, most Saigonese considered their economic well-being, not the war, their top preoccupation. Saigon's boom-town atmosphere was infectious. Thousands of rural villagers packed their belongings and abandoned their rice fields to seek new lives in already overcrowded Saigon. Most newcomers endured poverty and menial jobs, but few were willing to give up electricity and television to return to a village where such amenities were lacking.

Kept afloat by U.S. dollars, the Saigonese for a while could even afford the luxury of demonstrating against the United States, yet at the same time hoping that the Americans, and their money, would

Morning traffic jam. GIs in cyclos and Saigonese wait for a light to change on Cong Ly Street in Saigon. Inset. A young entrepreneur displays his selection of Vietnamese dolls.

Two views of Saigon. Elegant and comfortable French-style homes (inset) often bordered Vietnamese slum districts.

always be around. Only in 1969, when U.S. troops began withdrawing from South Vietnam, did the buoyant Saigonese find cause to reflect. For the first time, the people of Saigon had to confront a question they had so long ignored: What would be the fate of their city once the Americans were gone?

Hearts and Minds

Visitors to Saigon were often surprised at how swiftly the city ended and the countryside began, how suddenly the scene changed from urban to rural, from houses and cars and crowds and clamor, to fields and water buffaloes and vegetation and quiet. This was a different world from Tu Do Street, from the American base at Da Nang, or the concrete fastness of the American embassy. This was the true home of the Vietnamese people, of the peasants who made up the majority of South Vietnam's population. This was the world of the villages, a world seemingly of another century: rooted in the land, enclosed in thick hedgerows, isolated, autonomous, self-contained and self-reliant, a place of thatched huts and winding dirt paths, of Buddhist altars and ancestral tombs, of village elders and barefoot farmers. A world of tradition: timeless, changeless, and enduring.

But all was not what it seemed. In fact, a great deal had happened to village life over the pre-

vious century. War and revolution, colonial rule, and economic depression had profoundly shaken the traditional order. Decades of mounting disruption had set in motion social and political forces that were refashioning rural Vietnam even as the men of the 3d Marine Division cautiously left the protection of the air base at Da Nang in the summer of 1965 and entered the world of the "villes."

Tradition and revolution

Much of traditional life remained. The village continued to be an insular, family-centered world. Except for hamlets bordering main roads where small shops might be found, the physical appearance of the villages had changed little from what it had been generations before. Wherever the VC were unable to dominate, traditional landholding patterns persisted: A few resident farmers or absentee landlords owned the majority of hectares; the rest of the villagers had little or no land of their own. There continued to be a striking homogeneity in attitudes, values, and daily behavior, a shared world view rooted in the Buddhist-Taoist-Confucianist tradition. The level of technology in village

Preceding page. *An American marine offers a peasant girl a cigarette.*

production, like the level of specialization, remained low. The social horizon was still restricted to the events and people of the village itself, and the age-old patterns of livelihood—rice farming and fishing—still set the rhythms of life for the majority of peasants.

A social revolution had not yet overturned the Vietnamese village of the mid-1960s, but wherever one looked beneath the surface, change was evident. Kinship bonds loosened as individuals sought opportunities in urban areas. The spread of radios and government newspapers, like the arrival of teachers, connected isolated hamlets with the outside world. Challenged first by anti-French partisans and then by the growing political power of the central government, traditional hierarchies of authority were less secure. The village had become dependent on the national economy for an important part of its needs, and except for the most remote areas, individual fortunes had become enmeshed in an international economic structure. Technology in the form of fertilizer, concrete, rice mills, even tractors, had begun to suggest the broader possibilities of innovation. Improvements in transportation made it possible for wealthier villagers to engage in fruit or vegetable farming with an eye to the expanding urban markets, to travel more frequently to the cities, to become businessmen as well as farmers, and to sample the con-

Near a Vietcong village outside of Cu Chi, a straw roof camouflages a temporary shelter from American aircraft.

sumer goods of urban society.

These changes were in part a legacy of French efforts to exploit the resources of Vietnam. They were also the result of revolutionary innovations in landownership, taxation, and the distribution of local political power introduced by the Vietminh during the nine-year struggle against colonial rule. And in part they were a function of Saigon's attempts to develop the countryside and bring the peasant population under its control.

The government's efforts to improve communications, increase agricultural production, provide health care, and create a system of rural education were not without effect. But they rested on three faulty assumptions: that the peasants were content with their lot, when in fact they had serious grievances; that the way to gain their loyalty was by increasing the *amount* of material goods and social services available to them, when in fact many peasants were attracted to the Vietcong by the promise of a *redistribution* of wealth and power; and that the Communists' goal was to overthrow the government, when in fact they were intent upon overthrowing the entire social system on which the government rested.

These misconceptions help to explain why Saigon's development efforts, while slowly extending the benefits of modern life to rural hamlets, bore such little political fruit. But there were other reasons as well. The elimination of elected village councils, a land reform program that was reformist in name only, the corruption of local officials, the depredations of ARVN troops, as well as chronic political instability at the national level after 1963, were all symptomatic of a more fundamental problem: the failure of non-Communist South Vietnamese leaders to reach beyond class interest, political factionalism, and personal ambition to effectively govern their people. At the same time, the GVN's overheated rhetoric of change led to expectations that expanded more rapidly than the government's ability or desire to satisfy them, creating a "revolution of rising frustrations." Thus, even as new opportunities began to make their appearance in the villages, the brief years of peace evaporated in a renewal of insurgency.

By 1965 violence had become a brutal fact of village life. When the first American combat troops arrived in Vietnam, armed conflict had been going on in the countryside for seven years. The result was a state of almost perpetual insecurity. Few villages had been spared Vietcong incursions of one sort or another: propaganda, armed attacks, terrorism, demands for food and taxes, recruitment for political demonstrations or conscription into guerrilla units. As the insurgents grew stronger the government retaliated with military force and demands of its own: for men, for information on VC activity, for food, for public demonstrations of loyalty. But because the ARVN could not insure the villagers' safety, the peasants found themselves in an impossible situation.

Most villagers maintained an appearance of pragmatic neutrality. Outside the hamlet, explained one old man from a Mekong Delta village, "the people follow the Liberation Front, inside they follow the government. They follow whoever is strong. You see, they have two shoulders, so they can carry everything, so they follow both sides." But as the fighting escalated the dual burden grew heavier. "This war is much worse than the last one," said a refugee from Binh Dinh Province. "The fighting is far more widespread. ... People don't know which side to take to feel safe. There are so many families with relatives on both sides. I've seen government hamlet chiefs murdered by their own nephews. It breaks your heart to see Vietnamese families killing each other like that."

The seeming indifference the peasants often displayed to Americans obscured the terrible strains the war had created within the villages. With bands of armed men appearing at irregular intervals, deaths from fighting, families leaving to find some security elsewhere, and the influx of strangers relocated from other areas, the traditional cohesiveness of isolated hamlets gave way. There was great confusion and uncertainty about what was happening. "I don't think they know on whom they should put the blame," said one elderly farmer about his neighbors. "They only see that this war is miserable. ... They never put into their minds either nationalism or revolution. They do not see that this form of government behaves this way or that philosophy behaves in another way. They only say it is due to the war."

Meanwhile, pressures from both sides led to mounting division, accusations, and betrayal. The American anthropologist Gerald Hickey reported on this kind of social deterioration in the delta village of Khanh Hau, in the late 1950s, citing incidents of violence between villagers and even suicide—heretofore almost unheard of. The result was to turn the individual villager ever more inward, his concern limited to survival for himself and his family. Alienated from the government, fearful or unsure of the Vietcong, largely indifferent to the geopolitical issues at stake, most peasants only wanted the shooting to stop. "I would like the war to end because I hate hearing shooting and artillery planes and bombs," said a peasant woman from Long An. "I don't like to find bullet holes in my walls. I'm very much afraid of getting killed when there is shooting. ... I'm always anxious and tense. I can't sleep well at night. When there's shooting, you never know if you'll get hit or killed."

Thus when American soldiers and American pacification teams, American AID workers and American development experts entered the Vietnamese village they encountered a complex world in which revolution and counterrevolution were at work side by side; a world where age-old social arrangements were declining or under attack; where new possibilities were being shaped and new opportunities being seized—a world of superstition and innovation, of stability and insecurity, of violence and a desperate longing for peace. This was the world the United States set out to protect, to develop, to democratize, to save.

The Americans

"To rural South Vietnamese," wrote two of South Vietnam's former military leaders, "the United States was a total stranger." Although American professors, government workers, missionaries, and military advisers had been in contact with the world of the Vietnamese village since the late 1950s, their numbers were small and for most peasants they remained an unknown quantity.

To some, the Americans appeared much like the French, an association the Vietcong put to good use. "They say the Americans follow on the French heels, to replace the French," reported a village schoolteacher. "So they persuade the people to oppose the Americans." Not everyone was convinced. "Oh, we could never get close to the French," observed a man from Duc Lap Village in Hau Nghia Province. "But since the American advisers came here I could see they were all kind; they like the people and the children like them too." For others, like a platoon of Hoa Hao militia, the Americans were a welcome source of help. Recalled the platoon leader: "When we saw the Americans we had much affection towards them. When they saw that we did not have enough supplies they gave us cigarettes and ammunition. They gave us a telephone to contact their battalion, and when we went on combined operations with them the advisors always paid more attention to us than to the [ARVN]."

But for many peasants the Americans were an enigma. "When I see an American soldier I feel very sorry for my people," a peasant woman from the delta told an interviewer. "We are so small, and dark, and underfed compared to Americans. Life must be very good and the work must be very easy where they come from. I wonder why they want to come to this poor place."

At a meeting of U.S. and South Vietnamese leaders in Honolulu in February 1966, President Johnson insisted that the answer to that question was more than just defeating Communist guerrillas in battle. The war "must be won on two fronts," declared the president. Beyond the military effort "is the struggle against social injustice: against hunger, disease and ignorance, against political apathy and indifference," a struggle that "cannot wait until the guns grow silent and the terrorism stops." Pledging U.S. resources "to meet the people's need for larger output, more efficient production, improved credit, handicrafts and light industry, and rural electrification," Johnson vowed to push forward the work of "social revolution."

GVN propaganda posters on the wall of a government facility, flanked by the pages of a Playboy calendar, call upon the villagers to "Enter the army, kill the Communists and save our nation."

An American officer and USAID advisers examine the remains of a village house demolished by U.S. shelling.

In a U.S. funded school in the Mekong Delta, a young girl points to letters on the blackboard as her classmates sing out the sounds.

The focus of these efforts would be the 12,000 villages of the countryside. By 1966 the village had already been extolled as the key to pacification, the key to economic and social reform, the key to the stability of the GVN. There were U.S. military commanders who argued that the war could not be won unless operations were mounted directly against North Vietnam; and there were U.S. civilians who questioned what role development could play in the countryside when the primary demand was military security. Nonetheless, Honolulu reaffirmed a fundamental tenet of American involvement in Indochina: Whatever military victories the allied forces might achieve against the VC/NVA, the ultimate contest would take place in the hearts and minds of the people of rural Vietnam.

The programs and projects that emerged from this consensus were breathtaking in their scope and bewildering in their variety. The largest investment of money and manpower was made through USAID, which sponsored programs in education, agriculture, public health, public safety, land reform, local government, public works, and refugee relocation. By 1967 AID had hundreds of men and women in the field allocating over $300 million a year for development and relief. But they were not the only Americans at work in the villages. USIS Field Service teams showed films on agricultural innovations, health, and sanitation to millions of peasants, distributed leaflets, broadcast radio programs, and published a monthly magazine in simple Vietnamese called *Rural Spirit.* American servicemen labored on village civic action projects while dozens of private American voluntary agencies operated schools, supplied agricultural equipment, experimented with new crops, and conducted family planning clinics.

All of this effort produced some notable accomplishments. When the French left Vietnam in 1954 only 400,000 children had received primary school education. By 1970 this figure had risen to 2.3 million. During the intervening years some 40,000 teachers had been trained and more than 30,000 classrooms built. Newly constructed hospitals treated peasants whose parents had never seen a doctor, while their children were protected from smallpox, cholera, and the plague by a program of immunization that had reached the rate of more than 2 million a month in 1968. The introduction of "miracle" rice increased production by more than 40 percent to 7 million tons in 1974 which, along with successful programs to upgrade hog, poultry, and fish production improved the general availability of food and the amount of protein in the diets of ordinary Vietnamese. More than 2,500 miles of paved roads were completed between 1967 and 1971 alone, while village/hamlet radio systems brought communication to the local level and provided the foundation for a national telecommunications network.

Behind the impressive statistics and the bold pronouncements were individual Americans who came to work in the villages of South Vietnam. What they found there, what they were able to achieve, and what they left undone is in many ways the most lasting measure of what the United States was able to accomplish for the people of Vietnam. Here are the stories of four such Americans.

Hoa Hiep

Clustered along Route 1 twelve kilometers north of Da Nang, the village of Hoa Hiep was an island of green paddies and vegetable gardens surrounded by sand. "It was all dirt streets, dirt paths actually," remembers former U.S. Marine Sergeant John Large. Neither particularly prosperous nor desperately poor by Vietnamese standards, the village was still "a lot poorer than what I had anticipated, a lot more war torn than what I imagined it would be."

Large had come to Hoa Hiep in November 1966 to join a thirteen-man Combined Action Platoon (CAP) called Echo Two, one of seventy-five such units scattered along the coastal plain of I Corps. The CAPs were an innovative attempt to win the loyalty of villagers to the GVN. Working with two dozen Popular Forces soldiers, each CAP was charged with defending and pacifying a single village, simultaneously training the PFs and helping the peasants and fishermen build a better life.

What brought Large from Corpus Christi, Texas, to Vietnam in the first place was "a patriotism for my country. I thought my country needed me." It looked as if the people of Hoa Hiep did too. Deceptively peaceful during the day, at night the countryside around the village belonged to local-force VC who roamed out of the nearby foothills to burn down a house, murder an informer, or attack the Popular Forces garrison. The men of Echo Two set out to change that. They began by building a barbed-wire enclosed compound on the edge of the village to house the combined marine/Vietnamese unit, then settled into a wearying and sometimes nerve-wracking routine of day and night patrols, setting ambushes, gathering intelligence, and trying to instill in the PFs a more aggressive posture toward the enemy.

Making Hoa Hiep secure was the most important job of Large's platoon. But their mission also called for a heavy emphasis on civic action. "After we got the compound built, we got into social relationships with the villagers, gathering rice, building water wells, dikes, bridges, anything that we thought would help the Vietnamese." The men scrounged materials, offered guidance and sweat. It was a way of getting to know the Vietnamese in a casual atmosphere.

Lieutenant Rex Fore, a member of the province advisory team, teaches English to villagers in Cai Lay.

Large met a number of villagers when he turned his civilian builder's skills to the construction of a four-room high school. "There were a lot of people involved in that. We hired local bricklayers, local plaster people. There was more involvement between Americans and Vietnamese in the school than anything.

When I was building the school there was a fisherman across from me, working on a fishing boat. We would josh one another about our different ways of doing things. The school was being built with mechanical tools, power tools, and his boats were all built by hand. They were using tools that I've seen in museums in the States.

Large and the old man hit it off and the two would sit for hours talking about what was happening to the world of Hoa Hiep.

"Vietnam was changing rapidly while I was there. I'd guess you'd say the Vietnamese were becoming more and more Westernized. In terms of dress, in terms of business dealings, in terms of machinery. You'd go out to some of these villages, way out in the boondocks, see a Singer sewing machine sitting out there, old foot pedal model—

they were picking up on an easier way of doing things."

But for all the currents of westernization, for all the easy banter and the times he would be invited to a villager's home to share a family feast at Tet, Large found Hoa Hiep a difficult and deeply frustrating place. "We never did figure out why we didn't get a better reception than we did. You know, we'd go on patrol at night, the VC would be in the area, and people would never relate to us."

Yet this was, after all, Vietcong country and had been during most of the past twenty years. For some villagers the Americans were a source of danger. Going through the hamlets "you'd see where a house was burned out, where the VC had picked out one family and murdered it. If they related too closely to us and the VC found out about it, they would do away with them." For others, it was a matter of allegiance. It was estimated that from the main hamlet of Xuan Thieu alone, 100 young men and boys had left to join the guerrillas in the year before Large came to Hoa Hiep. Even so, Xuan Thieu was reasonably friendly. In other hamlets the marines were definitely unwelcome. "When I went to Vietnam, I thought we were going over to help a bunch of people who needed help, wanted our

Corporals Ron Schaedel and Rick Foreman attract a crowd on Hoa Hiep as they help line a well with cement in August 1967.

help, were doing all they could. But after I was there for awhile I got the feeling that they didn't want us over there. It became very frustrating. It got so you felt like all the Vietnamese were your enemies."

Relations with the Popular Forces soldiers were also tenuous. Poorly trained and motivated, they were not always dependable. "The attitude toward the PFs by I'd say the majority of the Marines there was mistrust, with good reason." They were too apt to spend a firefight with their heads to the ground and their guns silent. And there were disturbing incidents: a PF caught fooling around with a light one night—was he signaling the VC? A booby-trapped grenade found in the Americans' truck and three PFs unaccountably absent—were the guerrillas going to attack? It got so Large could tell if there were VC around by the way the PFs acted. "Be ready to go on patrol and they were casual about it, haphazard, you knew that the VC weren't in the area. But if they were very serious and half of them didn't show up, we knew there were VC." Even a PF who volunteered information, "you never knew whether or not he was telling the truth. You never could put a hundred percent faith in one of them."

There was corruption as well as hostility, indifference as well as fear. When the village chief asked the marines for cement, they gladly arranged to have some delivered. Only later did they discover he had used it to build himself a new house. Nor did the villagers always seem to want what the marines had to offer. "When you first joined the CAP unit you were enthused about what we were doing as far as showing them our modern ways because they were so backward over there. But after you were there for awhile you began to feel frustration because they didn't want to adapt to our ways, they wanted their own ways."

I can remember one time when we were showing them about outdoor latrines. We built them ourselves, and came back to the area later. But instead of using them for what they were intended, they used them to keep their hogs there.

The "rich" Americans became an unintended source of gain. "They wouldn't steal among themselves, but it was all right in their way of thinking to steal from the marines. I got the impression that they were out for what they could get from the marines or the Americans. Not all of them but the majority. I got very disgusted when I was over there. I really did."

The Americans did not make it easier. Some of their troubles came from outside: a marine in a passing truck who, for no apparent reason, threw a tear gas grenade into the village; a carelessly fired illumination flare that burned a peasant's house to the ground; a marine from another unit firing his .45 to drive off some pesky children and accidentally hitting a middle-aged woman. Too often, Large acknowledges, "the American put himself above the Vietnamese." Most of the men chosen for Echo Two were positive about the people, but a small percentage "were very bit-

ter, they had no liking for the Vietnamese. And it was that individual that made it difficult for the rest of us. The relationship with the Vietnamese it took us six months to build they could tear down in one day with their attitude."

By the time Large got ready to leave Hoa Hiep at the end of 1967, some of the resistance had dissipated. But there was never a sense of wholehearted trust between the marines and the villagers. "We got the feeling at times the Vietnamese people wished that we weren't there or didn't care if we were there. We got the impression that most of them felt like if we'd leave the war would be over, that we were more concerned about the war than they were. Then again," Large adds, "when you get to thinking about how long they had been at war, how many of them had died, you could understand their feelings, why they weren't enthusiastic about it. You have to consider that they had been at war for twenty years. They were really ready to quit."

With all the frustrations, Large felt he was accomplishing something in Hoa Hiep. The marines did not see their role as simply providing a temporary means of protection for the village. "We looked at it more long-term. Like the water well, that was something that would be there after we left. Or the school." He even considered extending his tour six months. Later he was glad he did not. Not long after Large left Hoa Hiep the CAP compound was overrun during the Tet offensive. Everyone in the platoon was killed. During the fighting the new schoolhouse was destroyed.

It was still a bitter memory, more than fifteen years later. "If it turned out different, it would all have been worthwhile. I think while we were there we did good things for the Vietnamese. Had we gone in there with the intent of winning that thing, what we did with the CAP unit would have been a very profitable move. But the way it ended up, it was just a waste."

DaMpao

In the spring of 1965 when Don Scott was first approached about working in Vietnam, "I don't even think I knew where it was." He was even less interested in finding out. Recently returned from the University of California, working for the Boston YMCA, dabbling in local politics, Scott and his wife Marilyn were well ensconced in a Beacon Street townhouse and looking to their own private future. There was "no way I would go to Vietnam."

But Dr. Jim Turpin, the founder of a medical relief agency called Project Concern and the one who told Scott about a new program for montagnard tribesmen in the central highlands, was a persuasive man. Twelve months after their first meeting, Don Scott climbed out of a dusty jeep and looked around a small mountain clearing in Tuyen Duc Province. The place was called DaMpao.

Although the terrain and vegetation reminded him of

Vermont, "I had never seen anything so rural in my life." To get to DaMpao Scott had to drive for hours over dirt roads "without seeing anybody but maybe a couple of small villages on the roadside." What he saw when he did arrive was hardly more impressive. An abandoned Special Forces camp, it consisted of two small cinder block buildings with tin roofs. One served as office and dormitory, the other housed an outpatient clinic, fifteen beds, and a small operating room. There was no sanitation, no hot water, no electricity. "There was no glass in the windows. Dust would come in during the dry season, rain would come in during the rainy season." Scott and his coworkers used candles and kerosene lanterns, "lived on malaria pills," and built a toilet system "on the gravity principle which more or less worked."

Neither their isolation nor their living conditions seemed to matter very much to the small but dedicated international staff of doctors, dentists, nurses, and other Project Concern volunteers at DaMpao. Even so, the first months after Scott's arrival were difficult ones. As the project's "chief cook and bottle washer," the new director found himself doing everything

from meeting with Nguyen Cao Ky to working with village chiefs and sorcerers; from high-level discussions with American Ambassador Ellsworth Bunker to "going into villages after attacks had taken place and working right next to the doctors." There was money to wrangle from Project Concern headquarters, a warehouse in Da Lat to oversee, food for distribution to the villages to be begged or borrowed from the U.S. government, and a mass of paperwork Scott gratefully turned over to his wife Marilyn, who followed him to DaMpao from Boston.

"The program grew very fast. We increased our budget several-fold in the first month and I think by the end of 1967 we probably had seventy-five or eighty people, including montagnards, working for us." By 1969, a second more elaborate facility had been constructed, "a great big modern hospital with operating theaters, X-rays and generators and deep freezes and all kinds of cold storage for medicine stuck way up in the mountains."

The new hospital only emphasized the gulf between the project and the people it was meant to serve. Scott's first reaction to the Koho tribesmen who lived in the villages around DaMpao was not unusual. "I was horrified. Here

was a race of people that were rapidly leaping into the year 1,000 as far as I could figure out, with horrendous problems." One of the worst problems was the state of their health. "I remember being told that if a child ran through the age of two he'd make it to five, and if he made it to five he'd make it to thirty-five, and then he'd die. I think that was pretty true." Hygiene was virtually nonexistent, malnutrition omnipresent. To his surprise Scott discovered that a growing number of the Koho suffered serious stomach ulcers brought on by anxiety, "and the anxiety was caused by the war."

The Project Concern compound never came under direct attack, but Scott remembers "evidence of war all around us. Every single night you would hear bombing. There was gunfire all the time." So pervasive was the war that even if a villager had not been directly affected, "he knew somebody who had, someplace he had a relative that had been killed or captured or who had just disappeared." Of those who came to DaMpao for help, 25 percent were casualties of the constant fighting.

Scott and his staff simply rolled up their sleeves and got to work. Word of their presence spread quickly. "I don't

girls—sixteen, eighteen, nineteen—and create a training program where they could work with us for six to twelve months. Then they would go back into their own villages and provide some of the same kind of service we were providing." Backed by the medical staff at DaMpao, the young montagnards built village clinics, dispensed drugs, and held classes on hygiene and sanitation, creating a medical network that reached thousands of people in an area that had never before received any kind of medical care.

The impact the project had on the montagnard villages, however, was broader than matters of health. "It wasn't our point in being there, but I think we tended to modernize the montagnards." There were the jeeps, the medical equipment, the specialized training. And inevitably the volunteers undermined the influence of the traditional tribal authority figures. "We often worked with sorcerers. Sorcerers did their thing, we did ours and somehow or other the person lived. And that was great because last time the sorcerer did it the person may not have lived, so the two of us now had really powerful medicine. But we also brought a lot of them

Montagnard children in DaMpao line up for vitamins supplied by Project Concern.

know how they found out about us. We had people that would walk four or five days from places that were on nobody's map." As long as the tribesmen had to come to DaMpao for medical care, however, there was a limit to what Project Concern could do. So they began holding clinics in the villages on a regular basis. Staff members would pile into jeeps—or, if it were not safe to drive, get a lift from an American military helicopter—and spend the day patching wounds, assisting with births, dispensing medicine, and providing advice on sanitation.

Eventually, DaMpao was servicing as many as twenty-five villages—perhaps 50,000 people—over an area of 100 square miles. The results were gratifying. "No matter what you did, there was always a thank you. Bloody mouths, horrible gashes in their arms or legs, operations of all sorts and people were always very grateful." But occasional visits could not fill the enormous need for medical care in the villages. "I think it was in early 1967 that we really decided that we ought to take young Koho boys and

around to realizing they shouldn't be dealing with sorcerers at all; they should only be dealing with doctors."

In fact, the men and women of Project Concern were only one of many forces hurling the montagnards into the twentieth century. "They were beginning to sell rice and wheat to the Vietnamese government. They were making things and taking them into the markets in the provincial capitals. They were buying cloth that they used to make themselves and bringing it back. We didn't even have a radio in 1966, and in 1971 you could drive ten miles down the road and go past four or five villages and hear portable radios blaring." Young montagnards started going to school. "Their dress suddenly was plaid shirts and Levis and boots. When I first got there they were running around in loin cloths with an axe or a crossbow over their shoulders. And when I left it was hard to find a young montagnard without a pair of slacks and a shirt on."

Less positive changes were also overtaking the Koho. The war had been with them for years, but it was only after the Tet offensive of 1968 that the allied pacification effort reached the highlands. When it did it transformed the boundaries of montagnard life. "The soldiers came in and built perimeters whether the montagnards wanted it or not. They had guardhouses and gates built to regulate going in and out of the village." Or whole villages would be relocated miles away. "They had always run their own lives and their own village structure, their own communities. But as the war increased and they got moved about they had the U.S. Army and the Vietnamese army and province chiefs and what have you telling them what to do. And they didn't have much to say about it."

The buffer that Project Concern could maintain between the montagnards and the war was limited at best. In 1969 relocation began in earnest, and within three years many of the villages near DaMpao had been consolidated into a single unit. To get to their fields, the Koho now had to walk four or five kilometers. "They'd get caught up in fire fights; there'd be napalm; there'd be trucks rolling through their crops." The result was less food harvested and more malnutrition. Like the war it was

a situation beyond Project Concern's capacity to remedy.

Looking back years later Scott believed that what he and his people did to ease the suffering of the Koho, what they did to teach them how to lead healthier lives, what they did to train them to care for one another, changed things in the villages for the better. But he also conceded, "There was very little permanence to anything there. The war made it impossible. Once it became our war there really wasn't any room left for humanitarian programs."

The delta

"We had a sometimes naive, often optimistic view that if you convince the rural population who were sitting on the fence that they had a stake in remaining loyal and throwing in with the central government, they would not only be protected, but assisted in their efforts at self-development and self-government."

A montagnard village chief and his people await the decision of Vietnamese authorities who are planning to remove the villagers from a Communist–controlled area.

By the time Tim Bertotti reached South Vietnam in March 1967 as USAID chief of New Life Development for Ba Xuyen Province, the name of the game was pacification. Nation-building, the watchword of the fifties, "fell down at the bottom of the scale," Bertotti recalls. "For us it was development, assistance, and security. We were concerned about how many villages and hamlets were under government control. We felt that if we could get a foot-hold then the development would take off a lot faster."

The development Bertotti became most involved with, first in Ba Xuyen and then from 1969 to 1970 in Kien Hoa Province, was a multitude of individual hamlet self-help projects. "At one time in 1969 I think there were more than 800 small self-development projects underway in Kien Hoa." Varying from "a cement bridge over a small canal to a pigpen built and stocked with AID funds," they were selected by the hamlet itself and monitored by province officials and AID advisers. Bertotti's role was that of a

"catalyst" who "tracked the projects, checked them out, and approved the commodities and funding that went into them." The job put him in frequent contact with village officials. They impressed him with their "tremendous conviviality and openness, their friendliness and their willingness to take risks."

Bertotti also took risks, regularly traveling around the villages unarmed and unescorted. But he was not unused to conditions in the Third World. A veteran of the Peace Corps, he had been "very confused" about the war effort. "I had been to forums in the States where they were debating pro and con, but both sides seemed more emotional than very clear or cogent about it." The combat death of a friend's fiancé finally propelled him to go to Vietnam "and make up my own mind" about the U.S. involvement there.

He quickly discovered that for many delta peasants the most visible form the American presence took was the dozens of AID workers in the field. In some provinces "we were very, very active. We had some fluent Vietnamese speakers and these guys got around all the time. They knew all the village chiefs. They would spend nights in the villages and talk about local problems or what was going on nationally with various programs." There were those for whom Vietnam was just a short assignment to get behind them, but by 1970 the proportion of experienced people really began to pay off. "We had two or three guys that came back for their third tour, and they were extremely effective. These guys wanted to be there. They knew the province and the programs. They had five times the impact of the adviser who just came and started checking off the days as soon as he got there."

That impact could be considerable. "We had, in one sense, more money than we could spend. It's not that we could have built a hydroelectric dam down there, but we never had any problems funding the projects we did have." It was more than just the money, however:

Nearly every developmental program in the villages was a reflection of American concern or advice, albeit from a distance. Maybe it was a public administration advisor in Saigon who'd written procedures for elections, or specified how hamlet councils would advise the hamlet chief. There was the fertilizer that the peasants bought or were given money to buy, the loans that were made, the insecticides, the experimental rice crops. . . .

There was no doubt in Bertotti's mind that the American involvement in many villages was significant. "Communications projects had high impact. When a small bridge was built or a road improved it had a lot of economic benefit in terms of access to markets. Electrification projects had a lot of pizzazz, too. We put a few generators into very remote areas. People having lights, being one of ten hamlets in some small area having lights was a big deal." Yet the real contribution for Bertotti was in terms of "people who prospered, whose lives became better. The infant

A rural electrification project sponsored by USAID brings a new standard of living to the people of Duc Tu. This village shop now has to stock light bulbs, electric pumps, even TV sets.

mortality rate dropped tremendously while we were there. Medical care in many areas improved markedly. Productivity of rice went up. Tenant farmers and people who worked the land were generally better off."

The commitment of the Americans was apparent. So were the limitations created by the war. "We were reminded of the war everyday, by coffins and casualties, by choppers and gunfire and B-40 rockets. We tried not to let it impede us. We felt that if we kept pushing hard then even when we lost a few projects—a bridge blown, or people frightened from carrying on—we'd get somewhere in the long run. But the war obviously slowed us down. One day's bombing cost more than a year of the money that was spent at the province level." Nonetheless, funds were available, and Bertotti felt that South Vietnam "could've been an economic miracle within a few short years" were it not for the war. More than simply diverting resources, "the war dictated the nature of development." It became not so much a means to long-term growth, as a method to promote security and win the local people for the government in the shortest possible time.

"Our own impatience helped do us in. We really wanted to get results fast, when all logic would indicate

that we were in it for a long haul." Bertotti saw "some American development experts who tried to upstage the Vietnamese by creating 'model villages,'" and on occasion he found his own role an anomalous one:

I was a young twenty-eight-year-old guy here with Vietnamese service chiefs who'd been to the Sorbonne, had excellent minds and technical credentials. *I* could barely follow the language, *they'd* been around the situation twenty-five or thirty years, and here's the new man on the scene who's supposed to be telling them what their next move should be in pacification programs. It was a little bit presumptuous on my part.

Americans—the good ones, the dedicated ones—could make an important contribution, "but it took the efforts of the Vietnamese," Bertotti soon realized, "to accomplish whatever good that was done."

If Americans could seduce themselves into believing that the only way to get the job done was to do it themselves, they could also be seduced by the Vietnamese. One of the biggest challenges Bertotti faced was "the tendency of the Vietnamese to say: 'The greatest thing the Americans can do for us is to come in and make things, build things, give us things, because that's what Americans do best. Don't come in and advise us how to do it, because it's so much easier for you to just do it for us.' "

The heavy priority placed on the security component of pacification (Bertotti himself had nominal charge of Vietnamese RD cadres in Kien Hoa), the relatively large amount of money and commodities available, the impatience of the Americans to get things done, and the willingness of Vietnamese officials to let them try, may have had short-term merit, but it made for long-term problems. From Bertotti's point of view "we were setting up the framework for whatever was needed to develop rural Vietnam, but we provided too few of the necessary institutional commitments and too little long-term training. When you're talking about institutionalizing something you have to look at the grassroots level. The Vietnamese had talented people who could push the paper in Saigon, and they had people who could formulate a decent plan. Even at the province level we had some very astute tech-service chiefs. But the talent had to stretch down a little further. It had to be a little thicker than it was."

Yet how appropriate to the Vietnamese situation was the whole concept of nation-building? "It made sense to us, but I'm not sure it made complete sense to the Vietnamese," Bertotti concedes. "They still placed a tremendously strong value on the family, on loyalty to the people they knew, their friends. There was suspicion about the central government." And how much American advice was meaningful in the Vietnamese context? "We often told them that they should work harder and be careful or they were going to lose their country, and it made a dent on them. But to the young kids in the military, even young men in their twenties, war was all they'd ever known." In an environment in which people accepted armed conflict as a permanent condition of life "you could talk about nation-building, and it may have made a little sense—surely some of the Vietnamese understood this better than the Americans—but maybe it was just that our model wasn't exactly what they wanted."

Hau Nghia

When Captain Stuart Herrington came to Hau Nghia Province in March 1971 as adviser to the Vietnamese intelligence officer in Duc Hue District, "I was as well prepared as I think anyone could have been." Familiar with the French debacle in Vietnam from studies at the University of Florida, a graduate of the U.S. Army Intelligence School at Fort Holabird, Maryland, Herrington had spent two years as an intelligence officer in Germany and six weeks at Fort Bragg, North Carolina, as a student in the Military Assistance Training Advisor course, before traveling to Fort Bliss, Texas, for three months of Vietnamese language training. Even so, he quickly learned "you could never really be prepared for what you would encounter over there."

What he discovered in Hau Nghia was "the eighteenth century world" of the Vietnamese countryside. "If an American walked into a village children would come running up yelling 'My, My'—'American, American.' They'd gawk and stare, come up and run their hands down your arm to feel the hair." It was a world that occasionally startled him with its incongruous juxtapositions.

I have a vivid memory of one village where I went on an operation with a South Vietnamese unit. During the noon hour we stopped at a home that looked like any other peasant home, except for a little barn with horses in it. The owner, an old peasant, took me in and inside a stall were two beautiful chestnut race horses. He not only owned them, but transported them to Saigon and raced them at Phu Tho racetrack every now and then. And when we went into the mud house, and it was still a mud house, he had a Sony television set running off of four Delco batteries.

Most surprising of all to Herrington was "how peaceful it was. I had conjured up in mind a hot war area, and I guess I thought it would be battle-scarred and ugly, and it wasn't that way, it was really beautiful."

In fact, Hau Nghia was not as peaceful as it sometimes seemed. The Vam Co Dong River, which bisected the province from west to east, was a sharp line of demarcation. The territory across the river belonged to the enemy—a blasted terrain of ruined homes and empty villages from which the VC made regular incursions into the more populated districts of the province. But these guerrilla bands were only the tip of the iceberg. As Herrington began to probe beneath the placid surface of Hau Nghia, he discovered a deeply rooted Communist presence that had penetrated virtually every hamlet in the province. The Vietcong infrastructure levied taxes, mounted propaganda campaigns, recruited village youth, and terrorized village officials. Unless this "shadow government" was destroyed, the insurgents would retain their influence and control over the people of Hau Nghia.

Using information gleaned from lengthy interrogations of Communist defectors, slowly establishing networks of sympathizers within the villages, working with his Vietnamese counterparts to put the bits and pieces together, Herrington began to identify the cadre who made up the revolutionary government of Duc Hue District. Once individuals had been pinpointed, he accompanied South Vietnamese forces on military operations designed to capture or kill them.

It was a laborious, and occasionally dangerous, process—one of Herrington's most valuable agents was shot by Vietcong guerrillas as he slept—but it worked. Within months of turning his attention to the village of Tan My, until then so tightly controlled by the insurgents that enemy documents referred to it as a "model revolutionary village," careful investigation and steady military pressure had thrown the local Communist organization into disarray. Aided by a new province chief who actively backed the U.S. adviser with military support, Herrington pressed his campaign throughout the district. A year after he had arrived in Hau Nghia he could see "real progress in breaking the hold of the insurgents on the peasantry."

Despite this progress—and despite apparently successful development efforts like the distribution of fertilizer and the introduction of miracle rice, innovations that had "changed things dramatically" for the farmers of the province—Herrington had to face a grim truth: "The battle for the so-called hearts and minds of Hau Nghia's villagers was far from over. There was simply no evidence to support a conclusion that the Vietcong's losses had been the government's gains."

No matter what their opinion of the Communists, virtually no one had much good to say about the government. The most visible source of discontent was corruption. With notable exceptions, "it seemed that there was no limit to the imagination of the people who worked for the GVN on how to make money for themselves. It was *rampant*. And it led to a universal cynicism about the government." But the ultimate cause of the GVN's difficulties, thought Herrington, lay with the Vietcong themselves. "The people who represented the South Vietnamese government in the villages—the village and hamlet officials, the police in particular—were lousy. They were lousy because the VC had

assassinated all the better people in the sixties. The kind of people who would have made the GVN a popular government by representing the people in the way they needed to be represented, that talent wasn't there. In many cases the older people who would have been the good civil servants, who might have made the kind of impression on the people that would have won their respect—those people were VC."

What this meant most immediately to Herrington as his extended tour drew to a close in the summer of 1972, was the prospect of an enormous vacuum in the countryside after the Americans departed, especially in the area of intelligence. "We Americans could manage the Phoenix Program into working by sheer force, by bludgeoning the Vietnamese and then going out and doing it ourselves. But what would happen when we left?" It was a problem that extended far beyond Duc Hue. "The American effort was so all-encompassing, so omnipresent, that if you pulled it away the Vietnamese couldn't take up the slack and do it themselves. We were running the train; we weren't showing *them* how to run the train."

Yet there was an even bleaker reality with which Herrington and all the Americans who worked in the villages of Hau Nghia had to contend, "a situation that was always gnawing on our minds.

The Vietcong Presence

As these captured Communist photographs demonstrate, beneath the calm surface of Hau Nghia Province a highly organized Vietcong infrastructure made its presence felt in scores of hamlets and villages.

Right. *Peasants from one village raise vegetables to feed Communist guerrillas.*

Far right. *The farmers of Loc Hung respond to the exhortations of local VC cadres.*

We could manage our programs, we could build a dike, repair the village bridge, clean out a well, pave a road or two, develop the territorial forces to where they could run a good ambush patrol, kill the VC cadres, scare the VC guerrillas—we could do all that. And we could escort people from Saigon on a tour of the province, take them to every district and almost all corners of all the districts, and be proud as hell of everything that had been accomplished. But hanging over it all, at all times, was the spectre of the Cambodian border right there. What that meant to us was that the entire favorable economic and military balance, the whole damn thing could be overturned in a matter of hours.

That was exactly what happened in Hau Nghia when the Communists launched their 1972 Easter offensive, saturating the province with regular NVA troops. "To force them into leaving required a major series of battles: air strikes, helicopter gun-ship attacks, mortars, artillery, and a lot of destruction and refugees—a major setback."

The proximity of Hau Nghia Province to the Communist base camps made it somewhat more vulnerable than other areas of the country, but Herrington was convinced that the American effort throughout the Republic of Vietnam suffered from the same problem. "No matter what we did from the Ben Hai River to the Camau Peninsula, no matter how many schools we built, no matter how many social programs we sponsored, no matter how well

we tried within the funding limits to equip and train the ARVN and the local militia, in the end the equation could be locally or massively overturned by a determined North Vietnamese army."

As his DC-8 "Freedom Bird" lifted off the runway at Tan Son Nhut air base, Herrington found himself leaving Vietnam with mixed feelings. He had become committed to the struggle against the Communists that he and his South Vienamese counterparts had waged in Hau Nghia Province, and he believed that his efforts had had effect. "There's no doubt about it, by 1972 the situation was so vastly improved compared to several years earlier that it astounded people who came back after having been there before." Herrington had learned, however, that the enemy was enormously resilient. He had learned that disrupting the Vietcong infrastructure could buy time, but it "could not in any way eliminate what the Communists called the 'contradictions' of South Vietnamese society that nourished the revolution." And he had learned that the task of winning the hearts and minds of the Vietnamese peasants "was not something that Americans could do. You couldn't manage this into happening. It was either going to happen by enlightened leadership and well-managed programs by the Vietnamese themselves, or it wasn't going to happen. And it didn't happen."

Two wars

During the height of U.S. military involvement in Indochina, thousands of Americans waged another war in the villages and hamlets of South Vietnam, a war against hunger and disease, ignorance and corruption, terror and subversion. Struggling to help effect a peaceful economic and social revolution of the countryside, they made a real difference to the world of the villages.

But were individual development and assistance projects an answer to the chronic problems of rural Vietnamese society? Jeffrey Race, a former U.S. Army adviser in Phuoc Tuy Province, maintained that the United States made the same mistakes in the countryside as the Saigon government: conceiving of "security" as a suppression of opposition rather than an absence of opposition; and ignoring issues of redistribution while concentrating on a program of development that, however humane, was both insignificant in scope compared to the military effort against the insurgents and irrelevant to the roots of the conflict. The problem for America in Vietnam, said Race, was not "How do we get the people on our side?" but "How do we get on the people's side?"

One of the things that made such an alliance difficult to achieve was a profound misunderstanding on the part of many Americans of the dynamics of the revolutionary movement in the villages. "There were those who had the simplistic notion that the Vietcong were bandits, criminals, and terrorists," observed Stuart Herrington.

They had no sense that the Vietcong frequently were family members of some of the villagers, or if not family members they were still Vietnamese. ... There seemed to be a notion that the Vietcong were not a part of southern society, that they were some alien force, so why don't the villagers just rat on them and be done with the whole thing.

Trying to understand the Vietnamese village, Herrington discovered, was like developing a photograph in a tray of chemicals. "And the red light in the darkroom was the ability to talk to the Vietnamese and to handle yourself in a way that they would talk to you." Without that "red light" there was no way of seeing the picture come into focus. Dependent upon interpreters, "The Americans were shielded from what was really going on by the language barrier and by not understanding the culture."

An even more important obstacle between the Americans and the people of the villages was the GVN. Through all the changes in government the presidential palace remained in the hands of men drawn from the military, professional, and landlord classes, whose interests scarcely coincided with those of the peasants. Yet they were also divided among themselves. Fearful of coups by ambitious military officers, those who did assume authority refused to concentrate power anywhere but in their own hands, careful to keep their own men in local control, putting per-

sonal loyalty above competence or even honesty. The corruption and bureaucratic inertia that resulted proved enormously frustrating to Americans whose "advisory" role and inexperience with Vietnamese rural society gave them relatively little leverage with district and province chiefs. At the same time, because Americans were visible in the countryside, the peasants frequently blamed them for not correcting the failings of their own government.

What made it triply difficult to "get on the people's side" was a military strategy ill-adapted to the fundamentally political nature of the war. It was one of the terrible ironies of the American presence in Vietnam that even as some were digging wells and building schools, providing medical assistance and keeping terror at arm's length, other Americans were participating in what two former South Vietnamese military commanders have called the "unspeakable destruction" of rural South Vietnam.

Wrote Major General Nguyen Duy Hinh, former commander of the 3d ARVN Division, and Brigadier General Tran Dinh Tho, former chief of operations for the Joint General Staff:

The participation of U.S. forces with their tremendous firepower added to the destruction. Many villages were completely obliterated from the surface of the earth. ... The end result was that houses were reduced to rubble, innocent people were killed, untold numbers became displaced, riceland was abandoned, and as much as one-half of the population of the countryside fled to the security of cities, province capitals, and district towns at some time during the war where most languished in abject poverty. ... Their way of life, which was considered as reflecting the traditional values of Vietnamese society, had been shaken to its roots. The ancient order seemed to have disintegrated.

The scope of that destruction—up to three-quarters of South Vietnam's villages damaged or destroyed, estimates of between 1 and 1.5 million civilian casualties—led many Americans and Vietnamese to charge that the United States had not come to protect the Republic of Vietnam but to guard its own interests, that the American military had waged war not only against the Communists but also against the entire rural population, that for all their strength and all their programs and all their dollars the only way the Americans finally found to "save" the villages of South Vietnam was by burning them to the ground and scattering their people to the winds.

In the end, the attempt to "build a nation" did fail. The effort to protect the villages often did lead to their destruction. And the struggle to win the hearts and minds of Vietnamese peasants did seem to engender more hostility than friendship. But this was neither the result of evil intentions nor a wanton disregard for human life. The truth was far more complex, and far more tragic.

113

The Peasants

When large numbers of Americans first encountered it in the mid-1900s, the world of the Vietnamese peasant seemed in most respects as ageless, and alien, as the land itself. Clustered in small hamlets beside the narrow canals of the delta, or scattered in fishing villages along the sandy coast of the South China Sea, the peasants lived the lives their parents and grandparents had lived before them—measured by the endless cycle of birth and death, bound to the wheel of ancient tradition, and far removed from the modern urban civilization that most Americans had left behind.

Fishermen land their catch on a beach along the central coast. Inset. Women from a fishing village in Phu Yen Province sorting dried fish.

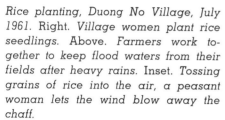

Rice planting, Duong No Village, July 1961. Right. Village women plant rice seedlings. Above. Farmers work together to keep flood waters from their fields after heavy rains. Inset. Tossing grains of rice into the air, a peasant woman lets the wind blow away the chaff.

A common enterprise

What joined the peasants together was not only the ties of family and in most cases a common religious tradition, but also a shared livelihood and way of life. Whether harvesting the sea or cultivating the land, virtually everyone in a given village—men and women, landlord and tenant, the old and the young—took part in a single enterprise whose demands shaped the contours of their days and bound them all in a mutual dependence.

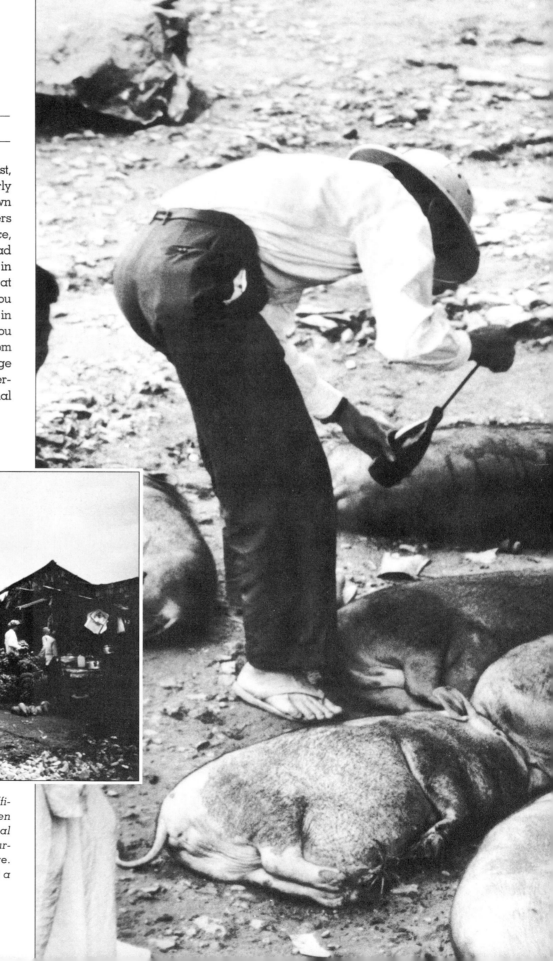

Ripples of change

For all its continuity with the past, peasant life was changing in the early sixties. New roads slowly broke down physical isolation, chemical fertilizers enlarged the margin of subsistence, village schools encouraged the spread of literacy. The changes were visible in the food stalls along the new road at the edge of the village where you might be able to buy a warm Coke, in the office of the village chief where you could listen to a radio broadcast from Saigon, and in meetings of the village council where government civil servants had supplanted the traditional leadership of the village elders.

Right. By the late 1960s the self–sufficiency of individual peasants had given way before the demands of a national market economy. Here middlemen purchase pigs from local farmers. Above. Ox carts and trucks jostle for space at a roadside fruit market.

Modern complexities

In fact, the forces of modernization were accelerating more rapidly than traditional peasant life could easily contain. New patterns of authority, wider discrepancies of wealth and poverty, as well as new opportunities for education and mobility had created a social environment in rural Vietnam far more complex than many Americans realized and far more difficult to deal with than anyone had foreseen.

Left. *The gap between wealthy and poorer villagers was a more visible part of Vietnamese life by the 1960s. The new cement house of a prosperous farmer stands in sharp contrast to the thatch home of the family on the left. Above. During the late 1950s and early 1960s, education expanded for most peasants. But landowners' children, like those pictured here at their lessons, could afford additional schooling that would lead them out of the village entirely.*

The American Way of War

Convening in Stockholm on May 2, 1967, the International War Crimes Tribunal was a curious, if not outlandish, enterprise. Its existence had been inspired by one philosopher, the British pacifist and mathematician Bertrand Russell, and its plenary sessions chaired by another, the French existentialist Jean Paul Sartre. The tribunal "comes from nowhere, with neither constituency, mandate, nor customs," admitted one of the chief American participants, former SDS president Carl Oglesby, "announces its intentions in an anti-American broadside or two, is ignominiously booted out of Paris and arrives ruffled and internally disquieted in Stockholm to hear in public eight days of often polemical testimony which it in fact had collected by and for itself, and then produces on the ninth day a judgment which everyone supposed could just as well have been drafted a year before."

That judgment was a wholesale condemnation of the American way of war in Indochina. The

tribunal denounced the use of such weapons as fragmentation bombs, napalm, and white phosphorous and the employment of such techniques as saturation bombing, free fire zones, and the forced relocation of rural peasants. Declaring that the American military had purposely brought to bear unrestrained and indiscriminate force against a defenseless civilian population, the tribunal accused the United States of a conscious policy of genocide against the people of Vietnam.

Supporters of the war were quick to denounce the tribunal, claiming correctly that its members were either virulent anti-Americans or well-known critics of the war relying to an important degree on evidence drawn solely from North Vietnamese sources. Yet, whatever bias may have compromised the testimony offered at Stockholm, its overall findings were echoed throughout the war—in testimony of veterans before antiwar investigations like the Citizens' Commission of Inquiry, in statements by officers and enlisted men before Congressman Ronald Dellums's ad hoc hearings on war crimes in Vietnam, and in a flood of public confessions in the wake of revelations about a massacre of civilians at My Lai.

Taking into account exaggeration and discrepancy, stripped of sensational detail and hyperbolic denunciation, serious charges remained: that the weapons used in Vietnam by the United States were in many cases illegal; that they were frequently employed in a criminal manner; that American forces regularly engaged in brutal treatment of the civilian population of South Vietnam; and that American firepower had laid waste huge sections of the Vietnamese countryside in an indiscriminate frenzy of needless destruction. Critics of the U.S. war effort argued that such behavior was the direct result of conscious policy and deliberate neglect on the part of American policymakers and the American military command, and that such acts constituted war crimes within the principles laid down by the Nuremberg Tribunal and under the provisions of international law. More than a decade after the last American soldier left Vietnam such charges remained subjects of controversy and dispute.

The law of war

The international law of war consists of the specific provisions of several international agreements including the Hague (1907) and Geneva (1949) conventions, the precedents developed in the post-World War II Nuremberg and Tokyo trials of Axis leaders, and a number of customary rules of behavior considered binding on all states.

The Hague and Geneva conventions prohibit the bom-

bardment of undefended villages or towns, the infliction of unnecessary suffering, the mistreatment of civilians or disarmed combatants, and collective reprisals against persons not guilty of committing an offense. The conventions declare that the right of belligerents to adopt means of injuring the enemy is not unlimited, that the destruction or seizure of property is justified only if "imperatively demanded by the necessities of war," and that every party to the agreements must strictly enforce its provisions.

The principles that emerged from the Nuremberg trials, and were subsequently codified by the United Nations, specified that any person who "commits or is an accomplice in the commission of an act which constitutes a crime under international law is responsible therefore and liable for punishment," notwithstanding that the individual may have acted pursuant to orders of his government or a superior officer.

Command responsibility was further defined *In The Matter of Yamashita* (1945), in which the U.S. Supreme Court upheld a death sentence pronounced on Japanese General Tomoyuki Yamashita for acts of atrocity committed by his troops during the closing days of World War II. Despite the fact that Yamashita had no specific knowledge of the crimes, the court asserted that the general had an obligation to take responsible measures for the protection of civilians and prisoners of war.

Finally, beyond specific conventions or individual prohibitions stand four fundamental principles regulating armed conflict: the principle of necessity, which prohibits methods, tactics, and weapons calculated to inflict unnecessary suffering; the principle of distinction, which requires that care be exercised to distinguish between persons taking part in hostilities and civilian noncombatants; the principle of proportionality, which requires that loss of life and damage to property must not be out of proportion to the military advantage to be gained; and the principle of humanity, which prohibits methods, tactics, and weapons that are inherently cruel in their effects and violate minimal notions of humanity.

In 1965 MACV issued Rules of Engagement (ROE) that sought to incorporate the accepted law of war and apply it to the unique conditions of combat in Vietnam. Trying to find a balance between necessary military force and the compelling need to minimize civilian casualties and property destruction, the ROE dictated procedures for the control of air power, artillery and mortar fire, naval gunfire, the use of incendiary weapons and riot control agents, and the establishment of free fire or specified strike zones. Republished every six months to insure their maximum visibility among American forces and modified as circumstances dictated, the ROE made provision for the identification of hostile targets, securing approval for air strikes and fire missions, the adequate warning of inhabitants, and the avoidance of unnecessary destruction. Professor Telford Taylor, chief counsel for the prosecution at the Nu-

Preceding page. American military strategy in Vietnam was predicated on the availability of massive firepower. This M109 155MM howitzer guards a command post perimeter at Chon Duanh.

As U.S. Marines move in to clear My Son Hamlet of Vietcong guerrillas on April 24, 1965, villagers caught in the crossfire attempt to protect their children.

remberg trials and a critic of U.S. Vietnam policy, called the ROE "virtually impeccable."

The care with which the ROE were drafted was a reflection of a national commitment to international law. By virtue of Article VI of the U.S. Constitution the provisions of the Hague and Geneva conventions are part of the supreme law of the land. Moreover, the principles on which the law of war rests are embodied in the Uniform Code of Military Justice and in the field manuals of the several armed forces.

But perhaps even more compelling was the admonition delivered by Justice Robert Jackson, the chief prosecutor for the United States at Nuremberg. "If certain acts in violation of treaties are crimes," he declared, "they are crimes whether the United States does them or whether Germany does them, and we are not prepared to lay down a rule of criminal conduct against others which we would not be willing to have invoked against us." It is one of the ironies of history that the Americans who fought in South Vietnam were held by their critics to a standard of behavior their fathers established a generation earlier. In

1945 the United States had asserted its moral authority on the rule of law, and from this assertion there could be no appeal. But to what extent the principles enunciated twenty years earlier in a small German city applied to the war that raged in the villages and jungles of South Vietnam was a far more complicated question to answer.

The logic of firepower

U.S. military leaders, raised to command in World War II and Korea, believed in massive firepower as a means of maintaining morale and saving soldiers' lives. The enemy's initial manpower superiority, as well as domestic political considerations that precluded full U.S. mobilization, reinforced the predilection to be stingy with men but lavish with ammunition. Wrote Colonel Sidney B. Berry, Jr., describing the mission of the brigade commander, "He spends firepower as if he is a millionaire and husbands his men's lives as if he is a pauper."

He could afford to do so because American commanders at all levels in Vietnam had at their disposal conventional weapons of every conceivable kind in almost limitless amounts: automatic weapons, recoilless rifles, mines, mortars, artillery, grenades, incendiary devices, helicopter gunships, B-52s, propeller and jet fighter-bomber aircraft, naval guns, herbicides, defoliants, and gas. This arsenal of fire gave U.S. forces enormous advantages but also brought with it terrible problems.

When American combat troops first arrived in Vietnam, the task they faced was not primarily one of tracking down guerrillas but of defeating a field army on the threshold of victory. In this initial encounter firepower was decisive. When enemy units dispersed and U.S. soldiers had to seek them out in small unit patrols, firepower became the great equalizer. Firepower made it difficult for Communist troops to concentrate for major attacks, disrupted their movement, and hurt their morale. It punished the enemy for exposing himself to battle, restored the balance when American troops were outnumbered, and enabled U.S. units to extricate themselves from ambushes

and firefights with far fewer casualties than they otherwise would have sustained.

Firepower often prevented the insurgents from effectively utilizing their greatest asset—well-trained and highly motivated infantrymen. Noted one former commander: "Many Western military leaders described the difficulty of getting at the enemy. Yet the enemy has found it even more difficult to get at our soldiers." From the infantryman's point of view, the ready availability of firepower meant that "the last fifty yards" frequently did not have to be crossed. Whether it came from an M16 or a 105MM howitzer, from a helicopter gunship or a B-52, when the shooting started it was firepower that the ground troops depended upon.

Abuse of power

A typical infantry platoon might carry into the bush twenty M16s, two M60 machine guns, several M79 grenade

launchers, forty hand grenades, a dozen claymore mines, and twenty pounds of C4 plastic explosive. Depending on the situation they might also have with them semiautomatic shotguns, 106MM or 90MM recoilless rifles, M72 rocket launchers known as light antitank weapons (or LAWs), an M14 rifle with bipods, or a 60MM mortar. The combined destructive force was many times what a comparable group of American soldiers had fought with in World War II or even Korea.

Nothing exemplified the expansion of the killing factor as vividly as the M16, an automatic weapon capable of firing between 700 and 1,000 rounds per minute, with sufficient force to tear a man's arm off at 100 yards. Its light weight and smaller cartridge size (5.56MM) enabled an infantryman, without increasing his total load, to carry more than twice as much ammunition as a soldier equipped with the older semiautomatic M14. Moreover, the small-caliber, high-velocity ammunition fired by the M16 tumbled upon impact, ripping a wide path through muscle, bone, and internal organs, thereby causing much greater damage than conventional rifle bullets.

Some critics likened the effect of the M16's tumbling bullets to the expanding "dum-dum" bullets outlawed by the 1899 Hague Declaration for causing unnecessary suffering. Of much greater concern to others, however, was the effect of placing a weapon of such destructive capacity in the hands of inexperienced and potentially irresponsible young soldiers operating in an environment where it was difficult to tell friend from foe. "Terrified and furious teenagers by the tens of thousands," wrote an army psychiatrist, "have only to twitch their index fingers and what was a quiet village is suddenly a slaughter-house."

Helicopter gunships presented the same dilemma on a much greater scale. The first armed helicopters of 1962, the UH-1s, carried .30-caliber machine guns and 2.75-inch rocket launchers. Five years later the Huey Cobra was outfitted with 40MM grenade launchers, a six-barrel minigun capable of firing 6,000 rounds per minute, two

Armed with the automatic M16 rifle, the standard infantry weapon in Vietnam, a small group of American soldiers at Tan Son Nhut air base looses a torrent of fire against the enemy at the start of the Tet offensive on January 31, 1968.

7.62mm high-rate machine guns, as well as up to seventy-six 2.75-inch rockets. Other gunships carried 22-11 wire-guided missiles, 20mm Gatling guns, and .50-caliber machine guns.

Helicopters changed the face of war in Vietnam. They could put troops anywhere a commander wished with unprecedented speed, precision, and mobility and extract them just as rapidly. They ferried tons of supplies to isolated units and throughout the war performed an heroic lifesaving mission. As gunships evolved into a kind of "aerial field artillery" in the mid-1960s, they also became a lethal instrument of mobile death wielded with great skill against an elusive enemy.

Many of the helicopter pilots and gunners were young and very gung-ho. "How can you make people understand," asked one of them, "that I have a gun that can soak a football field with bullets in a few seconds." Carelessness led to mistakes, and mistakes could be costly. David Bressem, a pilot from Springfield, Massachusetts, testified before the Dellums committee that in his unit, the 1/9 Air Cavalry, the rule was that "anyone taking evasive action could be fired upon." During one patrol a group of peasants was spotted running across a field. Bressem's CO wheeled his helicopters over a tree line and attacked.

During the body count afterwards it turned out that thirty-three people had died, twenty-two of them were women and children. I remember very specifically there was one little boy, maybe ten years old, who was dead, but he still had the halter of a cow in his hand.

Helicopter pilots told of dropping rocks on sampans full of fishermen, of slaughtering elephants and water buffaloes, of mounting sirens on their choppers to frighten villagers, then gunning them down when they ran away. James Duffy, an Sp5 with the 1st Air Cavalry, found the rotor wash from the helicopters "a very sadistic weapon."

In the morning the people from hamlets and villages go out to a designated field to defecate and if we'd be on an early morning mission we'd spot them, make a swoop in. . . . And as you swoop in with the ship, just as you approach, the pilot would flair the ship on its tail, and the rotor wash would spin around and hit the people, blowing them over through the sand and their defecation. This was one of the things that we did for kicks.

Even before the arrival of large numbers of American ground forces, a memorandum was issued to all army aviation commanders warning of such episodes. Noting "incidents in all CTZs in which friendlies have been killed by fire from our weapons," the memorandum asserted that helicopter crews had "no unilateral hunting license. We must not permit a hidden sniper or a suspected shot in our direction to trigger a burst of haphazard and wanton fire into a general area from which the shot *may* have come." American soldiers "cannot afford to be criticized as indiscriminate killers. The argument for our weaponry has

always been that we have the capability to be very selective." There would be "no tolerance of 'zap happy' aviators or gunners" in the helicopter command. "If we are to have a populace which will join actively in our common struggle, we cannot alienate them by these actions."

Weapons like the M16 and the helicopter gunship were criticized for the irresponsibility with which they were sometimes used. Others were condemned as illegal under the provisions of international law. Among these were various gases collectively known as "riot control agents" and incendiaries, especially napalm.

Incendiaries

The use of fire as a weapon of war has a long history. In the twentieth century, military forces used petroleum fuels in flame throwers, bombs, and shells during both world wars. In World War II in particular, magnesium and white phosphorous bombs were widely employed, along with a newly discovered jelly-like mixture of 25 percent benzene, 25 percent gasoline, and 50 percent polystyrene called napalm. Altogether some 14,000 tons of napalm were expended during World War II and nearly 30,000 tons in Korea. But by far the most extensive use of napalm took place in Indochina where a total of 400,000 tons—fully 10 percent of all fighter-bomber munitions—were dropped during the course of the war.

MACV Rules of Engagement urged the avoidance of incendiary munitions "unless absolutely necessary." But the effectiveness of incendiaries against enemy troops hiding in bunkers and tunnel complexes, and the fact that it could be dropped from a low level with less danger to the aircraft or friendly soldiers on the ground than fragmentation or high-explosive bombs, encouraged its wide use. Napalm and other incendiaries were also employed to defoliate jungle areas and destroy crops. By late 1965 air strikes with napalm were considered routine.

White phosphorus was also popular, in part because of its visibility and destructiveness. WP was designed to be used solely as a marker, pinpointing enemy and friendly positions for air attack or evacuation, but its incendiary properties quickly made it a regular tool of combat. Helicopter pilots called white phosphorus rockets "our favorite ammunition. With them you could see what you were hitting and it was no problem to burn an enemy ville." Soldiers on the ground also made widespread, even routine use of white phosphorus, but not without cost. "To avoid going into a village if we thought it might be VC infested," recalled Sergeant Fred Nienke of the 1st Marine Division, "we'd send in Willie Peter mortars that explode throwing white phosphorus on different hootches in the village. Start the hootches burning and also kill people. One of the worst sights I've ever seen is a person that's been burned by WP because it doesn't stop. It just burns completely through your body."

A helicopter door gunner scans the Vietnamese countryside below on an operation out of Bien Hoa in 1966. The M60 7.62MM machine gun by his side could fire up to ten rounds a second.

The permanent disfigurement of those who came in contact with incendiaries, and the fact that many victims suffered agonizing pain before dying, prompted protest against white phosphorus and especially napalm from early in the war. *Ramparts* magazine charged in 1967 that infants and small children burnt by napalm were littering Vietnamese hospitals. In 1971, the International Commission of Inquiry into U.S. Crimes in Indochina denounced the use of napalm and white phosphorus as prohibited methods of warfare. These and other critics claimed that such incendiaries were illegal weapons causing suffering not justified by military necessity. The 1972 photograph of a small, naked child fleeing in terror from a napalm strike near An Loc shocked Americans and lent credence to the accusations.

That incendiary weapons caused civilian casualties—including children—was beyond dispute. But investigations into the number of such casualties differed widely in their findings. Against some eyewitness testimony of "thousands" of victims burned by napalm, separate inquiries by government and independent physicians during 1967 concluded that the number of war-related burn victims in South Vietnamese hospitals was minimal—far less, for instance, than burns caused by domestic accidents—and included only a handful of children. Hospital statistics, however, may have told only part of the story. Napalm burns are severe and sudden death from shock and respiratory failure is common, especially among children, suggesting that many victims could have died before they reached a hospital.

Disagreement also exists with regard to the severity of incendiary wounds compared to those caused by conventional weapons. Whatever the relative suffering brought about by napalm or white phosphorus, however, contentions of illegality are difficult to sustain. On the one hand, no specific prohibition exists in international law against either substance. At the same time, the use of incendiary weapons such as flame throwers and fire bombs

throughout the twentieth century prevented the establishment of any customary rule against their employment. And in fact, as one historian of the Vietnam conflict has pointed out, "no militarily decisive and effective weapon has ever been regarded as causing 'unnecessary suffering' " no matter how painful the reality.

What was harder to justify than the employment of incendiaries against enemy soldiers was their use against inhabited villages. Some military officers argued that it was no kinder "to blast a man's head off than to fry him to death;" but most observers reporting on the aftermath of napalm strikes described scenes of special horror: "a woman who has both arms burned off by napalm and her eyelids so badly burned that she cannot close them"; "charred bodies of children and babies [in] pathetic piles in the middle of the remains of market places"; "an old man lying on a cot, burned to death with his hands stiff in rigor mortis, reaching for the sky as if in prayer or supplication forgiving us for what we had done." Regularly

dropped on hamlets reported to be, or more often suspected to be "friendly" to the enemy, napalm was scarcely calculated to gain anything but hatred from those who suffered its effects. "I have seen my faithful burned up in napalm," grieved a Vietnamese Catholic priest. "I have seen all my villages razed. By God, it's not possible. . . . They must settle their accounts with God."

Gas

Controversy over the use of tear gas in Vietnam was rooted in the same concerns that sparked the debate over napalm. First introduced for humanitarian reasons under strict restraints, it quickly became a standard weapon of American ground forces who employed it in ways that renewed a muddled controversy that had gone on since the Germans first used mustard gas during World War I.

In mid-1962 the U.S. supplied South Vietnam with three "riot control agents" (RCA)—DM, CM, and CS—for domes-

Left. *After a napalm strike outside Da Nang, flames and smoke envelop the terrain.*

Inset. *One of the war's terrible moments. Victims of an accidental napalm drop by GVN planes, South Vietnamese children flee down Route 1. This photograph provoked worldwide outcry.*

tic use. In 1963 CS was tested on the battlefield and received its first combat employment on December 23, 1964, when gas grenades were used as part of an attempt to rescue U.S. prisoners held in An Xuyen Province.

In February 1965 General Westmoreland informed his senior commanders that U.S. policy permitted use of RCAs only in self-defense. But based on increasing evidence that the destruction of underground fortifications by explosives was causing unnecessary civilian casualties and depriving U.S. forces of potential intelligence, MACV authorized the use of CS in offensive operations. By the middle of 1967 riot control agents had gained wide acceptance in combat, and from that point on gas was treated as a routine weapon in Vietnam.

Between 1965 and 1969 the amount of CS used by American troops rose from 93,000 to 2,334,000 pounds per year. The tear gas was employed to flush tunnel complexes and render them uninhabitable for months at a time. It was dropped or sprayed from aircraft to contaminate large areas of terrain not accessible to friendly ground forces. Gas was credited with aiding in the rescue of downed fliers, with neutralizing the enemy's firepower during house-to-house fighting in Hue and Saigon during the Tet offensive of 1968, and with allowing U.S. forces to overcome enemy units occupying villages without creating unnecessary civilian casualties or damage to civilian property.

Despite the apparent effectiveness of CS, and notwithstanding the military's claim that it would reduce the number of people killed, its use by the United States ignited an international uproar. The Political Committee of the UN General Assembly insisted that "the generally recognized rules of international law" prohibited the use of "any chemical agents of warfare in international armed conflicts." American legal scholars, like Northwestern University's Anthony D'Amato and Harvey Gould, declared that the gases used by the United States in Vietnam were "in violation of the laws of war," and the *New York Times*, reflecting a revulsion shared by other American newspapers, observed that "no other country has employed

An American marine waits for the smoke to clear after hurling a CS gas grenade into the opening of a tunnel.

such a weapon in recent warfare."

The question of legality rested in large part on the Geneva Protocol of 1925, adopted as a result of the universal horror engendered by the use of phosgene, chlorine, and mustard gas in World War I, and credited by many with preventing gas warfare in Europe during World War II. Although the U.S. did not sign the agreement, the protocol had long since become a part of customary international law and therefore was informally binding on all parties to the Vietnam conflict. The United States had on numerous occasions officially denounced the use of gas and had refrained from its employment during the Korean conflict.

Nonetheless, the wording of the protocol was ambiguous, prohibiting either "asphyxiating, poisonous or other gases," or "asphyxiating, poisonous or other *similar* gases," (emphasis added) depending upon the translation from the original French, a source of confusion that had resisted clarification despite several international reviews. The United States defended the use of RCAs in Vietnam on two grounds. First, it made no sense to ban substances numerous governments employed against their own citizens during domestic disorder. Second, the State Department interpreted the protocol to read "other similar gases," thus prohibiting only lethal gases. Since "riot control" gases are neither asphyxiating nor poisonous, per se, it cannot be said that their employment was illegal.

Some critics replied that the protocol made no such distinction. Others argued that despite MACV protestations that the use of gas was justified on "humanitarian grounds" by reducing the number of casualties, CS was frequently used in combat with "lethal intent": to drive enemy soldiers into the open where conventional weapons could kill them before they recovered from the effects of the chemical, something that took place at the battle of Tam Quan on December 8, 1967.

But the most severe criticism of the use of gas had to do with its effects on civilians. Official assertions that CS was only temporarily incapacitating—"for five or ten minutes after exposure to fresh air"—ignored the frequency with which it was used in tightly enclosed underground shelters. This lethal potential was borne out by the death of an Australian soldier killed by smoke and gas in a tunnel, even though he was wearing a gas mask, and by the observations of a Canadian doctor in Quang Ngai Province who treated peasants suffering from exposure to CS.

The patient usually gives a history of having been hiding in a cave or tunnel or bunker or shelter into which a canister of gas was thrown in order to force them to leave. . . . Patients are feverish, semicomatose, severely short of breath, vomit, are restless and irritable. . . . The mortality rate in adults is about 10%, while the mortality rate in children is about 90%.

This, and similar reports, have never been substantiated by independent inquiries, and the official American position continues to be that there was "no known verified instance" of civilian deaths caused by CS. The legal status of RCAs during wartime remains equally uncertain. Perhaps more important than questions of legality, however, was the evolution of gas warfare in Vietnam. Originally introduced for limited, "humanitarian" reasons, the use of RCAs rapidly became widespread in spite of the hard-won international principle of "no gas"—one of the few effective prohibitions to emerge from a century of total war.

Ways of war

The concept of warfare that the American military brought to Vietnam had been developed over the years by military strategists studying conventional battles between two armies, usually fighting on one another's soil. Within this context international law emerged to insure that civilians were adequately protected, destruction kept to a minimum, and suffering confined as much as possible to soldiers on the field of battle.

But Vietnam did not conform to the rules. Instead of large conventional battles Americans were usually engaged in small, widely dispersed firefights. Instead of recognizable armies arrayed along recognizable "fronts," the enemy was anywhere and everywhere. And instead of an opponent who protected the civilian population on whose behalf he was supposedly fighting, Americans encountered a callous and often vicious adversary with no compunctions about using children as human shields or luring allied reprisal on defenseless hamlets, then threatening with death any villager who tried to escape. That the same Vietcong would then turn around and point to the resulting destruction as proof of evil American intentions was testimony to the cynicism with which he was prepared to wage war.

Yet, at least through 1968, the American command remained wedded to a strategy of attrition, to the removal of the physical and human shield behind which the enemy hid. More than the destructiveness of the weapons themselves, more than doubts about their legality, it was U.S. tactics—harassment and interdiction fire, aerial bombardment of populated areas, the creation of free fire zones, defoliation, the generation of refugees—that provoked questions about military utility, questions of legality, and questions about the morality of the American way of war.

"From the South China Sea to the Cambodian border," declared *Army Digest* in May 1967, "a rain of steel descends day and night" on South Vietnam. No longer centralized at battalion level, but dispersed in small groups to fire support bases, artillery in Vietnam became the constant protector of the soldier on the ground. The new deployment meant tactical changes that brought with them considerably more, not less, artillery activity.

The amount of artillery ammunition expended during the Vietnam War was staggering. Between June 1967 and

June 1969, U.S. Army batteries fired more than 7 million shells in South Vietnam, an average of nearly 10,000 rounds a day over an area slightly larger than the state of Florida. Half of this ordnance was fired in direct support of combat missions, frequently after the enemy's presence had been determined by actual contact. And in that role it gave infantrymen a marked advantage over their adversaries. But a full 30 percent more was devoted to "Harassment and Interdiction" (H&I) fire, with much less useful results.

Designed as its name suggests to harass, interdict, and generally disrupt the enemy, H&I fire was directed toward "major base areas, known or suspected unit locations, supply areas, command and control installations, and infiltration routes." Taking the form of programmed fire into

likely areas of enemy activity, H&I shelling went on intermittently day and night across wide areas of rural Vietnam. Targets, which had to have the approval of Vietnamese authorities, were supposed to be selected so as to minimize civilian casualties and damage to civilian property. In reality, the information on which most targets were chosen was what one marine officer called "yesterday's intelligence," and approval from Vietnamese authorities was virtually automatic.

"When I was working with H&I fire ... the only clearance you'd have would be from battalion," recalled Lieutenant Mark Leniz of the 9th Infantry Division.

You'd call them, give them a grid square, and they'd say, "Sure, there's nothing there. Go ahead and shoot." Well, on one in-

stance that I can remember, there was nobody there and we went ahead and shot. The next day a papa-san brought in his dead wife and wounded baby. There was nobody there.

Even when strict controls were maintained, there was simply no way to guard against people wandering through zones cleared for H&I fire or violating night curfews.

Major General R. McTompkins, former commander of the 3d Marine Division in Vietnam, told a Congressional committee that in his view "most H&I fire is utterly worthless. It is a great waste of ammunition." In 1967 the Pentagon calculated that during the previous year 350,000 tons of unobserved air and artillery strikes had accounted for not more than 50 to 100 enemy KIA. Meanwhile, the 27,000 tons of dud bombs and shells resulting from such fire pro-

vided the VC with a wealth of munitions they readily transformed into mines and booby traps that killed or wounded more than 6,000 GIs during the first half of 1967. Estimates of civilian casualties from enemy mines and booby traps ran as high as 40,000 per year.

A source of civilian casualties and property damage when villages were inadvertently hit, such strikes had negative effects even when they did not, encouraging the enemy to hide in the hamlets and increasing the probability that firefights would develop in populated areas. A study made by the Pentagon's Systems Analysis Office concluded that H&I fire "doesn't interdict, and according to our evidence, doesn't harass very much." Worse, to the civilian population "It is a constant, noisy menace, creating an image of indiscriminate, unthinking use of force."

Bombardment

More calculated, and far more destructive, was the deliberate bombardment of South Vietnamese villages by U.S. artillery, naval guns, and aircraft. Firepower was directed at populated areas for a variety of reasons: on the basis of intelligence about the presence of enemy units in a village; in response to sniper fire; or the location of a village within a free fire zone. Although aerial bombardment was ostensibly conducted under the safeguard of elaborate rules of engagement, critics condemned it as a strategy that completely ignored the distinction between military and civilian targets. Moreover, charged opponents, since the desire was usually not to occupy an area but rather to prevent its use by the enemy, the tendency to destruction was unrestrained.

As with other aspects of the war, the rule of law and the situation on the ground did not always make for clear application. The Hague Convention of 1907 prohibited "the attack or bombardment, by whatever means, of towns, villages, dwellings, or buildings which are undefended." On the other hand, if a village is occupied by the enemy, used for the storage of war materiel, or fortified, it becomes a "defended place" and thereby subject to attack. According to the U.S. Army's *Law of Land Warfare*, however, even when attacking a "defended" village the rule of proportionality must be observed: "loss of life and damage to property must not be out of proportion to the military advantage to be gained."

What made the situation even more problematic was the Vietcong's practice of "clutching the people to their breast," occupying villages whether the inhabitants wanted them to or not and converting hamlets into fortified positions that invited allied attack. To the extent that situations of insurgency are dealt with by international law,

An M132 self-propelled flame thrower sets fire to the jungle in an effort to deny the Vietcong cover during Operation Cedar Falls in 1966.

such behavior is patently illegal. But it left American military commanders with difficult judgment calls to make. Some officers, like Colonel Daniel B. Williams, artillery commander of the 25th Infantry Division stationed near Cu Chi in 1966, exercised real caution. Williams identified three types of artillery wars in Vietnam—against Main Force Communist units and installations, against Local Force guerrillas, and as an adjunct to the pacification program—and insisted upon the utmost accuracy from each of his guns to avoid civilian and friendly troop casualties. Three years later the 25th's General Ellis Williamson adopted a policy of returning 1,000 shots for every one received. After sniper fire had been taken from An Thinh, artillery shells cascaded into the doomed village. "The captain in charge had clearance from the general to level the village," wrote an American reporter accompanying the operation, "and level it they did."

Artillery was a destructive element in the Vietnamese countryside, but it could not compare with the force let loose by American warplanes. Stationed initially at Guam, B-52s carrying up to 60,000 pounds of high explosives began regular sorties over South Vietnam in June 1965. The giant bombers, flying at heights of 30,000 feet, could attack regardless of the time of day or weather. Their large loads could pulverize wide areas, yet their flexibility and accuracy enabled them to be used in direct support of ground forces. B-52s prevented enemy forces from massing for offensives, interdicted their movement, destroyed their base camps and supply bases, and put enemy soldiers under constant fear of abrupt annihilation. When the enemy did concentrate his forces, as at Khe Sanh in 1968 or An Loc during the 1972 Easter offensive, B-52s were judged by many to have carried the day. Other American aircraft hunted their prey in the heavily populated delta and central coast. There the lavish use of firepower, the inadequacies of intelligence, overreaction, and even indifference led to considerable destruction of property and a large number of civilian casualties.

One of the most widely used aircraft was the A-1 Skyraider fighter-bomber, a World War II-vintage propeller plane capable of carrying 8,000 pounds of napalm and high explosives and armed with four 20MM cannon. The French journalist Bernard Fall flew in an A-1 on a 1965 raid against a Mekong Delta fishing village that intelligence identified as a "Communist rest center."

As we flew over the target it looked to me very much as any normal village would look: on the edge of a river, sampans and fish nets in the water. It was a peaceful scene. Major Carson put our plane into a steep dive. I could see the napalm bombs dropping from the wings. . . . As we peeled back from our dive [there was] an incredibly bright flash of fire as napalm exploded at the tree

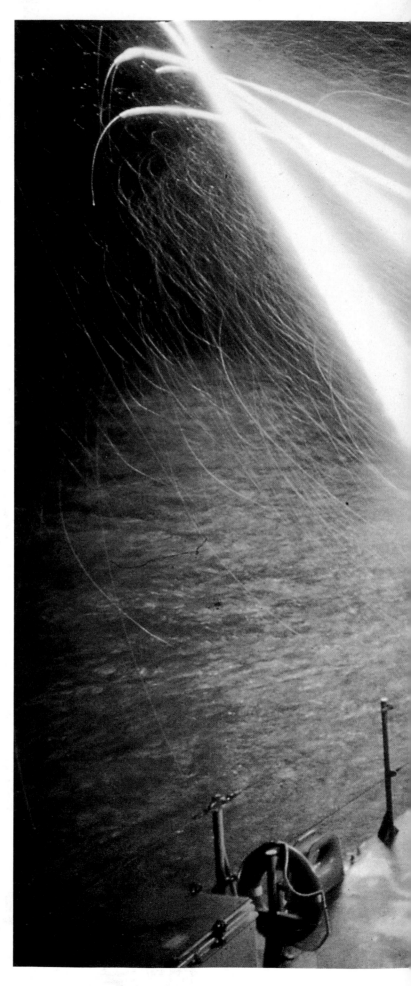

Rockets from the U.S.S. St. Francis River *streak into the night toward suspected VC position. Vessels such as this one patrolled the heavily populated delta region.*

136

level. ... The napalm was expected to force the people—fearing the heat and the burning—out into the open. [Then] our wingman followed us in and dropped his heavy explosives. Mushroom-like clouds drifted into the air. We made a second pass and dropped our remaining 500-pound napalm bombs. Our wingman followed. Then we went in a third time and raked over the village with our cannon. We came down low, flying very fast, and I could see some of the villagers trying to head away from the burning shore in sampans. The village was burning fiercely.

Fall estimated that there were probably "between 1,000 and 1,500 people in the fishing village we attacked. It is difficult to estimate how many were killed. It is equally difficult to judge if there actually were any Vietcong in the village, and if so, if any were killed."

Testimony from the military itself gave weight to Fall's doubts. There were complaints about the identification of "suspected" enemy targets and the elastic definition of "eligible" targets. As a former intelligence officer told a Congressional subcommittee, "unverified and in fact unverifiable information was used regularly as input to artillery strikes, harassment and interdiction fire, B-52 and other air strikes, often on populated areas."

During the course of the war aerial bombardment became a daily part of life in many rural areas. By 1969 more than 15 billion pounds of U.S. munitions had fallen on South Vietnam. Some of it was observed, much of it was not. Some of it had been in support of troops engaged in combat operations, much of it had simply been designed to harass and interdict. Some of it had been dropped on unpopulated jungle. But most of it had been expended against places like Gia Huu. One of fifteen hamlets clustered along the coast of Binh Dinh Province, in 1966 Gia Huu was occupied by VC and NVA troops who endured days of air attacks, naval shelling, and artillery barrages. The Communists eventually withdrew, leaving behind a thousand peasant homes blasted apart by bombs and shells or incinerated by napalm, bomb craters that pockmarked the hamlets and surrounding rice fields, coconut trees snapped in half by naval shells, hundreds of civilian casualties, and thousands of refugees. Because allied troops had no intention of remaining in the area after the operation, American officials wondered out loud whether it might not in the end prove to be "a pointless, bloody exercise."

Much the same question was raised a year later at a press briefing on how the 1st Air Cavalry "softened up" the Bong Son Plain at the start of Operation Pershing. The briefing officer informed the assembled journalists that before American forces had moved into the area it had been subjected to 365 tactical air strikes, 30 B-52 sorties, and more than 1 million artillery shells. Then he asked if anyone had any questions. "Well, only one," said a correspondent. "It appears you levelled virtually every village and hamlet, killed or driven more than 50,000 peasants off the land with your firepower. My question is, how do you intend to go about winning the hearts and minds of these people?" "I'm afraid you'll have to take that up with the S.5 [Civic Affairs] sir," replied the officer, "but, jeeze, it's a real good question."

Free fire

The "free fire zones" that proliferated in the countryside as the war grew in intensity were designed in part to place some measure of control over American firepower in rural areas. But their main purpose was to break the link between the insurgents and the general population. As General Westmoreland put it:

So closely entwined were some populated localities with the tentacles of the VC base area, in some cases actually integrated into the defenses, and so sympathetic were some of the people to the VC that the only way to establish control short of constant combat operations among the people was to remove the people and destroy the village. That done, operations to find the enemy could be conducted without fear of civilian casualties.

As counterinsurgent logic it was impeccable. The effect of free fire zones on rural peasants was another matter.

The practice of designating "precleared" zones of attack was originally established in 1958 with "free areas" for jettisoning unexpended aircraft ordnance. Four years later ARVN created "open zones" subject to artillery bombardment and air strikes with the intention of driving the inhabitants of the area into strategic hamlets. By 1965 Bernard Fall was reporting on "free bomb zones" occupying hundreds of square miles of countryside in which "any target, any structure, any movement at all" was fair game for pilots with extra ammunition.

In theory, the Vietnamese province chief had to give permission for air strikes in free fire zones to insure that innocent civilians were not hit. In practice, many local officials proved less concerned than the Americans about civilian casualties. In theory, the designation of such zones did not relieve the attacker of his obligation to select only military objectives as targets. But such discrimination was not always possible, nor practiced.

In 1965 the *Washington Post* reported that American pilots were "given a square marked on a map and told to hit every hamlet within the area. The pilots know they are sometimes bombing women and children." For some soldiers and airmen the designation of an area or a village as a free fire zone meant, in the words of one GI, that "anyone seen there is a Vietcong; if he does anything suspicious, we shoot him."

Free fire or free strike zones shifted frequently, and despite allied warnings relocated peasants persisted in returning to their homes. Richard West, visiting the delta in 1967, asked an American commander who had just ordered a strike on a village in a free fire zone whether air attacks like this did not kill many civilians. "But people shouldn't continue to live there," replied the officer. The military changed the designation of precleared areas to the more neutral "specified strike zone" (SSZ) in 1967, but the original term—with its "anything goes" connotation—persisted. In 1968 senior Vietnamese officials were complaining that out in the provinces U.S. helicopters were "shooting at everything that moves."

Rescuers carry the body of a young woman from the wreckage of her home. Her village was reduced to rubble by U.S. air and firepower after VC troops had occupied the area and engaged nearby American ground forces.

Incidents of civilian casualties and reports of property destruction continued to mount. Nevertheless, the U.S. command denied "any laxity in adherence to the established rules of engagement" and insisted that the SSZs were an "essential element in the fight against the Vietcong." Civilian casualties were the unfortunate but necessary cost of defeating the insurgents. Some Americans outside the military, like Telford Taylor, viewed the situation differently, charging that the employment of free fire zones caused human suffering and loss of life wholly disproportionate to the military advantage gained and therefore violated the provisions of international law. Whether reasonable safeguards and adequate warning legally justified the existence of special zones of attack is unclear. "It's probably fair to say, wrote Robert E. Jordan III, general counsel of the United States Department of the Army from 1968 to 1971, "that, while the theory of such zones was consistent with the laws of war, the practices associated with them may not have been."

Ecocide

Another means employed by American forces to get at the enemy was the dual program of defoliation and crop destruction. Designated "Operation Ranch Hand," the project expanded rapidly from a total of 5,681 acres covered in 1962 to 1,796,758 acres in 1967, the year of heaviest spraying. By 1971, when the program was halted, nearly 5.5 million acres of South Vietnam's forest and crop land had been sprayed at least once.

Despite the size of the area attacked—some 15 percent of South Vietnam's total land area—U.S. military officials contended that the spraying was conducted almost entirely in remote regions inhabited by less than 4 percent of the population. Moreover, they said, the substances being used—Agent Orange, the principal defoliant, and Agent Blue, the principal crop-destroying herbicide—were entirely nontoxic to human beings. MACV was enthusiastic about the program's benefits, citing improved aerial observation, enhanced base security, the elimination of ambush sites, the denial of food to the enemy, the diversion of enemy units from combat missions to food procurement, an increase in VC defectors, a drop in enemy morale, and an overall reduction in the enemy's combat effectiveness.

Critics of the program, including a host of scientists, journalists, lawyers, and environmentalists, rested their case on three main points: that the use of herbicides and defoliants as weapons of war was illegal under international law; that the spraying had been destructive to the environment of South Vietnam out of all proportion to the military advantage gained; and that Operation Ranch Hand had created needless suffering among the civilian population of the countryside.

The legal case against defoliation looked to prohibitions against the use of "poison or poisoned weapons" in the

Hague Convention of 1907 and the prohibition against poisonous gases "and all analogous liquids, materials or devices" in the Geneva Protocol of 1925. The United States contended that these injunctions did not apply to chemical herbicides because no chemical substance is nonlethal under all circumstances and because the protocol was not meant to prohibit for use in war chemical agents that were commonly used in time of peace.

North Vietnam charged that the United States was deliberately using herbicides to wage war against the people of South Vietnam. But it was not until experiments undertaken by the National Cancer Institute revealed that dioxin, a component of Agent Orange, had caused malformations in laboratory animals, that any scientific evidence of the health danger posed by the chemical was recognized. The study came to the attention of the White House in the summer of 1969. The following April the use of Agent Orange was suspended. Reports of increasing numbers of stillbirths and birth defects among Vietnamese exposed to herbicides could not be substantiated by American physicians who investigated the situation in 1970. But given their inability to visit the heavily sprayed central highlands, and in the absence of long-term observation, they could not rule out the possibility.

Far more apparent was the effect of defoliation on the natural environment. Applied at an average of thirteen times the dose recommended by the U.S. Department of Agriculture for domestic use, with many areas receiving multiple applications, defoliants severely damaged the country's upland forest, one of Vietnam's most important natural resources. Ten years after the program ended large areas of jungle had given way to shrubby bamboo, making reforestation difficult. In some defoliated regions fire and erosion had exposed bedrock and raised the danger of laterization, a process that turns the soil into a hard, rock-like substance in which nothing will grow.

Even more striking was the impact of defoliation on the coastal mangrove forests. Over 40 percent of this extraordinarily productive habitat—an important source of firewood, timber, and thatch; the breeding ground for numerous fish and crustaceans; the home to a variety of birds, mammals, and other animals—was utterly destroyed. The American botanist Dr. Arthur H. Westing discovered in 1980 that some areas remained barren of vegetation with serious erosion depositing silt in the Mekong River and destabilizing sections of the shoreline. Shellfish had all but disappeared, and the interruption of natural food chains threatened the extinction of several rare species. A steady decline in Vietnam's fishery production reflected the loss of this vital breeding ground.

Herbicides were only one weapon—and not at all the most destructive—that the United States brought to bear against the land and forests of its ally. Bombing and shelling destroyed rice fields and irrigation systems and opened the land to encroachment by the sea. Estimates

Indelible reminders of a B-52 bombing scar a section of countryside.

placed the number of shell and bomb craters at more than 20 million, covering all together some 350,000 acres. Frequently as large as forty feet across and twenty feet deep, often filled with rainwater, they became a permanent feature of the countryside and a breeding ground for mosquitoes, malaria, and dengue fever. In areas of heavy fighting metal fragments and unexploded munitions were so ubiquitous that farmers could not risk their animals or themselves by returning to the fields. By the early 1970s large areas of forest had been burned out with incendiaries. Others had been bombarded so intensively that most of the trees were destroyed; those that remained were filled with metal fragments making them susceptible to rot and impossible to mill.

The most awesome weapon let loose on the forests was the giant Rome plow: a huge Caterpillar tractor fitted with a 2.5-ton plow blade and protected by fourteen tons of armor plate. Beginning in the mid-1960s, massed tractors organized into companies scraped clean 750,000 acres, leaving only bare earth, rocks, and the jumbled remains of smashed trees.

By the end of the war the combination of chemical attack, bombing, and tractor clearing had completely or partially destroyed over half the total forest area and approximately 10 percent of South Vietnam's agricultural land. Scientists estimated it might take as long as fifty years or more for the damage to be repaired by natural processes, and some regions might never fully recover.

The devastation did not affect all areas of South Vietnam equally. A substantial amount of bombardment and aerial spraying took place in forested regions along the remote Cambodian and Laotian borders. Moreover, the intensity of fighting was consistently heavier in some regions—I Corps, the II Corps provinces of Binh Dinh and Kontum, and in Tay Ninh, Dinh Tuong, and Kien Hoa provinces to the south—than in others. An army photographer remembered "a lot of areas devastated by saturation bombing or where tanks had operated extensively, but they would kind of leap out at you because they were sore thumbs on a landscape that was largely untouched." At the same time, regions like War Zone C northwest of Saigon, Quang Ngai Province in I Corps, and portions of the delta were repeatedly subjected to "scorched earth" tactics that left whole areas in ruins.

Despite official assurance that the military advantages of defoliation made it indispensable, there was more than a little room for doubt. The impact of herbicides on certain areas—like the Rung Sat Special Zone south of Saigon, a long-time Vietcong stronghold—was decisive. But in the central highlands and along South Vietnam's western border the defoliation of one area only forced the enemy to change his regular pattern of movement, usually no more than an inconvenience. Rather than an effective military weapon, charged opponents, defoliation and crop destruction were part of a strategy designed to drive peasants in VC areas away from their homes and into refugee camps and cities under allied control. As Donald Hornig, science adviser to President Johnson once admitted, "It's all geared to moving people."

Justification for crop destruction rested on two requirements mandated jointly by the Pentagon and the U.S. Department of State: first, that spraying would be "confined to remote areas known to be occupied by VC," and "not to be carried out in areas where VC are intermingled with native inhabitants and [the] latter cannot escape"; and second, that only those crops "intended solely for consumption by the armed forces (if that fact can be determined)" could be destroyed. But spraying regularly took place in areas populated by civilians sympathetic to or intimidated by the NLF and in situations where it was impossible to determine whether the crops were intended primarily for use by the enemy. International law stipulates that, lacking such assurance, the destruction of food is justified only where the military advantage to be gained outweighs the harm it may cause civilians.

In fact, there were few programs undertaken by the United States that did less damage to the enemy while steadily alienating the rural population. Since the VC confiscated what rice they needed regardless of the size of the harvest, the only ones who suffered were the peasants. Rather than denying food to the enemy, the spraying led to local food shortages, suspected health problems, the abandonment of farms, and in some montagnard areas near starvation. Studies conducted by the RAND Corporation for the Department of Defense found that 88 percent of those interviewed blamed the US/GVN for the destruction of their crops. There was also "considerable resentment and fear" that the herbicide spray was poisonous, especially to children. The RAND investigators found "an almost total absence of efforts by the US/GVN to educate people about herbicide spraying, to warn them of attack, or to assist those who have been affected." Unaware or unconvinced of the official rationale of the program, the peasants had come to believe that the spraying was directed as much against them as against the VC. Crop destruction operations, concluded the report, "contribute substantially to a temper of mind consistently receptive to Vietcong propaganda designed to strengthen their control over the affected population and to discredit the GVN and the United States."

The extent of ecological destruction and its effects on the human population of the countryside led critics of the war to accuse the U.S. government of criminal assault against the environment and people of Vietnam. "It seems to me,"

declared Arthur W. Galston, a professor of biology at Yale University, and a member of the National Research Council, "that the willful and permanent destruction of environment in which a people can live in a manner of their own choosing ought to be considered as a crime against humanity," a crime Galston labeled *ecocide*. International law has yet to identify environmental destruction as a crime of war, and some, like the historian Guenter Lewy, have objected that in a situation where casualties were at stake, "the preoccupation with environmental issues demonstrated a certain callousness and indifference to the value of human life."

Yet environmental concerns ultimately have to do with the people who live in the environment. Commenting in 1972, Wisconsin Senator Gaylord Nelson asserted that there was "nothing in the history of warfare to compare" with the program of environmental destruction carried on by the United States in Indochina. "The cold, hard and cruel irony of it all," said the senator, "is that South Vietnam would have been better off losing to Hanoi than winning with us. Now she faces the worst of all possible worlds with much of her land destroyed and her chances of independent survival after we leave in grave doubt at best." On April 8, 1975, President Gerald Ford issued Executive Order No. 11850 renouncing the first use of herbicides in war. Crop destruction and defoliation as they were carried on in Vietnam were no longer considered by the United States to be permissible military tactics.

Population relocation

To one degree or another, all these measures—H&I fire, aerial bombardment of populated areas, free fire zones, defoliation and crop destruction—induced or compelled large numbers of rural peasants to leave their native villages. By 1971 estimates of refugees produced by the war ranged from 4 to 6 million out of a total population of between 17 and 18 million people. "It is probably safe to assume," concluded a Department of Defense report on refugee problems in South Vietnam, "that one-third of the population has been displaced by the war at one time or another."

Some of the people represented by these figures were urban dwellers whose homes were destroyed during the 1968 Tet offensive. Some were the victims of natural disasters, and some had fled from Communist terror and repression. But according to the U.S. Army chief of staff's 1966 PROVN study, the vast majority left their homes as a direct result of American and South Vietnamese bombing, artillery fire, and ground operations. Also, many peasants were forcibly moved as part of a deliberate policy adopted by U.S. civilian and military leaders.

Refugees flee An Loc during bitter fighting in June 1972. During the war as many as 6 million civilians were driven from their homes.

The generation of refugees was never officially authorized by MACV, but the tactic was well known and widespread. A September 1966 message from the State Department to the U.S. Embassy in Saigon recommended coordination between military operations and population relocation, including "military operations specifically designed to generate refugees." Leaflets dropped over the countryside in conjunction with military activities urged the people to move to government areas, and MACV issued instructions that specified strike zones "be configured to eliminate populated areas." American military operations themselves were the surest way to clear the countryside. Remarked one pacification official: "Search and destroy operations produced tactical conditions in which the civilian population could not live—sometimes in which they could not be permitted to live. Hence the refugees."

Eventually the swelling number of displaced persons became a much heralded index of military and political progress. Removing the population from the countryside was to deny the enemy vital manpower, food, and taxes. Without a civilian population in the way, allied firepower could be made more effective, and the flight of peasants from VC areas to those under government control would represent a political victory for Saigon.

The military's enthusiasm for the program was reflected in the escalating scope of relocation sweeps that directly removed at least one hundred thousand villagers from rural areas in 1967. What the refugees quickly discovered, however, was that neither their own government nor the Americans had any idea what to do with them. According to a United States official investigating conditions in I Corps at the end of 1967, "many Vietnamese officials do look upon refugees as a cursed nuisance and feel that if the Americans are so concerned let the Americans care for them." The result—despite considerable sums of United States aid, and the labor of numerous American and international voluntary agencies—was too often squalid camps that became breeding grounds for disease, huts built of rubbish, children ill fed, families disrupted, employment nonexistent.

By the end of 1967 the refugee problem had become so severe that MACV reversed itself and officially discouraged the relocation of any more civilians. But the old policy continued to be widely implemented at lower levels of command. Meanwhile, U.S. and GVN officials had finally devised a coherent program of relief and resettlement. Then came Tet, and with 1 million new war victims it was not until 1969 that efforts got under way in earnest to

U.S. soldiers of the 1st Battalion, 5th Artillery, fire a 105MM howitzer into War Zone C in Tay Ninh Province, 1967.

return long-term refugees to their homes or resettle them.

The U.S. role in creating the refugee problem was condemned by Americans working in Vietnam like Don Luce, the director of the IVS, by Congressional critics like Senator Edward Kennedy and Representative Paul McCloskey, and by journalists like Henry Kamm and Frances Fitz-Gerald. In 1967 a group of American theologians including Harvey Cox, Abraham Heschel, Robert Drinan, and Martin Luther King, Jr., called population relocations a "flagrant violation" of international prohibitions against forcible transfers of civilians in time of war.

Such prohibitions do exist, but the legal situation as it applied to Vietnam was ambiguous at best. Article 49 of the Geneva Convention permits "total or partial evacuation of a given area if the security of the population or imperative military reasons so demand." One may fault individual relocations ordered by the U.S. command, but the right to initiate such evacuations appears certain. On the other hand, the party conducting civilian evacuations must "ensure, to the greatest practicable extent, that proper accommodation is provided to receive the protected persons, that the removals are effected in satisfactory conditions of hygiene, health, safety and nutrition and that members of the same family are not separated," requirements that frequently were not met.

Still, it was difficult to assert with authority that the policy of civilian relocation was in serious violation of international law, and there was reason to believe that American forces had a duty to remove civilians from situations of potential danger. Yet, as many observers pointed out repeatedly, the forced relocation of large numbers of peasants had serious drawbacks. To "pacify" an area by removing its inhabitants was meaningless. Since most refugees were women, children, and old men, relocation had only a minor impact on VC recruitment, at the same time removing an important potential source of intelligence on enemy movements and significantly reducing the amount of land under cultivation. Relocation failed to prevent many peasants from returning to their homes while creating in the refugee camps ideal conditions for VC propaganda and infiltration.

Ultimately, forced relocation was a tactic that accomplished precisely the opposite of what it set out to achieve. "For a people as pragmatic as Vietnamese peasants appear to be," concluded a trio of U.S. government investigators in 1967, "the message implied in refugee movement is a clear one—'The GVN is not able to protect even its supporters from the insurgents so one had best withhold making any overt commitment to the government.' " Nor did relocations win Americans many friends among the people of rural Vietnam. As a pair of IVS volunteers toured one newly established refugee camp they asked an old woman what she thought of her situation. "We were forced to come here," she said. "The enemy came to our old village four times. Twice it was the men from the

jungle and twice it was you foreigners. Each time we suffered. You came last and brought us here. You ask me what I want. I want to be left alone. I want to grow rice."

A confusion of purpose

"The solution in Vietnam," declared Brigadier General William C. DuPuy, commander of the 1st Infantry Division, "is more bombs, more shells, more napalm . . . till the other side cracks and gives up."

"It is my contention," wrote Richard A. Falk, professor of international law and practice at Princeton University, "that the methods and tactics relied upon by the United States to conduct counterinsurgent warfare in Vietnam during the period 1962 to 1973 cannot be reconciled with customary law or the treaty rules governing the conduct of international warfare . . . and amount to crimes under international law."

The gulf that separates these two passionate convictions is a measure of the anguish that Americans have endured in their attempt to understand what went wrong in Vietnam. Yet the reality of U.S. participation in that bitter conflict cannot be so simply confined to assertions of force or accusations of criminality.

The problem was not that the United States systematically and deliberately violated international law, but that international law frequently provided too little guidance for the kind of war being fought in Vietnam. The problem was not so much that American tactics were militarily inefficient, but that too often they were counterproductive of the larger goals the U.S. had set out to accomplish. The problem was not that MACV was unaware of this difficulty—the army's own 1966 PROVN study cogently outlined the disabilities of the American way of war in Vietnam—but that for too long responsible military and civilian leaders failed to act on that knowledge. The problem, in the end, was not with the rules that were established to prevent the indiscriminate use of military force, but the fact that too often those controls broke down.

In determining how this came to be, four factors stand out in sharp relief: a failure of training and preparation; a failure of leadership and command responsibility; the irreducible complexities U.S. soldiers encountered in a situation of revolutionary war; and an abiding difficulty in distinguishing friend from foe. So great was this difficulty, and so onerous were the conditions to which American combat troops were subjected, that sometimes not just the Vietcong or the NVA, but the people of Vietnam seemed to have become their enemy.

If this was a concept that American military and civilian leaders rejected out of hand, it was nonetheless a fact of life for many of those called upon to fight the war. The result was a profound confusion of purpose, a disturbing loss of restraint, and a journey for some into their own heart of darkness.

"Body Count"

"I abhorred the term," wrote General William C. Westmoreland. "The only time during several years in my office that [my secretary] ever heard me swear was when somebody mentioned body count."

Part of Westmoreland's exasperation came from the baldness of the phrase; in part it was a response to Washington's constant prodding for numerical evidence of progress. Others had more serious problems with the body count, questioning its reliability, its utility, its legality, and its capacity for abuse. Yet as a tool of war it was not without a persuasive logic of its own, especially in Vietnam.

Every war has had its calculation of casualties; rarely have such statistics provoked unfavorable comment. During World War II, casualty figures were regarded as one of the most important measures of success. In Korea, General Matthew Ridgway declared on more than one occasion that the task of American soldiers was not to take real estate but to kill Chinese, a perspective that elicited relatively little public complaint. A careful compilation of enemy killed in action seemed even more vital in Vietnam where American forces were committed to a strategy of attrition without territorial objectives and with few major battles. "In a war without fronts, such as the war in Vietnam, and particularly in one as frag-

mented and atomized as it was," observed Pentagon analyst Thomas Thayer, "quantitative analysis was essential to fully understand what was going on. In no other way was it possible to keep track of the slowly changing patterns and movements that were so characteristic of this war, and to relate them to the achievement of U.S. objectives."

According to a 1967 MACV directive, only the bodies of "males of fighting age and others, male or female, known to have carried arms" would be considered "confirmed" kills. Body counts made from the air would be "based upon debriefings of pilots or observers which substantiate beyond a reasonable doubt of the debriefing officer that the body count was, in fact, KIA." Westmoreland claimed in his memoirs that the count received by MACV "probably erred on the side of caution," and a 1968 report by the MACV inspector general concluded that "personnel at all echelons visited were performing body count in a manner characterized by professional integrity."

But testimony of other officers cast serious doubt on the reliability of the casualty figures. In a 1969 study conducted at the Army War College among former commanders of combat units in Vietnam, more than 60 percent reported that a significant portion of the count was routinely "estimated," with the figures regularly "upped" during subsequent evaluation both for honest and dishonest reasons. When General Douglas Kinnard, former II Field Force chief of staff, surveyed the opinions of 173 general officers with service in Vietnam, he found that only 26 percent had confidence that body counts were "within reason accurate." A 1971 review by the Systems Analysis Office of the Department of Defense concluded that the body count was overstated by at least 30 percent.

The inflation of the body count was the result of numerous factors. The conditions of battle and terrain made bodies difficult to locate and often precluded careful searches, leading to a heavy reliance on estimates. Aerial observers frequently could not distinguish actual casualties from enemy soldiers only pretending to be dead or discriminate between the body of a pajama-clad guerrilla and the similarly clothed body of a farmer killed

in crossfire. Even on the ground it could be impossible to distinguish dead combatants from innocent bystanders. And despite the requirement that only the bodies of those "known to have carried arms" be counted, the fact that the VC frequently carried off the weapons of those who had died during an engagement made this a difficult rule to apply.

There was also the constant problem of duplication. "Whenever several agencies combined in a single operation," reported a U.S. pacification official in 1969, "it appears to be common practice for each to claim 100 percent of the results." Captain Brian Jenkins, a former Special Forces officer and later a member of the Long Range Planning Group at MACV headquarters, recalled one operation that resulted in nineteen confirmed enemy dead and a total estimate of thirty KIA. As the estimate made its way through reporting channels, however, it "accumulated" additional bodies "so that a relatively small engagement, in this particular case perhaps involving thirty casualties, would by the time it had been briefed at headquarters and entered in the books, begin to approximate the Battle of the Bulge."

Exaggerated body counts also took place as a result of command pressure and because of the ambitions of individual officers. "The incentives for field commanders clearly lay in the direction of claiming a high body count," noted Alain Enthoven, Robert McNamara's assistant secretary of defense for systems analysis.

Padded claims kept everyone happy; there were no penalties for overstating enemy losses, but an understatement could lead to sharp questions as to why U.S. casualties were so high compared with the results achieved. Few commanders were bold enough to volunteer the information that they had lost as many men in an engagement as the enemy—or more.

Said marine Corporal Matt Martin, "The more regular you were—regular Marine, regular army—the higher the body count was." On one occasion, Martin's platoon watched as an artillery barrage blasted a village suspected of harboring Vietcong troops. Scarcely had the last shell exploded when the colonel of Martin's battalion was on the radio demanding a body count.

Well this second Louie we had with us—he'd come up through the ranks—and he yelled "Over 300." So the radio man said, "You can't give them an even number." So he said, "Well, okay, 311." Three hundred eleven flat out deaths, sure kills. Well this officer loved it. He started yelling "Great, great, you did a great job."

In fact, the only casualty of the engagement was an old man who died when an American jeep turned over and accidentally killed him.

Investigating the experiences of Charlie Company, 1st Infantry Division, during the years 1968 and 1969, a team of *Newsweek* journalists found that the men of the company put little store by the numbers. Motivated less by a desire to record kills than to keep the brass off their backs, they found themselves in an Alice-in-Wonderland world where appearance often counted for as much as reality. Once, when a single misfired shot brought an immediate request from the battalion commander for a body count, the soldiers rooted around until they found a decaying two-week-old corpse they could claim as a KIA. On another occasion they came upon a rusty cache of rifles apparently abandoned years, if not decades, before. But a rifle counted as a kill in Vietnam. Three rifles counted as three bodies and were tallied accordingly.

Equally corrosive in their effect on discipline and restraint were other practices associated with the body count. Commanders determined to impress their superiors staged monthly competitions between battalions and companies, awarding soldiers who killed the most VC/NVA during a given period with passes to Saigon or even a five-day R&R to Hong Kong or Hawaii. The 9th Infantry Division instituted the practice of awarding a *Sat Cong* ("Kill Vietcong") badge to any soldier who personally killed a VC. Those who accumulated a prescribed number of badges were rewarded with time off from combat. Some units made cash awards to soldiers who had run up a high body count. "It was always better if you had a good kill count," said one marine grunt, "'cause everything would come your way. You'd get better supplies; steaks and booze once in a while. Everything would come your way."

Given the penalties for failure to record a high count, and the advantages of success, there was a strong tendency to forget about the difference between the enemy and the civilian population of the countryside. "A body count is a body count," testified Sergeant Michael Hunter during the Winter Soldier hearings on

The total measure of achievement. War Zone C, March 21, 1967.

Vietnam atrocities. "When a battalion commander calls up and says he wants a body count, if there are men, women, children laying out there, he gets a body count of that many people." It was in populated areas that the discrepancy between weapons captured and enemy casualties reported was the greatest, suggesting, according to Vietnam historian Guenter Lewy, "that the number of villagers included in the body count was indeed substantial."

Thus, while some challenged the body count as unreliable, others claimed it was illegal—clearly violating the principles of discrimination and proportionality that underlie the law of war. But defenders of the body count insisted it was a legal and necessary practice. Lieutenant General Julian J. Ewell, who, as commander of the 9th Infantry Division, won the sobriquet "The Butcher of the Delta" and who was accused of establishing body count quotas for his officers, later asserted that his critics misunderstood the nature of the war. "It's true that we kept track of body count," the general admitted, and for good reason. "It was about the only way you could deal with the VC/NVA. They wouldn't surrender. The number of prisoners you got was miniscule. The only way you could damage a VC/NVA unit was to kill them."

In fact, what was disturbing to many about the body count was not its legality or even its questionable utility, but its tendency to be abused and the message it implicitly sent to combat soldiers operating in a hostile, populated environment. To one GI who had served with the Americal Division during 1968, the soldier boasting of a high body count "was sort of saying how much I hate the gooks—in terms you can actually understand. I hate them a whole lot. I hate them more than a whole lot ... so, wow!, I killed 121 of them. That means I hate them worse than anybody does. ..." Concluded another infantryman: "If it's dead it's VC. *Because* it's dead. If it's dead, it *had* to be VC."

Counting the enemy's losses is a standard and necessary convention of war. But in Vietnam tallying the dead became an obsession that obscured the true extent of enemy casualties, eroded the professional ethics of the officer corps, demoralized whole units, and created an attitude among ordinary soldiers that contributed to acts of atrocity. "I know of no greater corruption than this phenomenon," wrote the psychiatrist Robert Jay Lifton. "The amount of killing—any killing—becomes the total measure of achievement. And concerning that measure, one lies, to others as well as to oneself, about why, who, what, and how many one kills."

An Environment of Atrocity

"My name is Jack Regald. ... My testimony is
about the indiscriminate murder of innocent civilian women and children, torture of prisoners for
fun and other reasons...."

"My name is Joe Bangerd. ... My testimony
will cover the slaughter of civilians, the skinning
of a Vietnamese woman...."

"My name is Scott Camille. ... My testimony
involves the burning of villages with civilians in
them, the cutting off of ears, calling in artillery on
villages for games, napalm dropped on villages,
women being raped, women and children being
massacred, CS gas used on people, animals
being slaughtered, bodies shoved out of helicopters...."

The year was 1971. The men were veterans—
officers and enlisted men, volunteers and
draftees—who had come to Detroit under the aus-
pices of the newly formed Vietnam Veterans
Against the War to tell the nation and the world
what they had seen and done in the uniform of

their country. For three days they related with grisly redundance a chilling pattern of atrocity and criminality: the murder of unarmed civilians, the abuse of women, the random destruction of entire hamlets.

Vietnam was not the first place that American soldiers were involved in illegal acts of violence. During the Civil War, Union commanders executed Confederate guerrillas on the spot, burned towns, and threatened civilians with retaliation for acts of resistance. Charges of brutality marked American suppression of the Philippines insurrection in 1901 and the pre-World War II marine occupations of Haiti, Nicaragua, and the Dominican Republic. Atrocities occurred on both sides during World War I, and in World War II the U.S. Army court-martialed and executed ninety-five American soldiers for acts of misconduct against civilians or POWs in Europe. In the Pacific, and later in Korea, racial animosity provoked torture and mutilation of enemy soldiers and a frequent policy of "no prisoners."

Between January 1965 and July 1975, 242 formal allegations of war crimes were made against U.S. Army personnel who had served in Vietnam. These charges ultimately resulted in the conviction by court-martial of 32 men. Similar statistics were not kept by the other services, but in the period 1965 to 1973, 201 soldiers, 78 marines, 9 sailors, and 7 airmen were convicted of serious crimes against Vietnamese victims, including murder, rape, assault, mutilation of a corpse, and kidnaping. These figures represent all crimes committed by American servicemen in Vietnam, including traffic accidents and the murder-robbery of a Saigon drug pusher. Only about 25 percent of those incidents resulting in death took place during combat operations. Nor were such incidents as common early in the war as they were later when the disintegration of morale and the decline of combat leadership made military discipline more difficult to maintain. Considering the number of Americans who served in South Vietnam, the length of time United States military forces were engaged there, and the history of other American conflicts, the proportion of substantiated war crimes in Vietnam does not appear remarkable.

Yet many argued that these figures represented only a fraction of the criminal abuse suffered by Vietnamese civilians at the hands of American troops. Beginning with the introduction of large numbers of American advisers, growing in step with each escalation of the American war effort, came first a trickle and then a torrent of accusations: from antiwar activists who charged that war crimes were not isolated acts but "a way of life in Vietnam"; from journalists who gave eyewitness accounts of the brutalization of peasants by American military personnel; and by

veterans themselves, who testified that mistreatment, assault, even murder of Vietnamese civilians was "standard operating procedure" in their units.

The vast majority of Americans who served in Vietnam did not commit crimes of war. Despite inadequate training, the fear and frustration of combat, and frequent provocation, most U.S. troops were neither "wanton perpetrators of atrocities, or proto-fascist automatons," as some have implied. To the contrary, for each example of hostility and mistrust there were those of friendship and generosity. For every instance of illegality and cruelty there were thousands more of courage and compassion. Heinous conduct was the exception, not the rule, taking place most often in poorly led units and in direct violation of existing policy. The unrestrained ferocity of some American soldiers could not obscure the bravery and self-sacrifice of others who served their country under the most difficult circumstances.

It is also true, however, that atrocities did take place. Several hundred men were prosecuted by the military for such acts. Hundreds more cases of murder, rape, and terror were reported by veterans claiming to be participants or eyewitnesses to these events. That some of this testimony was the product of exaggeration or invention has been established by psychological studies and military investigations. Nonetheless, the number and detail of such charges—drawn from military documents and the findings of army commissions, from court-martial records and the reports of military psychiatrists, from accounts published in military journals, national periodicals, and major newspapers, and from disclosures by veterans in dozens of books and film documentaries—raised the question of whether U.S. forces engaged in widespread brutality toward the civilian population of the countryside. In the years since the war this issue has remained the darkest and least decipherable legacy of the American presence in Vietnam.

A continuum of terror

American servicemen, of course, did not arrive in Vietnam intent on abusing civilians. There was a continuum of terror from the casual to the deliberate, from horsing around to mass murder. Sometimes it was "just for fun"—GIs pushing "mama-sans" off the road as they roared by in a jeep, helicopter pilots knocking Vietnamese peasants off their bikes with the skids on the bottom of the chopper, soldiers throwing loaded C-ration cans at kids' heads or lighting smokeless blue heat tablets then tossing them to the children as if they were candy. One marine said it was common practice when his platoon was going through a village for somebody to rip the top half of a woman's blouse off, "just because they were female and they were old enough for somebody to get a laugh at." Specialist 4 Sam Schorr of the 86th Combat Engineer Battalion remem-

Tan Binh, 1966. The body of a VC guerrilla is dragged to a burial site behind a U.S. armored vehicle.

bered how boring it could get being on bunker guard duty for a week at a time. "So we'd play little games.

The Vietnamese would be working out in their rice paddies with South Vietnamese flags stuck in the paddy so you would know they were there. And we would try and knock the flags down. I had a machine gun. My friend had a grenade launcher. We would shoot all over the area. . . . This was just out of sheer boredom and also because we just didn't give a damn.

In the diary she kept while serving as the administrator of the Canadian hospital in Quang Hay, Clare Cullhane wrote of:

Endless cases of women and children being run down by tanks, of GIs picking off children as they swam out to pick up food cartons from an overturned truck, of pilots inviting passengers for human "turkey shoots."

Helicopter crews had a particularly bad reputation. As early as 1963 veteran war correspondent Richard Tregaskis described the members of the 362d Helicopter Squadron as "wild men. . . . One chopper would go first," reported the journalist, "and when the people would go running, the second plane would spray 'em." James Duffy, a helicopter gunner with the 1st Air Cavalry, recalled that whenever a chopper had to make a crash landing "our company policy was to just keep on firing." Once when his ship was going down

I had fired at all the military targets I could spot and I looked out across the field and I spotted a Vietnamese woman peasant running away from the ship. I fired a burst of about six or seven rounds into her back before we hit the ground.

A couple of weeks later he and his company commander "had a good laugh about it." A year and a half after Duffy left Vietnam in April 1968, helicopter pilots based at Pleiku were still bragging openly in the company of officers about machine-gunning unarmed civilians.

"Squirrel hunting," as it was called, took place on the ground as well as from the air. Fred Laughlin, a former company commander, told the Dellums committee about a soldier "supposedly cleaning his rifle and he put a little boy in his sight and killed him." Patrick Ostrenga, a medic with the 25th Infantry Division, remembered the time he saw a "Vietnamese civilian, a pretty old man, riding down a road with a bicycle. The lieutenant that was with us took out his M-16 and aimed it at the guy and shot one round, and, well, killed the guy. . . . The lieutenant's comment was, 'Well, I guess I'm still a pretty good shot.'" According to the records of the army judge advocate general, in July 1968 PFC. Lex Gilbert was riding past a village in an army truck when, for no apparent reason, he fired his M60 machine gun into a group of houses killing a sixteen-year-old girl. A year later JAG investigators determined that PFC. Richard Gearity had taken pot shots with his M16 at

Responding to nothing more than "boredom," according to an eyewitness, soldiers of the 1st Cavalry (Armored) have some "fun" with a bayonet and a pair of Vietnamese villagers.

two boys as they passed by his guard tower at Lai Khe. One boy was killed, the other wounded.

Veterans back from the war told of popping mortars at peasants in the rice fields, stoning children, gunning down civilians and "collecting" their ID cards. The "worst thing" Sp4 Gary Keyes saw during his tour with the Americal Division occurred when "We were taking some grunts out on a beachhead. There were some fishermen out on the ocean and a couple of our sergeants thought it would be a good sport to use them as target practice. So they just swung their .50-calibers around and they just shot the shit out of them, for no reason, I guess."

Sometimes it passed beyond indifference to a more deliberate cruelty. In November 1966 five soldiers of the 1st Air Cav on a long-range reconnaissance patrol in the central highlands dragged a girl from her family's home where she was sleeping, forced her to accompany them on the patrol, gang raped her, then stabbed her to death. Three months earlier nine men of 2d Platoon, B Company, 1/5 Marines, had entered the small hamlet of Xuan Ngoc where for the next two-and-a-half hours they engaged in a private reign of terror. One young woman was raped while her husband, her mother, and sister were killed by gunfire. The woman's small son and five-year-old daughter were also shot down. The boy died immediately, but when the squad returned the following day the little girl was still alive. One of the men stood over the child and bashed her brains in with his rifle.

In March 1969 another marine squad set up an ambush a few hundred meters from the village of Cam Sa. When four young Vietnamese walked by—a boy aged eleven and three girls aged thirteen to nineteen—they were tied, gagged, and pushed down onto the trail. Two of the girls were taken to a nearby clearing where they were sexually abused by one of the men who then "stabbed them once in the throat and bashed their skulls in," according to court-martial records, before tossing the bodies into a nearby bunker. The remaining two captives were also killed and the bunker demolished with explosives.

An even more notorious incident took place in February 1970 when a five-man marine "killer team" patrol came upon the hamlet of Son Thang-4, a few kilometers north of Xuan Ngoc. The squad went to one hut and called out the occupants. When one woman suddenly ran toward a nearby tree line a marine shot her, then killed the others. From there the men went on to two more huts, ordered the inhabitants out, then cut them down with small-arms fire. In all, sixteen Vietnamese were killed that night—five women and eleven children.

That U.S. soldiers would commit acts of casual terror against helpless civilians was a disturbing discovery for many Americans. That they could be responsible for the annihilation of whole villages was incomprehensible. Yet the men who served in Vietnam were no different from those who remained at home. But they found themselves in a situation for which they had not been prepared, an environment of fear and uncertainty where restraint could mean death and the distinction between enemy and civilian could lose its reality, an environment of atrocity with its own logic of crime and punishment. "I gave them a good boy," despaired the mother of Paul Meadlo, one of those accused of participating in the My Lai massacre, "and they made him a murderer."

An environment of atrocity

The United States fought the war with teen-agers and paid a price for their immaturity. The average age of men in army and marine combat units was nineteen, compared to twenty-six in World War II. Vietnam was a dangerous place to be struggling with issues of manhood and identity common during late adolescence, a period of life typified by recklessness, instability, and sexual uncertainty. For confused young men, the war provided all too many opportunities for violent self-assertion. Even more problematic in a war in which contact with the enemy usually took place at squad or platoon level, a much greater degree of responsibility fell on the shoulders of men with little combat experience. Some individuals were able to mature rapidly in such circumstances, others were not.

U.S. military and political leaders compounded this gap between age and responsibility by lowering qualifications standards in two ways: retaining peacetime draft deferments and serving as an employer of last resort through Project 100,000. Despite the practice of hurrying units and individuals through curtailed training cycles, chronic personnel shortages still persisted, spreading experienced combat leadership much too thin while placing excessive demands on the often limited number of men in the field. Most units were in a perpetual state of turnover, making proper training and unit discipline difficult to maintain. It was no accident that the average marine involved in a serious crime in Vietnam was twenty years old, mentally below average on standard Marine Corps tests, the product of a broken home with a record of prior misconduct. Usually new to his unit, he had been in the country less than four months and was engaged in a mission involving a squad or less when the incident took place.

Whatever the deficiencies of some of the men in the ranks, far more crucial was a lack of adequate leadership from the officer corps, a problem rooted in the short duration and competitive nature of command assignments. The constantly expanding demand for first and second lieutenants outstripped the supply of junior officers and ultimately produced a steady decline in the quality of the officer corps. Limited to six months in the field, driven by their superiors to produce measurable results, marginal and inexperienced officers too often devoted themselves to raising their unit's "body count" with little attention paid to how those numbers were tallied up.

Fear and terror

The fear some Americans faced in daily village patrols could often make them look at any Vietnamese as the enemy. *Near right.* Men of the 1st Air Cavalry Division warily explore a suspected VC village near Bong Son during Operation Masher, January 1966. *Far right.* An American Division officer threatens a Vietnamese villager while a South Vietnamese interpreter at the right tries to explain that the man is mentally incompetent.

It was a situation ripe for abuse, made worse by the erosion of discipline during the latter years of the war, the failure of senior commanders to insure that junior officers understood their responsibilities toward noncombatants, and the generally cursory manner in which training in the law of war was carried out for officers and enlisted men alike. During much of the war recruits received one hour of instruction on the subject prior to deployment to Vietnam, a lecture on the Geneva conventions upon arrival in-country, and four wallet cards dealing with the rights of prisoners and noncombatants. Little attention was paid to what constituted a war crime or how to deal with illegal orders. The army discovered in 1969 that half of its personnel had not been given required annual training in the Geneva and Hague conventions. As to the cards, one platoon leader in the 173d Airborne spoke for most GIs: "Frankly I don't ever remember reading them."

Not only the general requirements of international law but also the detailed Rules of Engagement were often unknown or misunderstood by many U.S. servicemen. The majority of officers interviewed by the MACV Inspector General in 1967 exhibited a notable lack of familiarity with the regulations. Some officers said they were guided mainly by "common sense"; others suggested that "everybody had their own rules." Many veterans today profess ignorance of the ROE altogether.

Lack of knowledge of the ROE was one reason why possible war crimes were rarely reported. The difficulty of distinguishing combatants from noncombatants, the demand for body count, and the hostility of many soldiers toward the rural population were also important factors. Equally responsible were deficiencies in the reporting system, the pressures of careerism, and the loyalty of officers to their men. MACV directives specified that any military personnel "having knowledge or receiving a report of an incident or of an act thought to be a war crime make such an incident known to his commanding officer as soon as practicable." Until 1970, however, no provision was made for a situation in which the commanding officer himself was involved in such a crime. Even where he was an innocent party, a commander reporting a war crime by individuals in his unit would be admitting that he had not maintained control over his men. Cover-ups also resulted from more generous motives. Sharing the same dangers as those they commanded, junior officers in particular tried to protect their men by ignoring questionable behavior or dealing with it at the platoon or company level. Moreover, failure to report war crimes, even when detected, did not always result in substantial punishment. One company commander who stood by while two captured enemy nurses were raped and one of them murdered received only a reprimand and a $1,200 fine.

If American military personnel were confused about the way the war was supposed to be fought, they were even more confused about what it was they were fighting for. Instruction in the history and culture of Vietnam was min-

imal. Education about the political complexities of the situation was nonexistent. "My time in Vietnam," said former infantryman Tim O'Brien, "is the memory of ignorance. I didn't know the language. I knew nothing about the village community. I knew nothing about the aims of the people—whether they were for the war or against the war." It seemed to O'Brien, as it did to many GIs, that he was "a blind man wandering through a foreign land."

Young and inexperienced, without adequate preparation and sometimes without adequate leadership, American fighting men encountered in South Vietnam an alien culture, a ruthless opponent, and a frequently indifferent if not hostile population. Instead of grateful civilians happy to be liberated, soldiers met sullen, suspicious people who regarded them as intruders and often seemed to conspire in their destruction. The war the GIs waged in the villages was a counterpoint of boredom and terror, where contact was sporadic and casualties primarily the result of mines, booby traps, and hidden snipers. It was a combat environment that frequently made American soldiers passive targets: waiting for someone to fire at them; waiting for an ambush to be sprung; waiting for a land mine to explode under their feet.

For many men the source of terror became not simply the VC or NVA, but "Nam" itself. Testified Sergeant Michael McCusker of the 1st Marine Division,

The whole Vietnam thing is based on fear. You're scared to

death all the way over there. You're told continually that you're going to die if you don't do this, if you don't do that. That every Vietnamese is going to kill you; that boobytrapped babies are going to be sent against you and old grandmothers are going to throw bombs at you.

Alongside this fear was a steady toll of casualties and the maddening frustration of so little to strike back at. For some men the pressure to act could become so unbearable that eventually any Vietnamese they encountered would serve as a necessary target. Said one young sergeant matter-of-factly regarding the destruction of a village: "We took too many casualties; somebody had to pay." Worst of all, there was often no way of separating civilians from the enemy, no way of distinguishing by looks or dress who was a farmer and who a guerrilla, no way of convincing oneself that they were not, after all, one and the same.

Many of the stories were simply apocryphal—children wired like bombs, grandmothers hurling grenades—repeated so many times they gained a currency out of all relation to reality. But there could be no denying that women and children often cooperated with the VC by giving advance warning of approaching U.S. units, hiding weapons and ammunition, and preparing booby traps. One young GI who testified against men from his own platoon on charges they had raped and murdered a Vietnamese girl tried to describe the war that he and the defendants all found themselves caught up in.

Day after day, out on patrol, we'd come to a narrow dirt path leading through some shabby village, and the elders would welcome us and the children come running with smiles on their faces, waiting for the candy we'd give them. But at the other end of the path, just as we were leaving the village behind, the enemy would open up on us, and there was bitterness among us that the villagers hadn't given us warning.

"All that many of us could think at such times," he went on, "was that we were fools to be ready to die for people who defecated in public, whose food was dirtier than anything in our garbage cans back home." It was something that could change people. "It could keep them from believing that life was so valuable—anyone's life."

The callousness that developed was magnified by ra-

cism. "It developed in boot camp, it developed in [infantry training], it developed all the time we were in Vietnam," said Lance Corporal Kenneth Campbell, an artillery forward observer.

We hated these people, we were taught to hate these people. They were gooks, slants, dinks, they were Orientals, inferior to us. They chewed betel nuts, they were ugly, you know. ... [Our] instructors, the Vietnam veterans, these people we looked up to as like next to God, they always referred to all of these people as gooks and we picked up from them.

Some of it was simple prejudice but it was also a calculated kind of indoctrination. Said one recruit: "You are trained gook-gook-gook and once the military has got the idea implanted into your mind that these people are not

A Strategy of Terror

A truck carrying twenty teen-age girls of the Republican Youth Corps from a Saigon celebration is ambushed, nine of the girls killed in the attack.

A hamlet chief unsympathetic to the Vietcong is publicly disemboweled and then, while he is still alive, his eyes are punctured by the point of a bayonet.

VC troops blast a South Vietnamese Ranger post with mortars and automatic-weapons fire, then move forward behind a shield of peasant children. The Rangers then warn them to stop, but as the Communists continue to advance they open fire, killing ten children and wounding sixteen more.

One night a VC unit overruns a small garrison, killing the defenders and mutilating their bodies. The corpses are loaded into a sampan, along with surviving widows and children, and floated down a canal. In the morning light peasants along the waterway can just make out the slogan on the sampan's side: "Don't get in the way of the National Liberation Front or the same will happen to you."

The terrorism practiced by the Vietcong against the civilian population of South Vietnam took every conceivable form: harassment, kidnaping, assassination, execution, and massacre. VC terrorists mortared refugee camps, mined village roads, and hurled grenades into

crowded city streets. Between 1957 and 1965 an estimated 5,800 government officials were murdered and nearly 10,000 more abducted for varying lengths of time. Ordinary peasants and city dwellers fell victim to terror at even greater rates. The war that U.S. combat troops encountered when they first arrived in South Vietnam already contained an element of ferocity that few Americans could readily comprehend.

Some of the bloodletting was wholly indiscriminate but much of it was part of a calculated campaign of fear and intimidation. Initially a means of advertising the presence of the NLF, it became the insurgents' primary vehicle to power in the countryside. Striking at individuals of authority—hamlet chiefs, religious figures, schoolteachers—the VC eliminated virtually an entire class of Vietnamese villagers. In the process they isolated the peasants from the government that had promised them protection, leaving them only three alternatives: active support of the VC, passive neutrality, or death.

The men and women who carried out such acts were well trained, heavily indoctrinated, highly motivated, and willing to take great risks. During the early years of the war they were drawn from the "special activity cells" of the Guerrilla Popular Army. As the fighting grew more intense, terrorism in the South was centrally organized under the VC Security Service, an arm of the DRV Ministry of Public Security. Estimated to number 25,000 men by 1970, the Security Service operated in every province of South Vietnam, drawing up lists of potential targets, training assassination teams, and maintaining elite terrorist units. One of the latter was the infamous F-100.

Operating out of a secret base in the jungles of Binh Duong Province, F-100 carried the campaign of fear and disruption to Saigon and other urban areas. Between 1965 and 1967, F-100 terrorists bombed the National Police Headquarters, mortared the presidential palace, and attacked with rockets a Vietnamese National Day celebration. In between these spectaculars, the terrorists conducted countless assassinations, grenade strikes, and small-scale attacks that killed at least 250 people and wounded 1,400 more.

When American soldiers began to arrive in South Vietnam in force, the VC turned their strategy of terror on U.S. military personnel and civilians stationed in Saigon: bombs planted at a softball park and movie theater killing six Americans and injuring seventy others; another explosion at an American bus station leaving five dead and twenty-nine wounded; two American army billets attacked with demolition devices, killing seven servicemen and wounding thirty-seven more. In one of the worst attacks, the bombing of the My Canh floating restaurant, forty-four Americans and Vietnamese were killed and eighty wounded.

Urban terrorism reached stunning proportions during the Tet offensive of 1968 when VC and NVA troops methodically eliminated thousands of civil servants, police officers, educators, and religious figures during the twenty-six-day occupation of Hue. Throughout the remainder of the year the Communists rocketed Saigon, Da Nang, and other major cities, causing hundreds of casualties. During the 1969 post-Tet offensive in the delta, hundreds more fell victim to death squads.

human, it makes it a bit easier to kill them." Once they arrived in Vietnam this predisposition was fed by circumstance, by the resentment most American soldiers had for the often lethargic ARVN, by the pimps and prostitutes and drug dealers who were the only Vietnamese some GIs ever encountered outside the bush. "The way to win this war," went a common joke, "is to load all the dinks in the South on boats, kill all the ones in the North, and sink the boats."

The "mere gook rule," the attitude that the deaths of Vietnamese did not matter because, after all, "they're only gooks," helped justify a shoot first and ask questions later policy and made that much easier the process by which hostility toward the VC or NVA was transferred to the population at large. An available scapegoat for the enemy the soldier wished to confront but could not find, in extreme cases civilians came to be regarded as legitimate objects of combat.

The pressures that drove men to such conclusions were exacerbated by the constant demand for "body count" and by the absence of the normal restraints of civilian society. Most soldiers entered a village in small groups without an interpreter in what was in many ways an anonymous situation. Killing was made easier by the difficulty of fixing responsibility, the solidarity of the unit, and the implicit threat of retaliation against anyone who betrayed his comrades. It was made easier by the latitude that existed regarding who was to be considered the

Yet even as the insurgents made their presence felt in South Vietnam's cities, the campaign of terror in the countryside continued to mount. Assassinations of GVN officials, which had diminished after 1963 as the VC extended their influence over most of rural South Vietnam, jumped 500 percent between 1965 and 1966 and more than doubled again the following year. By 1969 nearly 250 civilians were being murdered or kidnaped each week. Meanwhile, as support from the peasantry grew less voluntary, the VC removed the velvet glove from its iron fist, launching full-scale attacks against villages and hamlets.

The most notorious incident of this type took place in Phuoc Long Province in December 1967. Fourteen months earlier more than 800 montagnard tribesmen had fled Vietcong control and resettled in the village of Dak Son. Fearing the effect of this exodus on the other 20,000 montagnards in the province, the VC first harassed the new settlement and then launched repeated attacks in hopes of overrunning it. On the night of December 5, Dak Son's luck ran out. The Vietcong began their assault at midnight with machine-gun, mortar, and rocket fire, then poured through the village defenses armed with sixty Russian flame throwers. The streams of liquid fire lit up the night burning everything in their path. But the attackers were not content merely to destroy the village. They turned their flame throwers on the refugees' homes, transforming the thatch-covered huts into roaring infernos that consumed the screaming inhabitants and asphyxiated those who had crawled into dugout shelters. Forcing 160 survivors from their bunkers, the VC shot 60 of them to death

on the spot, then marched the rest off into the jungle. When U.S. and South Vietnamese rescuers reached the smoking ruins the next morning, they found amid the rubble bloated, peeling remains of human beings, charred bodies of children locked in ghastly embraces, infants melted to their mother's breast. All told, 252 unarmed montagnards, most of them women and children, had been killed and 50 wounded, 100 kidnaped, and another 450 missing.

But if the Communists were willing to enforce their discipline on defenseless villagers by themselves, they found it even more useful to employ the Americans for the same purpose. Their technique was simple, cold-blooded, and chillingly effective: Occupy a village, provoke attack, then blame the death and destruction on the foreigners. In September 1965 the Japanese journalist Takashi Oka reported in the *Christian Science Monitor* what happened when a VC unit entered a village on the road from Saigon to Da Lat. They stayed only long enough to harangue the population and let word of their presence reach the district capital, then left. The next day American planes bombed the village and its Roman Catholic church. "The Communists, who had been hiding in the jungle," wrote Oka, "came back and told the villagers, 'Now you see what the Americans do to you.'" One year later U.S. Air Force jets killed twenty-four persons and injured eighty-four in an air strike on a village twelve kilometers west of Can Tho. Subsequent investigation revealed that the VC had held the peasants at gun point to prevent them from fleeing when they saw the first American planes.

A number of American critics of the

war contended that the terror employed by the Vietcong was in the main selective and justified, involving a relatively small number of victims. "I would suggest," wrote Richard Falk, "that the insurgent faction in an undeveloped country has, at the beginning of its struggle for power, no alternative other than terror to mobilize an effective operation." Yet Communist terror grew more intense as the war went on and was largely directed at civilians without connection to the government. It was often indiscriminate and generally in violation of the principles of military necessity, discrimination, proportionality, and humanity that are the basis of the law of war. The VC strategy of terror, in short, was a systematic, deliberate attack on the civilians of South Vietnam resulting in the death or injury of tens of thousands of noncombatants.

But the Vietnamese were not the only victims. The barbarity of VC terror, the seeming indifference of the enemy to the lives of their own countrymen, had a profound effect on the Americans who came to fight in Vietnam. The cruelty of the Vietcong toward the peasants reinforced the mistaken belief that life was cheap in the countryside. At the same time the inability of the peasants to defend themselves contributed to the contempt with which some GIs regarded them. Their refusal to risk their lives and those of their families by informing on the Vietcong helped nurture the idea that they were themselves the enemy. The strategy of terror employed by the Communists raised the level of savagery with which the war was fought and made the population of rural South Vietnam that much more negligible in the eyes of many who had come from so far away to protect them.

157

enemy. It was also made easier by the torrent of destruction an individual could let loose against the object of his anger or fear. In an environment of mutual hostility and distrust, a logic of brutality could come to prevail. The answer to VC activity, asserted an American officer serving in the delta, was terror. "The Vietcong have terrorized the peasants to get their cooperation, or at least to stop their opposition. We must terrorize the villagers even more, so they see that their real self-interest lies with us. . . . Terror is what it takes."

The psychiatrist Robert Jay Lifton has suggested that Vietnam was "an atrocity-producing situation." Fighting for a cause he did not believe in, for people who frightened and repelled him, in a hostile environment that offered "no honorable encounter, no warrior grandeur," the soldier's only goals became survival and revenge. It was a situation that created on the one hand intense feelings of guilt and impotence, and on the other a withdrawal into "advanced stages of brutalization and psychic numbing." To some it seemed as though they had been abandoned in a world of "absurdity and moral inversion," a world in which killing became a release, a world in which it was possible to believe that in gunning down old men, women, and children you had at last "engaged the enemy." This was the world that the men of Charlie Company wandered into one morning, at a place they called Pinkville, but that forever will be known as My Lai.

A contagion of slaughter

Like the helicopter gunship, My Lai has become a symbol of the Vietnam War—not because it was typical of American military behavior, but because so much of what made the war in the villages an "atrocity-producing situation" came together there in one terrible morning of death. Neither wholly exemplifying nor wholly isolated from the American way of war in Vietnam, it stands rather as the final step on a common path that a few men took to the end. My Lai is what happened when everything went wrong.

On the morning of March 16, 1968, the three companies of Task Force Barker launched a search and destroy operation into Son My Village, a collection of four hamlets ten kilometers north of Quang Ngai City. Their target was the 48th VC Local Force Battalion, which intelligence believed was using the village as a base of operations. Company C, under the command of Captain Ernest Medina, spearheaded the attack with a heliborne assault against the hamlet of My Lai–4. Contrary to expectations, the company encountered no resistance at the LZ and, after consolidating his forces, Medina ordered the 1st and 2d platoons into the hamlet.

As the Americans approached, some villagers began to flee across the open fields and were immediately shot down. The 2d Platoon, led by 2d Lieutenant Steven K. Brooks, swept through the northern half of My Lai–4 hurl-

ing grenades and setting fire to family shelters, calling the occupants out of their homes and gunning them down, raping and then murdering village girls, rounding up civilians and shooting them on the spot. After half an hour Medina ordered the 2d Platoon north to the hamlet of Binh Tay, where they gang raped several more girls before rounding up ten to twenty women and children and killing them on the spot.

Meanwhile, the 1st Platoon, commanded by 2d Lieutenant William L. Calley, Jr., was moving through the southern half of My Lai–4 shooting Vietnamese trying to escape, bayoneting others, raping women, destroying livestock, crops, and houses. Some civilians were killed when they emerged from their homes. Others were rounded up and moved toward a drainage ditch on the southeastern border of the hamlet where from 75 to 150 villagers were shot to death at Lt. Calley's command.

When Lieutenant Jeffrey LaCross's 3d Platoon entered the hamlet to "mop up" fifty minutes after the initial assault, they shot and killed several villagers trying to leave the area on an adjacent highway, burned houses, and killed what livestock had survived the other two platoons. At one point the men of the 3d Platoon herded together a group of women and children and sprayed them with M16 fire. A half-dozen other wounded villagers were killed "to put them out of their misery."

Altogether between 450 and 500 people died at My Lai–4, all of them unarmed, almost all of them old men, women, and children. But neither a bare chronicle of events nor the cold statistics of death can convey the horror of what took place that morning. For those involved the operation became a grotesque kaleidoscope of carnage. A group of GIs methodically pumping bullets into a cow then casually turning their fire on a woman who appeared nearby. "They just kept shooting at her," said photographer Ron Haeberle. "You could see the bones flying in the air chip by chip." A woman staggering out of a hut weeping, her dead baby in her arms. She took only a few steps before one of the men with Capt. Medina shot her down then "opened up" the dead baby with his M16. Soldiers setting fire to the hootches then shooting the Vietnamese as they tried to escape the flames. A GI stabbing a cow over and over as other men stood around laughing and commenting on his technique. A baby trying to open his dead mother's blouse to nurse, shot, then slashed with a bayonet. A GI raping a woman then putting his M16 into her vagina and pulling the trigger.

Larry Colburn, circling above the hamlet in a helicopter, watched infantrymen killing everything in sight. "The people didn't really know what was happening. Some of them began walking out of there and the GIs just started going up to them and shooting them all in the back of the head." Jay Roberts, an army reporter assigned to the operation, saw a "really tiny kid—he only had a shirt on, nothing else. He came over to [a pile of bodies] and held

My Lai-4

Above. "He's got ghosts in him" said one Americal GI as he watched the twitching body of a peasant in front of his burning home.

A small boy tries to shield his younger brother from the American bullets. Moments after this picture was taken they were both killed.

the hand of one of the dead. One of the GIs behind me dropped into a kneeling position thirty meters from this kid and killed him with a single shot."

"Some of the guys seemed to be having a lot of fun," said PFC. Herbert Carter. "They were wisecracking and yelling 'Chalk that one up for me.'" Others found the killing almost methodical. One witness saw two small children standing by themselves. "A guy with an M-16 fired at the first boy and the older boy fell over him to protect the smaller one. Then he fired six more shots. It was done very businesslike."

Not everyone took part in the madness. Some, like Sergeant Isaiah Cowen, simply wandered away from the killing. One soldier spotted three boys cowering in a field. He stared for a moment, then waved at them to hide. Others kept busy shooting animals to avoid having to shoot people. A few men refused direct orders to fire. When Calley instructed Robert Maples to "load your machine gun and shoot these people" in the ditch, Maples told him "I'm not going to do it." "I didn't shoot anyone," Tom Partch wrote in his diary. "Not even animals. I couldn't." Partch spent part of the morning with Michael Bernhardt who kept his rifle in its sling, pointing toward the ground. "It's wrong, it's wrong," he said over and over. But nobody tried to stop what was happening.

When the Americans first entered My Lai-4 they found the villagers peacefully eating their breakfast in front of their homes. Three hours later the hamlet had become a charnel house. "I was just coming into the middle of that ville," remembered one soldier, "and I saw this guy. He was one of my best friends in the company.

But honest to Christ, at first I didn't even recognize him. He was kneeling on the ground, this absolutely incredible ... I don't know what you'd call it, a smile or a snarl or something but anyway his whole face was distorted. ... He was kneeling there holding this grenade launcher, and he was launching grenades at the hootches. A couple of times he launched grenades at groups of people. The grenades would explode, you know, KAPLOW, and then you'd see pieces of bodies flying around. Some of the groups were just piles of bodies. But I remember there was this one group, a little distance away. Maybe there was ten people, most of them women and little kids, huddled all together and you could see they were really scared, they just couldn't seem to move. Anyway, he turns around toward them and lets fly with a grenade. It landed right in the middle of them. You could hear the screams and then the sound and then see the pieces of bodies scatter out, and the whole area just suddenly turned red like somebody had turned on a faucet.

Shortly after 1:30 P.M. Charlie Company marched off from the smoking ruins of the hamlet. By that evening Captain Medina had reported a total of ninety VC KIA. But the Peers Commission, which subsequently investigated the events of that day, determined that "only three or four" of the dead were in fact Vietcong.

Why My Lai?

In its assessment of the factors contributing to the My Lai incident the Peers Commission singled out the confused and unlawful orders issued prior to the operation. It is true that Lieutenant Colonel Frank Barker's instructions to burn houses, kill livestock, and destroy foodstuffs were illegal, and there was strong evidence that Captain Medina went even further, using language that was generally understood by his men to call for the destruction of everyone they encountered in the hamlet. These orders played a decisive role in the tragedy that unfolded. But in retrospect there can also be little doubt that Charlie Company was a disaster waiting to happen.

Virtually every problem that bedeviled U.S. forces in Vietnam was present in the company in abundance. The 11th Brigade of the Americal Division, to which the company belonged, suffered from major personnel deficiencies that left it 700 men short of authorized strength when it was committed to combat. Many of the soldiers were replacements whose training had been abbreviated and whose presence created more than the ordinary amount of turbulence. The men in Charlie Company were primarily draftees, ranging in age from eighteen to twenty-two with few having even a year of college. Ten percent of the company had failed the army's basic intelligence test, entering the service under Project 100,000. Although "better than average in infantry aptitude," according to the Peers Commission, "the inductees, as a group, had less education and were less trainable" than the average unit.

Army investigators reported that during training in Hawaii the men received at best "lackadaisical" education in the treatment of civilians. Almost immediately engaged in construction, guard, and patrol duties upon their arrival in Vietnam in December 1967, they were given no further instruction in the laws of war save for MACV's "Nine Rules" cards. The Peers Commission later discovered "they had put the cards in their pockets unread and never had any idea of their contents."

The situation was made worse by the failure of division, brigade, and task force commanders to disseminate such information to the soldiers, by Medina's aggressive pursuit of higher body counts and indifference toward civilians, and by the poor quality of the officers in charge of his platoons. This was particularly true of Lt. Calley, whose indecisiveness and chronic inability to follow instructions earned him Medina's constant criticism, and whose own defense attorneys argued during his trial that he would never have become an officer if the army had maintained its normal standards of selection. Calley, Brooks, and LaCross were neither comfortable nor confident about disciplining their men. Because of this, and because of a lack of correction from company and brigade levels, a dangerous permissiveness had been allowed to develop in the months before the My Lai incident.

Mine injuries were terrifying, and deadly. The mangled remains of a young American soldier hit by a VC mine are carried off a medevac chopper at the 93d evacuation hospital in Long Binh.

The men in the company had been shocked when they first saw a troop carrier driving by "with about twenty human ears tied to the antenna," but not long afterward some of them returned from a patrol with trophies of their own. "Medina was happy," they remembered, "it was his first kill." Michael Bernhardt recalled an escalating pattern of violence and brutality not only condoned by the officers but often committed by them: an old Vietnamese dumped in a well with a hand grenade tossed in after him; another old man pleading for the return of some possessions the Americans had just ransacked from his home until one of the soldiers lost his temper and gunned him down; a group of men interrupted as they tried to hang a villager; a woman gang raped in front of her child, then both shot. The only punishment ever meted out for any of these crimes was one man who was disciplined with a loss of rank after raping a girl.

None of this had anything to do with military objectives. It had a lot to do with the way the men felt about the villagers. They had been in-country for only a few weeks before the company developed a hatred for the Vietnamese, whom they treated "like animals," according to Michael Terry. "A lot of guys didn't feel that they were human

beings." Gestures of good will did not seem to be reciprocated the way the men expected. "In the beginning," remembers Fred Widmer, "we'd go to the villages, have a beer or two, talk and never show much hate," but it did not win them any friends. Instead, the peasants seemed to be in league with the Vietcong. Eusebia Santellana, home on emergency leave when the assault on My Lai took place, said the trouble was that "the people aren't straight like we are. We ask them something and they don't know. After we leave the VC hit us." So the men started striking back. "We would go through a village, tear up stuff, kicking it over, burning it down," said Charles Sledge. "You can't help knowing that they hate you," recalled Michael Bernhardt, "and [the soldiers] hated and feared them in return. So that a lot of these guys just wanted to kill every one of them."

It was a problem that grew worse as the men of Charlie Company experienced mounting casualties in a war against an enemy they hardly ever saw. For the first seven weeks when they operated out of Duc Pho there was virtually no action, just endless patrols, boredom, fatigue, and frustration. Then, in mid-February, they set up operations at LZ Dotty in northern Quang Ngai Province, a VC stronghold for over two decades. First, one member of Calley's platoon stepped on a mine and barely escaped with his life. A few days later the 1st and 2d platoons got caught in a sharp firefight on the northern edge of Son My Village. During the fighting Calley's radio man, Bill Weber, became the company's first KIA. For the next three days the company tried repeatedly to penetrate Son My and each time they were forced to retreat.

Things had begun to go sour and they would soon become much worse. The patrolling continued without letup. On February 21 they lost two more men to booby traps. On the twenty-third another man was hit by sniper fire. That night they blundered into a nest of booby traps. They managed to extricate themselves without damage only to see two more men felled by snipers; another became hysterical with fear and had to be evacuated. After weeks of inaction Charlie Company had suffered six casualties in three days and now was ordered north to take up a blocking position in a sweep operation planned for the following morning.

To get to their assigned location they had to rise before dawn and hack for hours through bushes and hedgerows. As they neared their rendezvous point they started walking up a small hill. Martin Gershen, a journalist who has chronicled the days leading up to My Lai, describes what happened next.

Suddenly there was an explosion that tore through the early morning stillness and a man screamed. Then there was another explosion, coming almost on top of the first, and another man screamed. Then there was another explosion, and another, and another, and another.

After a moment of stunned shock men rushed to help the wounded, setting off more mines. It was a scene none of them would ever forget: limbs torn off by the detonations, men screaming, medics crawling desperately from one wounded man to the next, and always, more explosions. It was not over for nearly two hours. In that time thirty-two men were killed or wounded. The psychological damage done to those who survived was incalculable.

After the minefield the company turned its anger on the Vietnamese, becoming, writes Gershen, "a danger to the Army and to U.S. policy in Vietnam." They began to cut a finger or an ear off Vietnamese corpses in a gesture of revenge, beat up children who came selling Cokes and beers, cut off the pigtails of Vietnamese girls to decorate their rifle barrels. But there was no rest from the VC. On March 4 the company was mortared at LZ Dotty and most of the men's personal possessions were destroyed. Ten days later, two days before the assault on My Lai, four more men were blown to pieces by a booby trap, including one of the company's last experienced NCOs. Forty-two casualties in thirty-two days from a company that operated in the field at a strength of 90 to 100 men, and they had scarcely seen the enemy.

The following day a memorial service was held and later Medina told his men they would have their chance for revenge. They would be attacking two companies of the VC battalion that had plagued them since the day Weber died. It would be a tough fight. But the company had a score to settle. He told the men that women and children would be out of the area, that nothing in the village was to be left standing. Medina "told us everything in the village was the enemy," remembers Robert Maples, a machine-gunner with the 1st Platoon. "The way I think he said it—and the way they took it—was that anything in the village was VC." One of the soldiers whispered into a companion's ear, "It's going to be a slaughter, you watch."

Afterward, when they had all come home, the men of Charlie Company had different feelings about what had taken place at My Lai. Henry Pedrick did not think it was anything unusual. Neither did Nicholas Capezza, one of the company's medics: "To me, it was just like another day in Vietnam." Some just did not care. "I haven't let it bother me," said John Smail. "I never wanted to go there in the first place. I hated those people, I really did." But others were more disturbed. Rennard Doines "knew it wasn't right." For William Wyatt, Vietnam was "some sort of fantasy-land." Even so, what happened at My Lai "wasn't like it was supposed to be."

Michael Bernhardt had never been able to make any sense out of what was going on while he was with Charlie Company. "Maybe this was the way wars really were," he thought. "Maybe what we saw in the movies and on TV wasn't so, that war was running around and shooting civilians and doing this kind of thing. I felt like I was left out, like maybe they forgot to tell me something, that this was the way we fought wars and everybody knew but me."

At one point during the massacre Herbert Carter shot himself in the foot—to escape having to join in the killing, according to some eyewitnesses. Nearly two years later he was still wondering "why human beings claim to be human beings but still conduct themselves as savages and barbarians." Thinking back on all the company had gone through it seemed to Carter that My Lai was simply the logical conclusion of the only war he knew. "The people didn't know what they were dying for, and the men didn't know why they were shooting them."

A question of responsibility

The subsequent conviction of Lieutenant Calley for the murder of "at least" twenty-two unarmed men, women, and children provoked charges that he had been made a scapegoat for policies that emanated from the highest levels of political and military command. Citing principles laid down during the Nuremberg Tribunals, some claimed that because they had knowingly instituted or permitted the employment of tactics that were in themselves illegal and that could lead to no other result but the murder of ci-

Like so much else about the war, the burden of its conduct fell ultimately on those who fought it. An American infantryman drops to his knee and fires into My Lai, March 16, 1968.

vilians, it was General Westmoreland and President Johnson who should be called to account for the war crimes the men of Charlie Company stood accused of.

The historian Guenter Lewy, who has maintained that U.S. military tactics in Vietnam were neither illegal nor in the main irresponsible, has suggested nonetheless that MACV knew that Rules of Engagement were "not applied and enforced as they should have been." As the commander of U.S. forces "Westmoreland *should* have known that in the Vietnam environment inadequate understanding of the ROE could and would lead to violations of the law of war." Failing to insure that the regulations were more rigorously enforced, he was guilty of "at least dereliction of duty or perhaps even criminal negligence. . . ."

Others have insisted that the responsibility for war crimes rested primarily with the nation's civilian leaders. Critics like the journalist Neil Sheehan, the historian Gabriel Kolko, and the legal scholar Richard Falk have argued that it was Secretary of Defense Robert McNamara, Secretary of State Dean Rusk, and presidential adviser W. Walt Rostow who supervised the war for President Johnson in the face of clear evidence of the consequences of their policies and that therefore it was they who should be subject to criminal liability under the provisions of international law. Or was it the case, as former Deputy Assistant Secretary of Defense Townsend Hoopes has claimed, that to single out civilian officials was to mistake questionable judgment for evil intentions and to ignore the broad mandate for military involvement in Vietnam that both Congress and the American public gave the Johnson administration in the form of appropriations and votes?

Whatever the merits of these various positions, they offered scant comfort to the men actually called upon to deal with the dark confusion of the Vietnamese countryside: a war of isolated encounters and sudden destruction; an enemy who wore no uniform and played by rules of his own invention; orders that were often ambiguous in pursuit of a mission that no one really seemed to understand.

Those whom America sent to Vietnam did not choose the terms of the struggle nor its place, they simply paid the price. "A war can only be fought with sound men," wrote the German novelist Jakov Lind. "The highest demands are made on every individual, it takes nerves of steel. We have to do things that may not be to our liking. Yes, sometimes we have to do violence to our own nature. Most of the duties a war imposes on us . . . are revolting, let's face it, insane, and yet the soldier who performs them has to be fully responsible. That's the way it is, it can't be helped."

Crime and Punishment

Several hundred U.S. Army personnel participated in, witnessed, or knew of the events that took place in Son My Village on March 16, 1968. On the basis of the findings of the Peers Commission, and as the result of lengthy investigations conducted by the army's Criminal Investigations Division, charges were ultimately preferred against sixteen officers and enlisted men for offenses ranging from murder to the failure to report possible war crimes. Preliminary charges against twelve other individuals were dismissed for lack of sufficient evidence. An even larger number of men were immune from prosecution because they had already been discharged from the service by the time the army's probe into the My Lai incident was underway.

Of the sixteen formally charged, five were tried by court-martial. Only one of those tried—Lieutenant William Calley, Jr.—was found guilty.

Escorted by military police, Lt. William Calley, Jr., leaves the court building at Fort Benning, Georgia, after his conviction for the premeditated murder of Vietnamese civilians at My Lai.

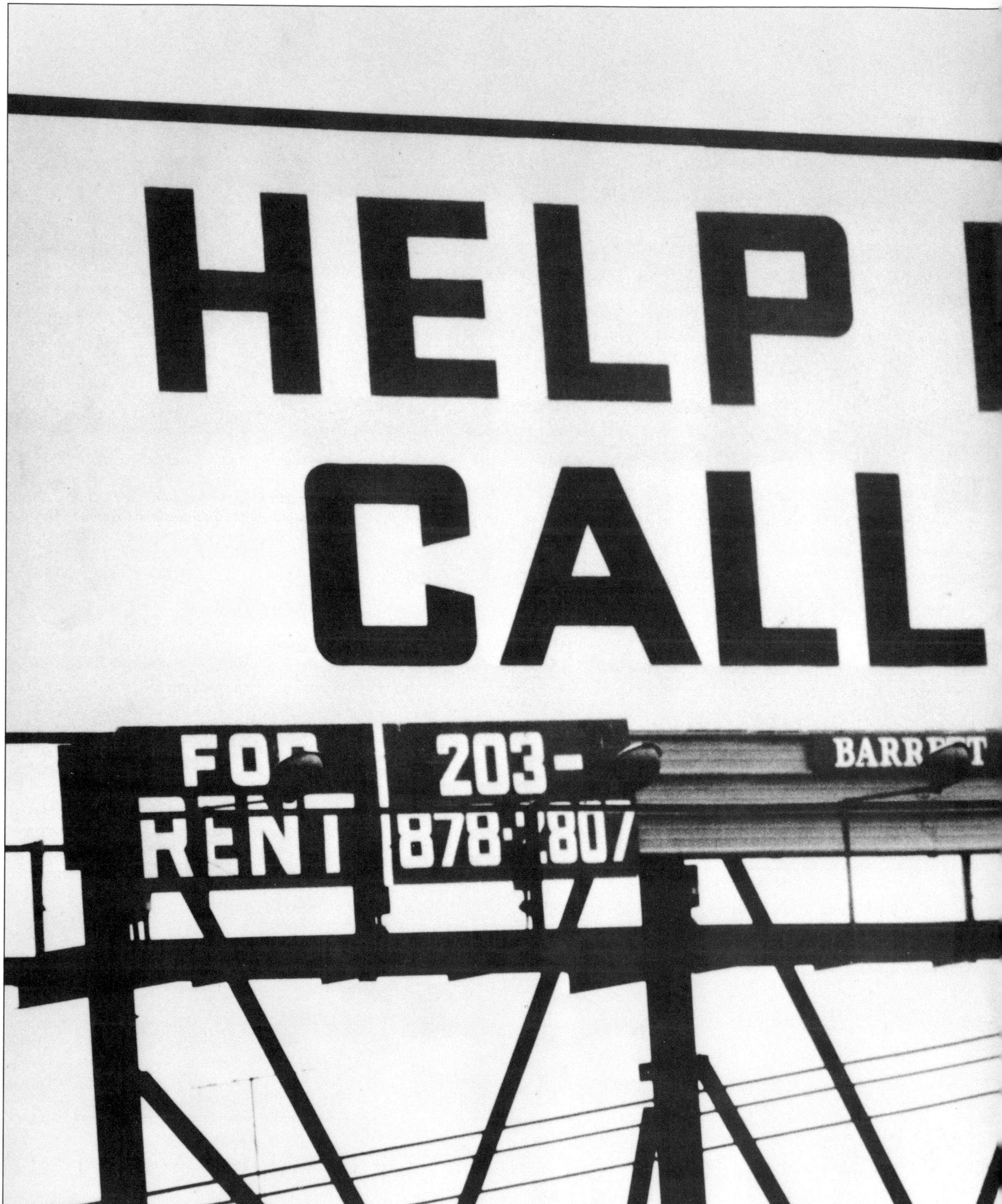
HELP
CALL
RENT
203-

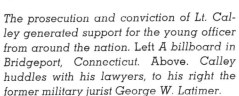

The prosecution and conviction of Lt. Calley generated support for the young officer from around the nation. Left A billboard in Bridgeport, Connecticut. Above. Calley huddles with his lawyers, to his right the former military jurist George W. Latimer.

The impassioned reaction of the American people to the My Lai prosecutions, particularly that of Lt. Calley, was overwhelmingly negative. Eighty percent of those polled were opposed to Calley's conviction. A sizable minority believed he had committed no crime at all. Others thought he was merely a scapegoat for the army command.

In the wake of the trial a flood of phone calls, letters, and petitions for his release inundated the media. Songs defending Calley were recorded, entire draft boards resigned in protest, and the White House received over 15,000 letters demanding a presidential pardon.

Conservatives asked how Calley "could fight for his flag and then be court-martialed and convicted for apparently carrying out his orders." Antiwar activists called the prosecution a hypocritical charade, singling out one instance of criminality in a war that was "totally criminal." Many Americans viewed the verdict as somehow an attack on themselves and their beliefs, a judgment against the nation and what it stood for.

Calley's original sentence of life imprisonment at hard labor was reduced upon review to twenty, and then ten years. He was ultimately paroled on November 19, 1974, after spending three-and-a-half years under house arrest.

The trial of Captain Ernest Medina began in March 1971. Originally charged with premeditated murder and commanding an unlawful act—homicide—he actually came before the tribunal accused of involuntary manslaughter for failing to exercise proper control over his men. Not convinced that Medina had "actual knowledge" of what his men were doing inside My Lai, the jury acquitted him.

A dozen officers were charged with participation in the My Lai cover-up, but none was convicted. Colonel Oran K. Henderson, commander of the 11th Infantry Brigade—Charlie Company's parent unit—was tried by court-martial and acquitted. Charges against Major General Samuel W. Koster, commander of the American Division, were dismissed, although he was subsequently censured, reduced in rank to brigadier general, and forced to resign as superintendent of West Point.

Captain Ernest Medina walks to court during the fifth month of his court-martial, accompanied by his wife.

Left. Major General Samuel W. Koster. Right. Colonel Oran K. Henderson.

A Parting of the Ways

At the conclusion of a conference with his South Vietnamese counterpart Nguyen Van Thieu in June 1969, President Richard Nixon announced his decision to remove 25,000 U.S. troops from Vietnam. After twenty years of escalating economic, political, and military involvement in Indochina, the American withdrawal had at last begun. Over the next twenty-four months 260,000 soldiers and marines returned to the United States. By December 1971, with the "Vietnamization" program in full swing, U.S. strength in South Vietnam had been reduced to 184,000 men. One year later only a "residual" force of 27,000 remained. With the departure of the final troop contingents on March 29, 1973, direct U.S. military participation in the Vietnam War came to an end.

Accompanying the redeployment of American military forces was a steady withdrawal of American advisers and economic aid. From a peak strength of 2,350 employees, USAID personnel in South Vietnam had dwindled to 735 by

The VIETNAMESE PEOPLE WILL FOREVER REMEMBER YOUR SACRIFICES

RVNAF IS STRONG ENOUGH TO ASSUME the RESPONSIBILITY OF DESTROYING the COMMUNISTS

BE PROUD of FIGHTING of FREEDOM and WORLD PEACE

1973. The AID budget declined as well, to $74 million in 1972, compared to $240 million in 1968. Overall U.S. economic assistance to South Vietnam, amounting to $575 million in 1971, shrank by 35 percent over the next two years, the value of the reduced aid package further diminished by the devaluation of the dollar in 1971 and a sharp rise in world prices.

American officials in Vietnam privately admitted that the pace of withdrawal, the reduction of aid, and the increase in defense expenditures that would have to be assumed by the GVN seriously endangered already vulnerable social and economic reconstruction projects. They worried that South Vietnam would no longer be able to continue its artificially supported consumer goods economy. Expressing little confidence in the ability of the South Vietnamese to take over U.S. programs, most observers gave the Saigon regime no more than a 50-50 chance of survival. Yet many Americans who had worked in Vietnam for years also believed that leaving the South Vietnamese to solve their own problems might be the best thing the United States could do. After a two-month investigation in 1971, journalist Norman Sklarewitz reported in *U.S. News & World Report* that the mood of Americans in Vietnam reflected "a sense of finality." The way most of them summed it up: "What happens from here on out is up to them."

Coming home to roost

American pessimism was well founded. The withdrawal of U.S. military forces meant the disappearance of a major source of national revenue. American spending, which once reached $450 million annually, had dropped to $100 million by 1973. Because of the devaluation of the dollar, the real purchasing power of that $100 million was further reduced by some 30 percent. Almost totally dependent on foreign imports for everything from toothpaste to rice, South Vietnam faced an annual bill of more than $750 million for foreign purchases. The precipitate decline in American consumption, which accounted for half of South Vietnam's foreign exchange reserves, was a balance of payments catastrophe.

It also translated into a cost of living rise of more than 50 percent for ordinary Vietnamese. Particularly devastating were sharp increases in prices for rice, pork, and *nuoc mam*, the staples of the Vietnamese diet. Those with the lowest salaries—ARVN enlisted men and civil servants—found their earnings sufficient to meet only one-third of their minimum needs.

Inflation also compromised the economic and political

strategies the United States relied upon to bolster South Vietnam in its contest with the North. The influx of consumer goods had greatly increased the demand for petroleum. Villagers had been introduced to water pumps, outboard motors, and motorbikes. They also needed large quantities of fertilizer to grow the "miracle" rice supplied by USAID. But the soaring cost of these commodities prompted some farmers to give up growing rice entirely in the face of drastically declining profits. Meanwhile, as the value of the piaster plummeted against the dollar wealthier Vietnamese found it increasingly difficult to obtain American goods. The attempt to contrast an affluent South Vietnam with its austere northern adversary had backfired. "We forcibly raised demand and consumption way beyond what the Vietnamese could ever afford to pay," admitted one U.S. official in Saigon. "We were trying to buy votes, not solve economic problems. Now the chickens are coming home to roost."

As the economic crisis worsened both Vietnamese and American officials took countermeasures. In 1969 President Thieu proclaimed a battery of economic reforms, including a revival of austerity taxes to reduce spending on consumer goods. The following year the Nixon administration established a foreign exchange level of $750 million in hopes of stabilizing the South Vietnamese economy and charged the Department of Defense with "meeting any shortfalls from this goal." In September General Abrams created a new Office of Economic Affairs to advise him on all matters pertaining to the stability and growth of the RVN economy. That same month the South Vietnamese legislature established a two-tiered piaster exchange rate designed to discourage the black market and make South Vietnamese exports more competitive.

Such reforms and adjustments, however, could not overcome the fundamental disabilities of the South Vietnamese economy. The U.S. departure had left a vacuum in economic research and planning. At the same time, many Vietnamese blamed the Americans for failing to produce long-term development strategies that the GVN could implement. The trouble with the Americans, complained one Vietnamese economist, was they "never thought of really teaching us instead of just building things."

But at least equally to blame were South Vietnamese businessmen and government officials. Many Vietnamese with money chose to invest not in industry but in quick-profit ventures such as hotels and nightclubs catering to Americans. The GVN also rejected U.S. advice to buy capital goods such as factory equipment, electing instead to import cosmetics, automobiles, fashion apparel, tape recorders, and jewelry. Indeed, even as Thieu reinstated aus-

---

Preceding page. Members of the South Vietnamese armed forces bid farewell to the first marine unit redeployed to the United States, the 1st Battalion, 9th Marines, at Da Nang on July 14, 1969.

Saigon, 1971. One of several handicapped veterans protesting his ineligibility for veterans benefits. Some of the demonstrators threatened to blow themselves up with hand grenades if their demands were not met.

terity taxes, he simultaneously lifted import restrictions to satisfy the Vietnamese addiction for luxury goods. Such items might soak up piasters and thereby serve as some check on inflation, but they did not build an economy geared for long-range development, a fact that became increasingly clear once the Americans began to withdraw.

The test of survival

Given these weaknesses, the departure of nearly 550,000 U.S. troops and the dismantling of the logistical system that supported them had a devastating effect on those Vietnamese whose livelihoods depended upon the Americans. Approximately 125,000 people worked directly for U.S. military or civilian organizations driving cars and trucks, holding clerical positions, acting as interpreters, or doing maintenance work on U.S. bases. Another 150,000 earned their living indirectly from the Americans as café operators, real estate agents, shoe-shine boys, black marketeers, or bar girls. In towns like Da Nang, Nha Trang, and Bien Hoa, which surrounded military bases, half of the population relied on GI spending—between $50 and $58 million per year—for most or all of their income. As American forces departed and one after another American bases shut down, tens of thousands of these people were dumped onto a labor market that had no way to absorb them.

Particularly hard hit by the U.S. redeployment were South Vietnam's thousands of prostitutes. "In 1969, the half million GIs in Vietnam were looked upon not as defenders of freedom but as consumers," wrote Richard Boyle in *The Flower of the Dragon*, and sex was the biggest product. Three years later Donald Kirk found Saigon's empty bars crammed with "waitresses" ready to ply their trade for customers who never showed up. Another sign of the times could be seen along Cach Mang Road where prostitutes who used to solicit GIs from the back seats of motorbikes now did their hustling on foot.

Small businessmen also saw the bottom drop out of their enterprises. Many bars, hotels, nightclubs, and restaurants simply closed. Some tried to stay open by changing their names from the "Tennessee Bar" or "G.I. Dolly" to Vietnamese street names or local movie heroes. Other adaptations were attempted. Writing in the *New Yorker*, Robert Shaplen described a woman who had once made herself wealthy finding girls for American servicemen. In 1972 she was trying to squeeze a few dollars out of her accumulated assets through newspaper advertisements: "Miss Lee: Needs to buy air conditioners and cars, top prices paid—Has car for rent monthly, weekly, daily with insurance: Toyota, Mazda, Datsun, Volkswagen, Jeep, Microbus, etc.—Servants, Cooks, Driver License [sic], Villas, Apartments, Houses for Rent." One American reporter saw Da Nang businessmen forced to do manual labor on city public works projects "or go hungry."

The economic dislocation that accompanied the withdrawal of American men and money tore at the social fabric of South Vietnam. As American jobs and dollars disappeared, whole communities collapsed. The U.S. military pullback also resulted in the forced relocation of thousands of Vietnamese and montagnard tribesmen from the central highlands to camps near the coast where the ARVN could keep an eye on them. Disintegration began to appear in the army itself, as incidents of theft, hooliganism, and financial extortion from civilians rose throughout the countryside. For those who had grown wealthy during the period of American involvement, the U.S. withdrawal precipitated an exodus of paintings, lacquer ware, heirlooms, jewels, and cash to foreign banks and long vacations for their families to such international gathering places as New York, Paris, London, and Switzerland. Meanwhile, desperate bar owners and drug dealers turned their attention from the Americans to the Vietnamese youth who emulated the GIs' lifestyle.

The Easter offensive of 1972 intensified the disruptive impact of the American troop withdrawal, multiplying the throngs of unemployed and hurling the economy deeper into recession. So desperate had conditions become that the Communists seemed less threatening than the collapsing economy. To a Saigon politician surveying the turmoil the war was "remote and we are used to it. But the cost of living affects everyone. It may well be that the real test of our national survival will not come on the battlefield but in the marketplace." After a decade of urban prosperity fueled by the war and by the Americans who came to fight it, the South Vietnamese economic bubble had burst. "The much talked about 'Honda Society,'" concluded *Newsweek* correspondent Loren Jenkins, "has virtually run out of gas."

A gathering storm

"I have a dream—call it a nightmare—that I am the last American left in Da Nang, and that is something nobody wants." The speaker was a U.S. official, the year was 1971, and the fear he expressed was shared by many Americans during the period of withdrawal. The impending U.S. military departure exacerbated long-standing grievances, raising tensions between Americans and Vietnamese to dangerous levels. Resentful of what they saw as American control of Vietnamese life, yet dreading the prospect of a complete break with American dollars and protection, Vietnamese wrestled with conflicting feelings of betrayal and relief that spilled over into public expressions of anger. As U.S. troops and civilian workers left Vietnam, those who remained witnessed a gathering storm of anti-Americanism.

Vietnamese-American relations had been deteriorating for some time when the multiple shocks of the 1968 Tet offensive, Lyndon Johnson's withdrawal from the presidential race, and his decision to halt the bombing of North Vietnam jolted South Vietnamese confidence in the American commitment. Offended by unilateral U.S. peace initiatives, apprehensive of American support for a coalition government, and fearful of a premature settlement, many Vietnamese saw in the unfolding events the threat of abandonment. "I do not ask the U.S. troops to stay here for 100 years," pleaded President Thieu. "I only ask the Americans to have the courage and the clear sight to remain here until we nationalists have enough military, economic and political strength."

By the summer of 1969 American reporters were discovering a new edge to the endemically difficult relations between the two groups. The young Honda-riding toughs called *cao bois* ("cowboys") had become so vicious in their taunts that few Vietnamese women liked to be seen walking with an American. Newspaper stories of happily married women corrupted by the Americans abounded, as did more bizarre word-of-mouth accounts of conspiracies between the U.S. and the Vietcong to annex South Vietnam to the United States and tales of mysterious sex-ual diseases deliberately spread by American troops. Educated Vietnamese blamed the Americans for turning the country into a gigantic garbage dump. They also took offense at what they regarded as the unwarranted cultural arrogance of the foreigners. "We consider your country too young, and there is not much we can learn from you, save for what we call modern development," said one intellectual. "We tend to equate you with machines for whom there is no deep thinking." Sneered another: "Americans have no culture, unless you call beer and big bosoms culture."

Over the next three years this growing resentment took more blatant forms. A 1971 editorial cartoon in the opposition newspaper *Hoa Binh* portrayed Lyndon Johnson and Richard Nixon literally raping South Vietnam. In August of the same year a man holding a poster of President Nixon with a Hitler mustache burned himself to death in downtown Saigon. At a 1972 art exhibition at Saigon University, one large panel pictured Americans as eagles, hawks, and wolves stalking the Vietnamese countryside.

By 1970 U.S. officials estimated that approximately 1,000

Teen-age cao bois *hang out on a Saigon street corner.*

The American Connection

The size of the U.S. presence in Vietnam created a special labor market to serve American needs and siphon off American dollars. Above. An American, trailed by her Vietnamese maid, takes her Pekingese for a walk. Left. A GI haggles with a Vietnamese street photographer over the price of his picture. Right. Prostitutes in front of a Saigon brothel called "The Flowers" on Tu Do Street.

confrontations between Americans and South Vietnamese occurred each month. Although many of these were minor incidents—*cao bois* yelling obscenities at American women—an increasing number were notably violent. Vietnamese teen-agers who used to beg for candy bars at the U.S. PX in Cholon began taking what they wanted from American women they accosted outside. Others enjoyed the "sport" of running down American pedestrians with their motorbikes. During a bar brawl in October 1969 a major in the Vietnamese Rangers chopped off the hand of a United States military policeman. Earlier that year, a lieutenant colonel who commanded the Vietnamese Airborne Battalion shot and killed two American MPs. In July 1970 a group of *cao bois* attempted to castrate an American civilian outside Tan Son Nhut air base. That same month the United States Army Command and the U.S. Embassy warned Americans "for their own safety" not to travel alone in Saigon.

Attacks on individual Americans occasionally merged into public demonstrations staged primarily by high-school and university students. Taking the form of marches, songs, sit-ins, and noisy motorcycle parades, these demonstrations rarely attracted more than a few hundred participants. Yet their small numbers belied their capacity for violence. On June 15, 1970, a U.S. jeep was set on fire in Saigon and its occupant, an American sergeant, beaten by Vietnamese as he tried to flee. Nearby the protesters scrawled "Down with the country-selling clique," "Peace Now," and "Bunker, Go Home" on the pavement. The fragility of the equilibrium that existed between Americans and Vietnamese was graphically demonstrated when a U.S. Army private accidentally shot and killed a Buddhist high school student in Qui Nhon on December 7, 1970, precipitating two days of violent anti-American demonstrations only temporarily brought under control by squads of police and militiamen. No sooner had a twenty-four-hour curfew been clamped on Qui Nhon than rioting broke out in Saigon, where protesters hurled rocks at American soldiers, burned trucks, hanged effigies of President Nixon, and bombed U.S. officer facilities. Violent out-

bursts continued to rock both cities for the next month.

The Vietnamese election campaign during the late summer of 1971 provoked numerous anti-American demonstrations by students, politicians, Buddhists, intellectuals, and disabled veterans. Demonstrators staged protests in front of the U.S. Embassy in Saigon, distributing leaflets and splattering red paint on the walls of the compound. In Hue, students carried posters labeled "Nixon's Vietnamization" showing President Nixon sitting on a pile of Vietnamese skulls, blood dripping from his fingers. One group threw plastic bags filled with gasoline and burning matches at American military vehicles, setting a number of trucks and at least one navy man on fire.

The students who staged these attacks condemned the United States for its support of President Thieu, whom they regarded as an arbitrary and indecisive ruler more concerned with his own reelection than in restoring peace to Vietnam. They also believed that United States involvement in South Vietnam posed as serious a threat to the stability and survival of their country as the Vietcong

or the North Vietnamese. When Ha Dinh Nguyen, a student leader at Saigon University, first saw Americans in his native village of Hoi An in central Vietnam, "I admired those soldiers. They seemed so carefree, so strong. I was moved to think that they would have come from so far away to die for something other than their own country." After he came to Saigon, however, Ha's attitude gradually began to change. "I saw how they interfered at all levels in Vietnamese society. I read about the massacre of Vietnamese civilians in My Lai. I saw myself how the lives of city people were disrupted by the American presence. I began to feel that the American presence itself is the reason the Communists continue the war."

The small number of student activists who led the demonstrations were the noisiest, but hardly the only group of South Vietnamese criticizing the United States. Politicians who had kept such sentiments in check during the American build-up now assailed their allies at every opportunity. Leading the onslaught was Vice President Ky, who denounced "colonial slavery" and blamed Vietnam's troubles on "erroneous and unreasonable meddling by the Americans." The Vietnamese people considered the Americans not friends, asserted the vice president, "but in the category of bad and unwelcome masters." Arguing that it was imperative to "greatly reduce the influence of the Americans—the sooner the better," Ky told the West German magazine *Stern:* "The Americans are here to defend their interests, which do not always correspond with those of Vietnam. They are here because they want to remain in Asia and to stop communism in Asia and not because they have any particular concern about us."

Other political leaders, including opposition deputies in the National Assembly, echoed Ky's suspicions. Ironically, rather than easing their resentment, the gradual process of disengagement only inflamed the politicians' anger. When the United States urged Thieu to raise taxes and devalue the piaster in order to counter inflation, South Vietnamese legislators warned against cooperating with American "schemes" to impoverish the country. Socialist leader Ngo Cong Duc charged that American policy in South Vietnam aimed at "Americanizing the Vietnamese people, transforming the Vietnamese into foreigners in their own country, into increasingly ignorant creatures stripped of their dignity." Anti-Americanism became the sole rallying cry of Tran Tuan Nham, a National Assembly candidate whose party symbol was a caricature of Richard Nixon designed to resemble Adolf Hitler.

Some Americans claimed that condemnation of the U.S. role in Vietnam was pure political demagoguery designed to discredit the Thieu regime. But criticism of the United States also swept Saigon newspapers loyal to the presi-

In the days before the 1971 South Vietnamese presidential election, explosions rock Saigon in protest of the Thieu government and the Americans who support him.

dent. Many felt that Thieu, who was not above blaming the U.S. for his country's woes, used the press attacks for his own ends. "You know I cannot always criticize the Americans," he told one group of Saigon journalists. "But I do not care if you do."

A mood to forget

Preferring to ignore verbal attacks, U.S. officials focused instead on anti-American demonstrations that they blamed on the Communists. And not without reason. A number of South Vietnamese peace and student groups had either been set up or infiltrated by the NLF. Moreover, the Communists were quick to "exploit the contradictions among the people," providing anti-American literature to student organizations and timing their own terror attacks to coincide with demonstrations in hopes of provoking civilian panic.

Concentrating on Communist connections with anti-American protest, however, only obscured the more fundamental fact that by the early seventies South Vietnam's urban population was highly receptive to negative portrayals of American purpose and behavior. It was a situation that became worse as the withdrawal progressed and GIs grew less careful about treating their hosts with respect. Many soldiers blamed the Vietnamese for having to serve in "Nam" in the first place and were increasingly disinclined to risk death in order, as one soldier put it, "to buy time for some dinks." Paradoxically, the boredom that resulted as combat responsibilities shifted to the ARVN only seemed to heighten anti-Vietnamese sentiment among the Americans. The result was a rising incidence of barroom brawls, reckless driving, public drunkenness, and plain discourtesy to which angry Vietnamese responded by blocking roads with coffins of traffic victims and beating U.S. servicemen involved in highway accidents.

Antipathy toward the Americans swept up even those who had little or no contact with GIs. Vietnamese blamed the Americans for corrupting the young, undermining the country's economy, using Vietnamese officials as "henchmen," disregarding South Vietnam's sovereignty, dignity, and customs. After years of pervasive foreign presence, the people of South Vietnam no longer believed they could control their future. They had become convinced that they were simply pawns of the United States and with fatalistic resignation waited for Washington to retain Thieu, depose him, make peace, or continue the war. That the Vietnamese had no ability to determine their own destiny was "the only point of complete agreement among all sides," *New York Times* correspondent David Shipler discovered, "and it has become a kind of national psychosis."

Refusing to accept responsibility for the scramble after profit, the failures of leadership, and the corruption that had so contributed to the situation they found themselves in, Vietnamese made America a scapegoat, portraying themselves as victims of a deliberate global policy to make small countries dependent on the United States. "Everything in Vietnam is planned by the Americans," explained a college professor. "If the Americans don't want Nguyen Van Thieu for President, he will leave—it is as simple as that. If they want to stop the corruption and the grasping, they can do it." In a poll conducted in five separate areas of South Vietnam, between 71 and 83 percent of the respondents thought that Washington controlled the Saigon government. A majority of all the people questioned said that the United States could have won the war but chose not to do so for perverse and selfish reasons, and 56 percent asserted they were pleased to see the Americans leave.

In fact, Vietnamese attitudes about the U.S. withdrawal were extremely ambivalent. Tired of advice, tired of condescension, tired of war, they were ready for a divorce from their American partner. Some Vietnamese looked forward to political and military independence; others longed for American withdrawal because they were convinced the presence of U.S. forces perpetuated the fighting. Many thought the U.S. departure would neutralize Communist propaganda and promote nationalism and self-sufficiency. Whatever their hopes, recalls Robert Shaplen, by the early 1970s a considerable number of Vietnamese believed "that nothing could be worse than the destruction of the country both physically, morally and culturally under the impact of the Americans."

Yet Shaplen also encountered a "near schizophrenia" regarding the American withdrawal. At first, explained Bui Diem, the Vietnamese ambassador to the United States, many of his countrymen simply refused to believe it. "The Vietnamese couldn't think in terms of Americans intervening in something and not succeeding ... they couldn't think that the Americans once having committed their troops in Vietnam, having spent so much money in Vietnam, could one of these days leave everything behind and quit." Once it became clear that the Americans were indeed going to leave, many Vietnamese feared for the imminent collapse of the government and army. By 1972 even bona fide nationalists had long since given up hope that the country could stand on its own. Stuart Herrington found that the presence of a handful of American advisers in Hau Nghia Province carried with it "a symbolic importance that was totally out of proportion to any contribution that the few of us could make to the war effort. But no matter how hard one tried to convince the South Vietnamese that they no longer needed us—that 1972 was not 1965—they weren't buying."

In the wake of the Easter offensive, and with negotiations in Paris between U.S. Secretary of State Henry Kissinger and North Vietnam's Le Duc Tho nearing completion, accusations of "sellout" and "betrayal" could be heard from Vietnamese officials and ordinary citizens alike. Herrington noticed that the Vietnamese word used by his counterparts to refer to the American departure was "bo," meaning "to discard" or "throw away," rather than "rat," which means "to withdraw." It revealed a bitterness that some made no effort to disguise. "Americans come like firemen to extinguish the fire, but they haven't done the job, and now they are going home. It's unbelievable," said a Vietnamese civil engineer. "Fine, we will put out the fire ourselves, but you have taken the water, the pump and ladder with you."

Others were more balanced in their repudiation. In an interview with an American reporter in 1971, a Vietnamese newspaper editor reflected on his disappointment with his country's ally. "At first, the Vietnamese thought the Americans were very generous, with idealism to fight Communism. But after years of seeing you behave in bars, driving recklessly and insulting our people, we know that we were wrong to put you so high." Yet the newspaperman also recognized that Vietnamese perceptions of Americans were often only half-truths. "If our people could see you in the States, they would have a far better impression. But here they see GIs running over innocent people and fleeing the scene of the accident." Condemning American assumptions of superiority, he rejected the self-selected title of "advisers." "To us, an adviser should be someone who is superior in every way, who can give you advice on all subjects, on life, on love. You are really just 'demonstrators.' You show us how to shoot the M-16 and fly the F-5, and we need you for that. But you are not 'advisers.' " Worst of all, thought the editor, the Americans' advice had been fundamentally flawed. "You thought that by giving us an easy life, a television, a washing machine, a car, that we could fight Communism better. That is not true. You must have discipline, you must make sacrifices to fight Communism. We have become bourgeois. . . ."

Zalin Grant first came to Vietnam in 1964 as an intelligence adviser. When he returned as a journalist in the spring of 1973 he found the Vietnamese by and large ready to say good-bye. Struck by the speed with which signs of the U.S. presence were disappearing, and the apparent indifference with which the Saigonese greeted the formal ceremonies marking the American departure, he concluded that most South Vietnamese were "in a mood to forget us." Perhaps after twenty years the United States had simply outstayed its welcome. "Everyone is happy to see the Americans go," said a hotel waitress in Hue as she watched the sun set over the Perfume River. "But we also know the Americans were happy to leave."

"Good-bye, and Good Luck"

What the United States left behind was a country profoundly altered by more than two decades of American involvement in its affairs. The cumulative impact of hundreds of programs, millions of men and women, and billions of dollars had worked changes of revolutionary scope on South Vietnamese society. What had been a nation of villages had become substantially urbanized. What had been an almost wholly agricultural society now boasted a technological infrastructure rare in the developing world. What had been an amalgam of Vietnamese, Chinese, and French heritage was now enriched by the influence of American language and culture. The United States had introduced a vast array of modern amenities to South Vietnam, woven together a network of land communications, and extended electricity into the countryside. In the process whole new classes had emerged in the swelling urban areas, while at the same time the physical gap between the cities and the countryside had narrowed. Endemic scourges such as tuberculosis were brought under control, and farmland, which had yielded only what traditional practices could wrest from the soil, now produced record crops thanks to mechanization, hybrid strains, and modern farming methods.

These changes brought with them not only great benefits but also serious social and economic dislocations. The distribution of population in 1972 resembled that of an industrialized country, but without the industrial base to support it. Nor were the cities capable of providing the most basic sanitation or health facilities to the majority of people clustered in the urban areas. Many of those lured to the city by the promise of a better life or driven there by the war would be able to return to their villages as the fighting waned, but millions of others would not: peasants whose land had been devastated or whose hamlets had disappeared; technicians trained for jobs that could exist only in the cities; children of rural families who had grown up in the cities, with a taste for urban society and little if any recollection of traditional village life.

At the same time, the rapid process of modernization and the impact of the American presence had unsettled traditional Vietnamese social relationships and standards of behavior. In a society of familial responsibility and strong parental authority there now existed a profusion of urban youth gangs, boys and girls neither disciplined by nor dependent upon their parents. In a society of puritan social mores there was now an entire class of prostitutes and bar girls, pimps and drug pushers whose very presence called into question the vitality of traditional social norms. In a society of limited resources and communal arrangements, a new materialism had emerged, an unfettered pursuit of wealth and luxury that strained families, fostered crime, and so accentuated the contrast between the cities and the rural areas that it seemed to many that the South Vietnamese people were living in "two separate worlds far removed from each other."

Along with such problems there were as well major tasks left undone. The forms of democratic government—a written constitution, political parties, an independent judiciary—had been created, but they existed more in form than in substance. The government remained the province

181

Bien Hoa air base, 1971.

of the military, ruling through extraordinary powers that made the National Assembly little more than a noisy sounding board for complaint. Political opposition was hopelessly fragmented and tightly restricted by the Thieu government. Elections had been introduced, but constant abuse had brought them into widespread contempt. Perhaps most important, the effort to democratize South Vietnamese society remained a process that was imposed from the top down rather than developed from the bottom up, so that what progress had been achieved made little impression on the bulk of the population.

In much the same way, for all the tangible advances that had taken place, economic and social development remained insecure. United States advisers and AID workers had initiated numerous thoughtful programs and shepherded thousands of projects to completion. But they had not succeeded in translating their individual accomplishments into a permanent process of growth. "We are not creating any lasting institutions over there," lamented an AID Rural Development officer in 1969. "We create a school, but we don't create within the GVN the means to continue creating schools after we leave. As soon as we leave it all collapses."

These disappointments were but symptoms of two problems at the heart of the American endeavor: a continuing inability to forge a productive partnership with the Vietnamese and a growing posture of dependence that by 1972 permeated South Vietnamese society. Eager to achieve results as quickly as possible, the United States had been too willing to take a guiding hand in virtually every aspect of Vietnamese life from administering the government in Saigon to supplying cement to individual hamlets, from training the police to preparing teachers for South Vietnamese universities. The United States never "controlled" the Republic of Vietnam, far from it. But the all-encompassing American initiatives left the country, according to one Vietnamese general, "utterly passive, dependent, subservient, and unable to make decisions for its own sake." It was a condition long nurtured by the French and a root cause of the bureaucratic inertia that so bedeviled American policymakers and advisers who first addressed themselves to the problems of the Vietnamese. During the American years, when South Vietnam sought to create the foundations of an independent existence, this dependent relationship had the additional effect of destroying the prestige and credibility of the Saigon government, not only internationally but also among its own people.

One of the most important reasons why this came to be was the failure of Americans and Vietnamese to establish a partnership that worked. Never before had the United States attempted such massive, detailed, and prolonged involvement in another nation's affairs. Perhaps because of the very novelty of the effort, Washington underestimated the difficulties inherent in such an enterprise,

difficulties compounded by enormous cultural and historical differences. The Vietnamese knew very little about the Americans when their joint efforts began, and Americans knew even less about the Vietnamese. What they did know derived mainly from books written by the French, carrying the biases of their colonial rule and political perspective. Nor did brief tours of duty, ignorance of the language, and lack of meaningful interaction enable most Americans who served in Vietnam to gain more than a superficial understanding of this ancient people.

The very real differences between them led to a gulf of misunderstanding that was never satisfactorily overcome. Americans believed in the necessity of action, while the Vietnamese tended to regard time as an eternal panacea. The Americans typically strove for a single, optimum solution to a given problem. The Vietnamese were more likely to follow several paths simultaneously. Although Americans were aware of the strong attachments that existed among Vietnamese families, the overwhelming importance these obligations had were outside the American experience, nor did they wholly appreciate how little attention most Vietnamese paid to the social organizations around which Americans had structured their own society. Most important of all, while the experience of war was for the Americans something episodic and limited, it had come to be regarded by most Vietnamese as a permanent part of their lives.

The difficulty of bridging the cultural-historical gap was one of the primary lessons that those long associated with the American involvement in Vietnam took from their experience. Analogous to this was the conviction that the United States had made a mistake in allowing the global dimensions of the Vietnamese conflict to override the importance of local factors. "Operating on this foundation of sand," declared Colonel Donaldson Frizzell, chief of Strategic Concept Studies at the Air War College, "our nation-building and military efforts were condemned to irrelevance and frustration." Frizzell was speaking at a 1974 colloquium also attended by Ambassador Robert Komer, the former director of CORDS, who believed that the United States had erred fundamentally in regarding the problem as primarily military rather than political, an emphasis that led to a greater Americanization of the war and a greater toll of death and destruction than might otherwise have taken place. It seemed to Komer that "we understood far better what needed to be done than we ever figured out how to do it," that the American attempt to build the South Vietnamese nation and rally the South Vietnamese people "just was not 'do-able'" without effective nationalist leadership in Saigon, that in the end the solution to Vietnamese problems could come only from the Vietnamese themselves.

A key element in the partnership American planners had envisioned was the necessity of capable leadership from the South Vietnamese. Without an effective and reasonably popular nationalist government in Saigon, there was little hope that a unified nation would emerge in the wake of the French departure, or the threat of Communist aggression be met. Yet capable leadership proved difficult to find and harder to sustain. Those who did rule South Vietnam, especially after Diem, were not truly nationalist in the broadest sense; nor were any of the republic's presidents, including Diem, representative of the majority of South Vietnamese. Less concerned with the welfare of their people than with maintaining the power and economic privileges of those they did represent, they demonstrated little commitment to forging a meaningful alliance with the peasants. Resentful of U.S. interference in their affairs even as they depended upon American aid and military support for their survival, they were convinced that the Americans did not understand their country, their culture, or its problems.

In this they were at least partly correct. It is safe to say that the South Vietnamese were as bewildered and frustrated with the Americans as their allies were with them. The result was a persistent and discouraging impasse in the relations between Washington and Saigon: continuing agreement on common goals; continuing disagreement on how those goals should be achieved. Because of this, because of their political insularity, their administrative inefficiency, and the limitations imposed upon them by the war, successive South Vietnamese governments adopted a revolving series of short-term approaches to such long-term problems as urbanization and economic development, proving unable to successfully integrate U.S. aid and expertise in the task of building a nation.

By the spring of 1973 the United States had come full circle. Nearly two decades earlier President Eisenhower had pledged to Ngo Dinh Diem American economic aid, political support, and military assistance. As the last American combat troops departed, this was once more the role the United States was prepared to assume in Vietnam. For the thousands of Americans who stayed behind—the shrinking corps of military advisers, the declining AID staff, the still numerous businessmen, missionaries, and volunteer relief workers—this role remained a vital and important one. If the prospects for the future were troubled, they were not hopeless. What so many Americans before them had tried to achieve might still be accomplished. But the long years of involvement were drawing to a close. In Tay Ninh Province a simple sign marked the site of a former U.S. Army installation that had just been turned over to the South Vietnamese government. Virtually everything else at the base had been removed by ARVN soldiers. But the sign remained, hanging crookedly in front of what had been. "Good-bye," it said in English, "and Good Luck."

A Vietnamese woman and her children walk through a deserted town near an abandoned U.S. base.

Bibliography

I. Books and Articles

Abrams, Arnold. "South Vietnam: Every boy U.S.A." *Far Eastern Economic Review,* February 12, 1970.

Adair, Dick. *Dick Adair's Saigon.* Weather Hill, 1971.

Adams, John Clarke, Harlan Cleveland, and Gerald J. Mangone. *The Overseas Americans.* McGraw–Hill, 1960.

Alsop, Stewart. "Vietnam: Whose War?" *The Saturday Evening Post,* January 28, 1967.

Amter, Joseph A. *Vietnam Verdict.* The Continuum Publishing Co., 1982.

American Council of Voluntary Agencies for Foreign Service. *Development Assistance Programs for Vietnam.* Technical Assistance Information Clearing House, 1976.

Anderson, Charles R. *Vietnam: The Other War.* Presidio Pr., 1982.

Anderson, Gerald H., ed. *Christ and Crisis in SEA.* Friendship Pr., 1968.

Arnett, Peter. "Reflections on Vietnam, the Press and America." *Nieman Reports,* March 1972, 6–8.

Baldwin, Hanson W. "The Information War in Saigon." *The Reporter,* February 24, 1966, 29–31.

Barber, Charles. "Business Boom in Saigon." *Far Eastern Economic Review,* March 10, 1966, 443–47.

Bonds, Ray, ed. *The U.S. War Machine.* Crown, 1978.

——. *The Vietnam War.* Crown, 1979.

Boyle, Richard. *The Flower of the Dragon.* Ramparts Pr., 1972.

Braestrup, Peter. "Covering the Vietnam War." *Nieman Reports,* December 1969, 8–13.

Brownmiller, Susan. *Against Our Will.* Bantam Bks., 1975.

Browne, Malcolm W. *The New Face of War.* Bobbs–Merrill, 1965.

——. "Vietnam Reporting: Three Years of Crisis." *Columbia Journalism Review* (Fall 1964): 4–9.

Browning, Frank, and Dorothy Forman, eds. *The Wasted Nations.* Harper & Row, 1972.

Buckley, Tom. "See it Through With Nguyen Van Thieu." *New York Times Magazine,* September 26, 1971.

Bullington, James R. "South Vietnamese Countryside Political Perceptions." *Asian Survey* 10(1970): 651–61.

Bunn, George. "Banning Poison Gas and Germ Warfare." *Wisconsin Law Review* 2(1969).

Carthew, Anthony. "Vietnam Is Like an Oriental Western." *New York Times Magazine,* January 23, 1966, 8–20.

Chandler, Robert. *War of Ideas.* Westview Pr., 1981.

Cincinnatus. *Self Destruction. The Disintegration and Decay of the United States Army During the Vietnam Era.* Norton, 1981.

Citizens Commission of Inquiry, ed. *The Dellums Committee Hearings on War Crimes in Vietnam.* 1972.

Clergy and Laymen Concerned About Vietnam in the Name of America. Turnpike Pr., 1968.

Coffey, Raymond R. "The People Beneath the War: The Vietnamese." *The Nation,* January 17, 1966, 61–63.

Committee of Concerned Asian Scholars. *The Indochina Story.* Bantam Bks., 1970.

Dickerman, Sherwood. "How the Marines Fight the 'Other War.' " *The Reporter,* April 6, 1967.

Duffett, John, ed. *Against the Crime of Silence.* Simon and Schuster, 1968.

Emerson, Gloria. *Winners and Losers.* Harcourt Brace Jovanovich, 1976.

Emery, Edwin. "The Press in the Vietnam Quagmire." *Journalism Quarterly* (Winter 1971): 619–26.

Erlich, Paul R., and John P. Holdren. "Starvation as a Policy." *Saturday Review,* December 4, 1971.

Evans, Barbara. *Caduceus in Saigon.* Hutchinson and Co., 1968.

Falabella, Robert. *Vietnam Memoirs.* Pageant Pr. International, 1971.

Falk, Richard A., ed. *The Vietnam War and International Law.* Vols. 1–4. Princeton Univ. Pr., 1976.

——, Gabriel Kolko, and Robert Lifton, eds. *Crimes of War.* Random, 1971.

Fall, Bernard B. "This Isn't Munich, It's Spain." *Ramparts,* December 1965, 23–29.

FitzGerald, Frances. *Fire in the Lake.* Random, 1972.

——. "The Tragedy of Saigon." *Atlantic Monthly,* December 1966, 59–67.

Flynn, John. "Young Civilian Tries to Win Fight on People Front." *Life,* November 27, 1964.

Fox, Richard D., M.D. "Narcissitic Rage and the Problem of Combat Aggression." *Archives of General Psychiatry* 31(December 1974).

Garms, David. *With the Dragon's Children.* Exposition Pr., 1973.

Gault, William Barry, M.D. "Some Remarks on Slaughter." *American Journal of Psychiatry.* 128(October 1971): 4.

Gershen, Martin. *Destroy or Die.* Arlington House, 1971.

Gloechner, Fred. *A Civilian Doctor in Vietnam.* The Winchell Co., 1972.

Goldman, Peter, and Tony Fuller. *Charlie Company: What Vietnam Did to Us.* Morrow, 1983.

Goldstein, Joseph, Burke Marshall, and Jack Schwartz. *The My Lai Massacre and Its Cover-Up.* Free Pr., 1976.

Grant, Zalin B. "Vietnam Without GIs." *New Republic,* May 19, 1973, 19–21.

Grose, Peter. "The 'Ordinary Life' of Americans in Saigon." *New York Times Magazine,* September 27, 1964.

Haas, Harry, and Nguyen Bao Cong. *Vietnam: The Other Conflict.* Sheed and Ward, 1971.

Halberstam, David. "Getting the Story in Vietnam." *Commentary,* January 1965, 30–34.

——. *The Making of a Quagmire.* Random, 1965.

——. "Return to Vietnam." *Harpers Magazine,* December 1967, 41–58.

Haley, Sarah A. "When the Patient Reports Atrocities." *Archives of General Psychiatry* 30(February 1974).

Hammer, Richard. *One Morning in the War: The Tragedy at Son My.* Coward–McCann, 1970.

Hasselbad, Marva. *Lucky–Lucky.* Fawcett, 1966.

Hefley, James C. *By Life or By Death.* Zondervan, 1969.

Hendry, James B. "American Aid in Vietnam. *Pacific Affairs,* December 1960, 387–91.

——. *The Small World of Khanh Hau.* Aldine Publishing Co., 1964.

Henry, Jules. "Capital's Last Frontier." *The Nation,* April 25, 1966, 480–83.

"Herbicides in Vietnam." *Christian Century,* February 10, 1971.

Herman, Edward S. *Atrocities in Vietnam.* Pilgrim Pr., 1970.

Herr, Michael. *Dispatches.* Avon Bks., 1977.

Herring, George C. *America's Longest War.* Wiley, 1979.

Herrington, Stuart A. *Silence Was a Weapon.* Presidio Pr., 1982.

Hersh, Seymour. *My Lai 4.* Vintage Bks., 1970.

Holbik, Karel. "United States AID to Vietnam." *Intereconomics* 8(1968).

Hostetter, Doug. "After the Debris Is Cleared." *Sojourners,* September 1978, 20–23.

——, and Michael McIntyre. "The Politics of Charity." *The Christian Century,* September 18, 1974, 845–50.

Hughes, Larry. *You Can See a Lot Standing Under a Flare in the Republic of Vietnam.* Morrow, 1969.

Jackson, Donald. "Confessions of the 'Winter Soldiers.' " *Life,* July 9, 1971.

Johnstone, Craig L. "Ecocide and the Geneva Protocol." *Foreign Affairs* 49(1971): 714.

Kahin, George, and John W. Lewis. *The United States in Vietnam.* Dial Pr., 1967.

Karnow, Stanley. "The Newsmen's War in Vietnam." *Nieman Reports,* December 1963, 3–8.

Kirk, Donald. *Tell It to the Dead.* Nelson–Hall, 1975.

Knightly, Phillip. *The First Casualty.* Harcourt Brace Jovanovich, 1975.

Knoll, Erwin, and Judith Nies McFadden, eds. *War Crimes and the American Conscience.* Holt, Rinehart & Winston, 1970.

Kroll, Jerome. "Racial Patterns of Military Crimes in Vietnam." *Psychiatry* 39(February 1976).

Kucharsky, David E. "Vietnam: The Vulnerable Ones." *Christianity Today,* March 1, 1968, 540–43.

Ladejinsky, Wolf. "Agrarian Reform in Asia." *Foreign Affairs,* April 19, 1964.

Langner, Herman P., M.D. "The Making of a Murderer." *American Journal of Psychiatry* 127(January 1971): 7.

Langguth, Jack. "Saigon Tries to Live in a Hurry." *New York Times Magazine,* August 8, 1965, 12–13.

Lawrence, Anthony. *Foreign Correspondent.* Allen & Unwin, 1972.

Lewallen, John. *Ecology of Devastation: Indochina.* Penguin Bks., 1971.

Lelyveld, Joseph. "The Story of a Soldier Who Refused to Fire at Songmy." *New York Times Magazine,* December 14, 1969.

Lewy, Guenter. *America in Vietnam.* Oxford Univ. Pr., 1978.

Lifton, Robert J. *Home From the War.* Simon & Schuster, 1973.

Lindholm, Richard W. *Viet-Nam. The First Five Years.* Michigan State Univ. Pr., 1959.

Littauer, Raphael, and Norman Uphoff, eds. *The Air War in Indochina.* Beacon Pr., 1972.

Luce, Don, and John Sommer. *Vietnam: The Unheard Voices.* Cornell Univ. Pr., 1969.

Ly Qui Chung. *Between Two Fires.* Praeger, 1970.

McCartney, James. "Can the Media Cover Guerrilla Wars?" *Columbia Journalism Review* (Winter 1970–71): 33–37.

Maclear, Michael. *The Ten Thousand Day War, Vietnam: 1945–1975.* St. Martin's, 1981.

Marr, David. "Political Attitudes and Activities of Young Urban Intellectuals in South Vietnam." *Asian Survey* 6(May 1966): 249–63.

Martin, Earl S. *Reaching the Other Side.* Crown, 1978.

"The Massacre at My Lai. *Life,* December 5, 1969, 36–45.

Mecklin, John. *Mission in Torment.* Doubleday, 1965.

Mohr, Charles. "This War and How We Cover It." *Dateline* Vols. 6–10, 1962–1966, 19–22.

Moser, Don. "Their Mission: Defend, Befriend." *Life,* August 25, 1967.

Montgomery, John. "Crossing the Culture Bars." *World Politics,* July 1961, 544–60.

——. *The Politics of Foreign Aid.* Praeger, 1962.

Moskin, Robert J. "USA in Asia." *Look,* May 30, 1967.

Nguyen Thai. "A Vietnamese Speaks Out." *New Republic,* June 1963, 14–17.

Nighswonger, William A. *Rural Pacification in Vietnam.* Praeger, 1966.

Norden, Eric. "American Atrocities in Vietnam." *Liberation,* February 1966.

Novak, Michael. "Latest Casualty in Vietnam." *Christianity and Crisis,* October 30, 1967, 250–52.

Oglesby, Carl, "The Bourgeois Gentlemen of Saigon." *The Nation,* November 15, 1965.

——. "Vietnam: This Is Guernica." *The Nation,* June 5, 1967, 714–21.

Paige, Jeffery M. "Inequality and Insurgency in Vietnam." *World Politics,* October 1970.

Palmer, Dave Richard. *Summons of the Trumpet.* Presidio Pr., 1978.

Peers, Lt. Gen. W. R. *The My Lai Inquiry.* Norton, 1979.

Pell, Walden II. "A Parson's View from Vietnam." *The American Oxonian* 3(July 1962): 160–65.

Pfeiffer, E. W., and Arthur H. Westing. "Land War." *Environment,* November 1971.

Pike, Douglas. *War, Peace and the Vietcong.* MIT Pr., 1969.

Pimlott, John, ed. *Vietnam: The History and the Tactics.* Crescent Bks., 1982.

Pisor, Robert. *The End of the Line.* Norton, 1982.

Poirier, Normand. "An American Atrocity." *Esquire,* August 1969.

Popkin, Samuel L. *The Rational Peasant.* University of California Pr., 1979.

Post, Helen. "Vietnam: Dilemma for Missionaries." *Japan Christian Quarterly* (Spring 1968): 98–100.

Prokosch, Eric. "Conventional Killers." *New Republic,* November 1, 1969, 18–21.

Purnell, Karl H. "Winning Hearts in Vietnam." *The Nation,* April 3, 1967, 434–35.

Race, Jeffrey. *War Comes to Long An.* University of California Pr., 1972.

Raymond, Jack. "It's a Dirty War for Correspondents, Too." *New York Times Magazine*, February 13, 1966.

"Religious Agencies in Vietnam." NACLA Latin America and Empire Report. 7, no. 10(December 1973): 3–31.

Salzburg, Joseph S. *Vietnam: Beyond the War*. Exposition Pr., 1975.

Santoli, Al. *Everything We Had*. Ballantine Bks., 1981.

Schell, Jonathan. *The Military Half*. Knopf, 1968.

_____. *The Village of Ben Suc*. Knopf, 1967.

Schell, Orville. "Pop Me Some Dinks." *New Republic*, January 3, 1970.

_____. "Silent Vietnam." *Look*, April 6, 1971, 55–58.

Schulze, Gene. *The Third Face of War*. Pemberton Pr., 1970.

Scigliano, Robert. *South Vietnam: Nation Under Stress*. Houghton Mifflin, 1963.

_____. "They Work for Americans." *American Sociological Review* (October 1960): 695–704.

_____ et al. *Technical Assistance in Vietnam*. Praeger, 1965.

Selby, Hope. "Vietnamese Students Talk About the War." *New York Times Magazine*, October 31, 1965.

Shaplen, Robert. "Profiles: We Have Always Survived." *New Yorker*, April 15, 1972.

_____. *The Road from War: Vietnam 1965–1970*. Harper & Row, 1970.

Sheehan, Susan. *Ten Vietnamese*. Knopf, 1967.

Shipler, David K. "What We Left Behind." *Harper's*, April 31, 1975, 31–34.

"Six Missionaries Martyred in Vietnam." *Christianity Today*, March 1, 1968, 37.

Smith, Desmond. "Saigon: Drowning in Dollars." *The Nation*, December 5, 1966, 602–5.

_____. "There Must Have Been Easier Wars." *The Nation*, June 12, 1967, 745–50.

Smith, Ralph Lee. "The Lessons of Vietnam." *Challenge*, November 1959, 7–12.

Snepp, Frank. *Decent Interval*. Vintage Bks., 1977.

Stafford, Ann. *Saigon Journey*. Taplinger Publishing Co., 1960.

Steinbeck, John IV. *In Touch*. Knopf, 1969.

Sterba, James. "The Hours of Boredom, The Seconds of Terror." *New York Times Magazine*, February 8, 1970.

Stockholm International Peace Research Institute. *Incendiary Weapons*. MIT Pr., 1975.

Streit, Peggy. "Go Ye Therefore and Teach All Nations." *New York Times Magazine*, March 22, 1964.

Summers, Col. Harry G., Jr. *On Strategy: The Vietnam War in Context*. Strategic Studies Institute, U.S. Army War College, 1981.

Sutton, Horace. "Saigon Is Bizarre Center for Come-and-Visit War." *Holiday*, February 1970.

Tanham, George et al. *War Without Guns*. Praeger, 1966.

Taylor, Milton. "South Vietnam: Lavish Aid, Limited Progress." *Pacific Affairs* 34(Fall 1961): 247–56.

Taylor, Telford. *Nuremberg and Vietnam*. Bantam Bks., 1970.

Thompson, W. Scott, and Donaldson D. Frizzell. *The Lessons of Vietnam*. Crane, Russak & Co., 1977.

Tran Van Don. *Our Endless War*. Presidio Pr., 1978.

Tregaskis, Richard. *Vietnam Diary*. Holt, Rinehart & Winston, 1963.

_____. "Why We Cover Wars." *Dateline*, Vols. 6–10, 1962–1966, 24–27.

Trooboff, Peter D., ed. *Law and Responsibility in Warfare*. University of North Carolina Pr., 1975.

Turpin, James. *Vietnam Doctor*. McGraw-Hill, 1966.

"U.S. Branch Banks Open in Vietnam." *Banking*, December 1966, 59.

U.S. Chemical Warfare and Its Consequences." *Vietnam Courier*, 1980.

"Vietcong Kill Young Missionary." *Christianity Today*, February 4, 1966, 48–49.

Vietnam Veterans Against the War. *The Winter Soldier Investigation*. Beacon Pr., 1972.

Warner, Denis. *The Last Confucian*. Macmillan, 1963.

Weller, Jac. *Fire and Movement*. Thomas Y. Crowell Co., 1967.

West, Richard. "The Captive U.S. Journalists." *Atlas*, December 1966, 23–25.

_____. "Eye-Witnesses in Vietnam: 1." *New Statesman*, March 3, 1967.

_____. *Sketches from Vietnam*. Jonathan Cape, 1968.

Westing, Arthur H. "The Environmental Aftermath of Warfare in Viet Nam." *Natural Resources Journal*, April 1983.

_____, and E. W. Pfeiffer. "The Cratering of Indochina." *Scientific American*, May 1972.

Westmoreland, Gen. William C. *A Soldier Reports*. Doubleday, 1976.

"When the War Ends: A World of Opportunities." *Nation's Business*, February 1968, 36–38.

White, P. T. "Saigon: Eye of the Storm." *National Geographic*, June 1965, 834–72.

White, R. K. "Conflict as Seen by the Vietnamese Peasants." *Journal of Social Issues* 22(July 1966): 19–44.

_____. "Misperception and the Vietnam War." *Journal of Social Issues* 22, no. 3 (1966).

Winburn, Thomas T. *The Vietnam Story of IVS, Inc*. Terminal Report, 1972.

Young, Gavin. "Stories From Vietnam." *Encounter*, December 1966, 86–90.

Young, Perry Deane. "Two of the Missing." *Harper's*, December 1972, 84–100.

Zasloff, Joseph J. "The Problem of South Vietnam." *Commentary*, February 1962.

II. Government and Government-Sponsored Published Reports

BDM Corporation. *A Study of Strategic Lessons Learned in Vietnam*. National Technical Information Service, 1980.

Betts, Russell, and Frank Denton. *An Evaluation of Chemical Crop Destruction*. RAND Corporation RM-5446-I-ISA/ARPA, October 1967.

Buckingham, William A. *Operation Ranch Hand*. Office of Air Force History, 1982.

Congressional Research Service. *Impact of the Vietnam War*. GPO, June 30, 1971.

Dunn, Lt. Gen. Carroll H. *Base Development in South Vietnam 1965–1970*. Department of the Army, Vietnam Studies Series, 1972.

Nguyen, Maj. Gen. Duy Hinh. *Vietnamization and the Cease Fire*. Indochina Monograph Series. U.S. Army Center of Military History. 1980.

_____, and Brig. Gen. Dinh Tho Tran. *The South Vietnamese Society*. Indochina Monograph Series. U.S. Army Center of Military History, 1980.

Ewell, Lt. Gen. Julian J., and Maj. Gen. Ira A. Hunt, Jr. *Sharpening the Combat Edge*. Department of the Army, Vietnam Studies Series, 1974.

Goodman, Allan E. *Government and the Countryside*. RAND Corporation P-3924, September 1968.

Grant, James P. "AID's Proposed Program for Vietnam in Fiscal Year 1969." *Department of State Bulletin* 58(May 6, 1968): 594–98.

Gravel Edition. *Pentagon Papers*. Vols. 1–4. Beacon Pr., 1971.

Hay, Lt. Gen. John H., Jr. *Tactical and Materiel Innovations*. Department of the Army, Vietnam Studies Series, 1974.

Higgins, J. W. *Temporary Villages for Refugees*. RAND Corporation RM-5444-ISA/ARPA, August 1968.

Jenkins, Brian M. *The Unchangeable War*. RAND Corporation RM-6278-1-ARPA, September 1972.

Komer, Robert W. *Bureaucracy Does Its Thing: Institutional Constraints on U.S.-GVN Performance in Vietnam*. RAND Corporation R-967-ARPA, August 1972.

McGee, Gale. "Vietnam: A Living Example for Implementing the American Spirit." Speech delivered before the U.S. Senate, February 9, 1960.

Ott, Maj. Gen. David Ewing. *Field Artillery, 1954–1973*. Department of the Army, Vietnam Studies Series, 1973.

Parsons, John et al. *American and Vietnamese*. Department of Defense and Human Resources Inc., 1968.

Pearce, Michael. *Evolution of a Vietnamese Village* (Parts 1–3). RAND Corporation RM-5442-I-ARPA (April 1965); RM-4692-I-ARPA (April 1966); RM-5450-I-ASA/ARPA (October 1967).

Russo, Anthony J. *A Statistical Analysis of the U.S. Crop Spraying Program in South Vietnam*. RAND Corporation RM-5450-I-ASA/ARPA, October 1967.

Shulimson, Jack, and Maj. Charles M. Johnson. *U.S. Marines in Vietnam: The Landing and the Buildup*. Department of the Navy, United States Marine Corps, 1978.

Stolfi, Capt. Russel H. *U.S. Marine Corps Civic Action Efforts in Vietnam, March 1965–March 1966*. U.S. Marine Corps, Historical Branch Headquarters, 1968.

Swan, Ellen J. *Small Industry in Vietnam: Present Development*. Contract Services to USAID, 1968.

Thayer, Thomas C., ed. *A Systems Analysis View of the Vietnam War 1965–72*. Department of Defense.

_____. *How to Analyze a War Without Fronts: Vietnam 1965–1970*. Journal of Defense Research 7B (Fall 1975).

Tolson, Lt. Gen. John J. *Airmobility 1961–71*. Department of the Army, Vietnam Studies Series, 1973.

U.S. Agency for International Development. *Debrief of an American Businessman, Vietnam, 1962–68*. No. 22687.

_____. *Debrief of a Program Economist, Vietnam, 1968*.

_____. *Debrief of a Province Representative, Vietnam, 1963–67*.

_____. *Debrief of a Representative in Vietnam/Laos, 1963–67*.

_____. *Debrief of a Rural Development Officer, Vietnam, 1967–69*.

_____. *Debrief of a Secretary in Saigon, Vietnam*.

_____. *Debrief of a Senior AID Official, Vietnam, 1962–67*.

_____. *Vietnam in Perspective. United States Economic Assistance in South Vietnam, 1954–1975*. Terminal Report.

U.S. Congress. House. Appropriations Committee. *Briefings on Vietnam Program*. 91st Congress, 1970.

U.S. Congress. House. Committee on Armed Services. Armed Services Investigating Subcommittee. *Investigation of the My Lai Incident*. 91st Congress, 2d sess., 1970.

U.S. Congress, House. Committee on Foreign Affairs. Subcommittee on National Security Policy and Scientific Developments. *Chemical-Biological Warfare*. 91st Congress, 1st sess., 1969.

_____. *Technical Assistance in the Far East, South Asia, and Middle East*. 84th Congress, 2d sess., 1956.

U.S. Congress. Senate. Committee on Foreign Relations. *Technical Assistance in the Far East, South Asia, and Middle East*. 84th Congress, 2d sess., 1956.

_____. *Vietnam: Policy and Prospects, 1970*. 91st Congress, 2d sess., 1970.

_____. *Impact of the Vietnam War*. 92d Congress, 1st sess., 1971.

U.S. Congress. Senate. Committee on Government Operations. Permanent Subcommittee on Investigations. *Fraud and Corruption in Management of Military Club System*. 92d Congress. 1st sess., 1971.

U.S. Congress. Senate. Committee on the Judiciary. *War-Related Civilian Problems in Indochina*. 92d Congress, 1st sess., 1971.

_____. Subcommittee to Investigate Problems Concerned with Refugees and Escapees. *World Refugee and Humanitarian Problems*. 92d Congress, 1st sess., 1971.

III. Unpublished Government and Military Documents

Department of the Army, the Navy, and the Air Force. *Marriage in Oversea Commands*. AR 600-240. June 1978.

Department of Defense. *Southeast Asia Analysis Reports*. Office of the Assistant Secretary of Defense (Systems Analysis), 1967–72.

Joint United States Public Affairs Office (Vietnam). *The PSYOPS-JUSPAO Role in Revolutionary Development*. October 24, 1966.

Office of the Judge Advocate General. *Talking Paper*. April 11, 1971.

Shulimson, Jack, and Maj. Edward F. Wells. *First In, First Out; the Marine Experience in Vietnam, 1965–71*. Marine Corps Historical Center, August 4, 1982.

United States Agency for International Development. *Vietnam in Perspective, 1954–1975*, n.d.

United States Information Agency. *USIA Psychological Operations in Viet-Nam*. June 11, 1965.

USMACV. *MACV Command Overview, 1969–1972*.

IV. Judicial Proceedings

United States v. Bumgarner. CM 421583 (1970).
United States v. Calley. 22 U.S.C.M.A. 534, 48 C.M.R. 19 (1973).
United States v. Crider. NCM 69–4114 (1972).
United States v. Duffy. CM 424795 (1973).
United States v. Griffen. CM 416805 (1967).
United States v. Keenan. 18 USCMA 108, 39 CMR 108 (1969).
United States v. Potter. NCM 67–1348 (1967).
United States v. Schultz. 18 USCMA 133, 34 CMR 133 (1969).
United States v. Willey and Carmeron. CM 423609 (1971).

V. Unpublished Journals and Nongovernment Reports

CBS. "The People of South Vietnam: How They Feel About the War." March 21, 1967.
Gracy, Doris. *Our Year in Vietnam: 1964.* Unpublished journal.
Hostetter, Doug. Unpublished journal.

VI. Newspapers and Periodicals Consulted by Authors:

Business Week (1965–1973); *Forbes* (1972–1973); *Fortune* (1965–1973); *New York Times* (1954–1973); *Newsweek* (1955–1973); *Saigon Daily News* (1965–1972); *Time* (1955–1973); *Times of Vietnam* (1955–1963); *U.S. News and World Report* (1965–1973); *Wall Street Journal* (1965–1972).
Air Force Magazine; Air Force Times; Air University Review; Army; Army Digest; Army Quarterly; Infantry Magazine; Marine Corps Gazette; Military Review (1963–1973 inclusive).

VII. Interviews

Charles R. Anderson, Lieutenant, Third Military Police Battalion, III Amphibious Force.
Peter Arnett, Associated Press correspondent.
Edward Bassett, United Press International correspondent.
Tim Berttoti, USAID Chief of New Life Development, Ba Xuyen Province, Assistant Provincial Representative, Kien Hoa Province, 1967–1971.
Ronald Bayless, Sp4, 519th Military Intelligence Battalion.
Patrick Bodden Sp5, 519th Military Intelligence Battalion.
Peter Braestrup, covered Vietnam for the *New York Times* in 1966–67 and the *Washington Post*, 1968–69.
Frank Bourne, Director of Research. Joint United States Public Affairs Office, 1968–69.
Norman Camp, Colonel, former member of Northern Neurological Psychiatric Team in Da Nang, 1970–71.
John Clancy, Sp4, 196th Light Infantry Brigade, American Division.
Ralph Crossen, 9th Marines, 3d Marines, 4th Logistics Command.
Larry Demeo, Captain, 1st of the 50th Infantry, 173d Airborne.
George Esper, Associated Press correspondent.
W. Eugene Evans, Christian and Missionary Alliance, Vietnam.
Raymond Flynn, former 1st Lieutenant, 503d Infantry, 173d Airborne Brigade.
Richard Frank, Captain, 2d of the 17th Cavalry, 101st Airborne.
John Gibney, Colonel, 1st Cavalry Division.
David Greenway, Vietnam correspondent for *Time* magazine, 1967–68, and the *Washington Post*.
Richard W. Grefrath, Sergeant, 101st Airborne Division.
Gerald Hickey, author of *Village in Vietnam* and former consultant on Vietnamese affairs for the RAND Corporation.
Stuart A. Herrington, Colonel, military intelligence adviser, Hau Nghia Province, 1970–72.
Doug Hostetter, Mennonite Central Committee, 1966–69.
Dr. Richard A. Hunt, Center of Military History.
Terry Jones, 1st Lieutenant, 20th Engineer Brigade.
Ward Just, covered Vietnam for the *Washington Post*, 1965–1967.
Harry W. O. Kinnard, Lieutenant General, Commander, 1st Cavalry Division (Airmobile).
Paul Lapointe, 1st Lieutenant, 1st Battalion, 52d Infantry, 198th Infantry Brigade, American Division.
John Large, Sergeant, 1st Marine Division.
Don Luce, Director of International Voluntary Services, Vietnam, 1961–67.
Hugh Manke, Director of International Voluntary Services Vietnam, 1967–71.
Earl Martin, Mennonite Central Committee.
Mike Mielke, Team Sergeant, Special Forces, AID public health worker.
Biff Morse, Sergeant, 1st Brigade, 5th Infantry Division.
Phillip Moulaison, 503d Infantry, 173d Airborne Brigade.
Tim Page, free-lance photographer.
Lindsey Phares, manager of Da Nang port construction for the construction consortium RMK–BRJ.
Dean Phillips, E–5, 101st Airborne Division.
Robert R. Ploger, Major General, Engineer Commander 1965–67.
Brian Price, Sergeant, 716th M.P. Battalion.
Marc Pritchard, E–5, 2d of the 20th Artillery Battalion.
John Ripley, Lieutenant Colonel, 3d Marine Division.
Don Scott, Director of Project Concern, Vietnam, and Executive Director of My Friend's House in Saigon.
Robert Shaplen, journalist, covered Vietnam for the *New Yorker*, 1946–75.
James Webb, 1st Lieutenant, 1st Battalion, 5th Marine Regiment.
Joanne Webb, member of Army Nurse Corps in Vietnam, July 1971–72.
William C. Westmoreland, General, Commander of U.S. Armed Forces, Vietnam, 1964–1968.
Barry Zorthian, Head of Joint United States Public Affairs Office in Vietnam, 1964–68.

Acknowledgments

Boston Publishing wishes to acknowledge the assistance of the following people: W. A. Anderson, Office of the Adjutant General, U.S. Army; Robert Aquilina, History and Museums Division, U.S. Marine Corps; Nan Borden, IVS; Frank Bourne, former Director of Research, JUSPAO; Heidi Gifford; Doug Hostetter, American Friends Service Committee; Don Luce, former Director, IVS; Mike Mielke; Jack Shulimson, History and Museums Division, U.S. Marine Corps; Paul Taborn, Office of the Adjutant General, U.S. Army. The map on page 4 was prepared by Diane McCaffery.

Picture Credits

Index

U.S. Military Units
(see note below)
Army
Marines

Note: Military units are listed according to the general organizational structure of the U.S. Armed Forces. The following chart summarizes that structure for the U.S. Army. The principal difference between the army and the Marine Corps structures in Vietnam lay at the regimental level. The army eliminated the regimental command structure after World War II (although battalions retained a regimental designation for purposes of historical continuity, e.g., 1st Battalion, 7th Cavalry [Regiment]). Marine Corps battalions were organized into regiments instead of brigades except under a few unusual circumstances. The marines, however, do not use the word "regiment" to designate their units; e.g., 1st Marines refers to the 1st Marine Regiment.

U.S. Army structure
(to company level)

Unit	Size	Commanding officer
Division	12,000–18,000 troops or 3 brigades	Major General
Brigade	3,000 troops or 2–4 battalions	Colonel
Battalion*	600–1,000 troops or 3–5 companies	Lieutenant Colonel
Company	150 troops** or 3–4 platoons	Captain

* Squadron equivalent to battalion.
** Size varies based on type of unit.

Names, Acronyms, Terms

Agent Orange—a chemical defoliant widely used in Vietnam to deny jungle cover to the enemy. Named after the color-coded stripe painted around the barrels in which it was stored.

ANZUS—a collective defense arrangement between Australia, New Zealand, and the United States. Similar to SEATO (see below), ANZUS was formed as a deterrent to Communist expansion in the Pacific.

ARVN—Army of the Republic of Vietnam (South Vietnam).

Cao Dai—religious sect formed in 1925 by a group of civil servants in southern Vietnam, known then as Cochin China. A spirit revealed itself to them as the "Cao Dai," or supreme god of the universe.

CAPs—Combined Action Platoons. Pacification teams consisting of a South Vietnamese Popular Forces platoon, a U.S. Marine rifle squad, and a medical corpsman.

CIA—Central Intelligence Agency.

Civic Action—term used by U.S. military forces for pacification programs in South Vietnam.

CORDS—Civil Operations and Revolutionary Development Support. Established under MACV in 1967, CORDS organized all U.S. civilian agencies in Vietnam within the military chain of command.

CS—tear gas widely used by the U.S. in Vietnam.

CTZ—combat tactical zone. See I, II, III, and IV Corps.

DRV—Democratic Republic of Vietnam.

firebase—artillery firing position, often secured by infantry.

IV Corps—Four Corps. The fourth allied combat tactical zone encompassing the Mekong Delta.

free fire zones—areas designated by the GVN to be completely under enemy control, thus permitting unlimited use of firepower against anyone in the zone.

Geneva accords—signed by the French and Vietminh on July 21, 1954, the Geneva accords marked the end of the French Indochina War. They established a provisional boundary at the seventeenth parallel between the DRV and the new Republic of Vietnam.

GVN—U.S. abbreviation for the government of South Vietnam. Also referred to as the Republic of Vietnam.

Hoa Hao—Vietnamese religious sect founded in the South in 1939.

ICA—International Cooperation Administration. The predecessor of the United States Agency for International Development (USAID). Also known as the Foreign Operations Administration (FOA).

IVS—International Voluntary Services.

KIA—killed in action.

LZ—landing zone.

MAAG—Military Assistance Advisory Group. U.S. military advisory program to South Vietnam beginning in 1955.

MACV—Military Assistance Command, Vietnam. U.S. command over all U.S. military activities in Vietnam, originated in 1962.

MEDCAP—Medical Civic Action Program. Established in fall 1965. MEDCAP units of several medical corpsmen escorted by an armed squad conducted regular sick calls in villages.

miracle rice—a short maturity rice, introduced to Vietnam through USAID programs in 1968, the new strain could yield two and a half times as much as local South Vietnamese varieties.

montagnards—the mountain tribes of Vietnam, wooed by both sides because of their knowledge of the rugged highland terrain and their fighting ability.

MP—military police.

MSUG—Michigan State University Group led by Dr. Wesley Fishel. Attempted in 1955 to reorganize Diem's administration, police, and Civil Guard.

napalm—incendiary used in Vietnam by French and Americans both as a defoliant and antipersonnel weapon.

NCO—noncommissioned officer.

NLF—National Liberation Front. Officially the National Front for the Liberation of the South. Formed on December 20, 1960, it aimed to overthrow South Vietnam's government and reunite North and South Vietnam. The NLF included Communists and non-Communists.

NVA—North Vietnamese Army. Also called the People's Army of Vietnam (PAVN).

Office of Rural Affairs—created in 1962, the Office of Rural Affairs represented USAID's decision to send more civilian advisers into rural areas. Referred to as the Office of Provincial Operations or the Office of Field Operations by mid-1964.

I Corps—"Eye" Corps. First allied combat tactical zone encompassing the five northernmost provinces of South Vietnam.

PF—Popular Forces. South Vietnamese village defense units.

piaster—Vietnamese form of currency. In the 1960s, the exchange ratio between piasters and dollars was 118:1. In September 1970, the piaster was devalued to 275 piasters to a dollar.

Project 100,000—a program introduced in 1966 that lowered the military standards for induction.

PROVN—Program for the Pacification and Long Term Development of South Vietnam.

RAND Corporation—a private, nonprofit institution engaged in research and analysis of matters affecting national security and the public welfare.

RCA—riot control agent. Starting in mid-1962, the United States supplied South Vietnam with three types of RCA gases, DM, CM, and CS.

RD cadres—Revolutionary Development cadres. South Vietnamese who were trained to use Vietcong political tactics to carry out GVN pacification.

RMK-BRJ—a consortium of four private U.S. construction and engineering firms—Raymond International, Morrison-Knudsen, Brown and Root, and J. A. Jones—contracted by the U.S. Defense Department to build logistical bases in South Vietnam.

ROE—Rules of Engagement.

RVN—Republic of Vietnam.

SEATO—Southeast Asia Treaty Organization. Organized in 1954 by Thailand, Pakistan, the Philippines, the U.S., Britain, France, Australia, and New Zealand to form an alliance against Communist subversion, especially in Indochina.

SSZ—specified strike zone. Term created in 1967 to replace the controversial "free fire zone."

Tet—Lunar New Year, the most important Vietnamese holiday.

III Corps—Three Corps. Third allied combat tactical zone encompassing area from northern Mekong Delta to southern central highlands.

II Corps—Two Corps. Second allied combat tactical zone encompassing central highlands and adjoining central lowlands.

USAID—United States Agency for International Development. Responsible for administering American economic aid to many countries around the world, including South Vietnam.

USIS—United States Information Service.

USO—United Service Organization.

USOM—United States Operations Mission. The name of the USAID mission in Vietnam (see USAID).

VC—Vietcong. Common reference to the NLF, a contraction of Vietnam Cong San (Vietnamese Communist).

Vietminh—founded by Ho Chi Minh in May 1941, the coalition that ruled the Democratic Republic of Vietnam. Absorbed by the Lao Dong (Communist) party in 1951.

Vietnamization—term given to President Nixon's phased withdrawal of U.S. troops and transfer of their responsibilities to South Vietnamese.

WP/"Willie Peter"—white phosphorus. Incendiary chemical employed initially to mark positions for attack or evacuation. Later used as an offensive weapon.